The Women of Rural Asia

Also of Interest

Women in Changing Japan, edited by Joyce Lebra, Joy Paulson, and Elizabeth Powers

Women and Technological Change in Developing Countries, edited by Roslyn Dauber and Melinda Cain

*The Underside of History: A View of Women Through Time, Elise Boulding

Scientific-Technological Change and the Role of Women in Development, edited by Pamela M. D'Onofrio-Flores and Sheila M. Pfafflin

The Liberated Female: Life, Work, and Sex in Socialist Hungary, Ivan Volgyes and Nancy Volgyes

Women and Work in Africa, edited by Edna G. Bay

India: Cultural Patterns and Processes, edited by Allen G. Noble and Ashok K. Dutt

Agricultural and Rural Development in Indonesia, edited by Gary E. Hansen

The Agrarian Structure of Bangladesh: An Impediment to Development, F. Tomasson Januzzi and James T. Peach

Burma: A Socialist Nation of Southeast Asia, David I. Steinberg

Burma's Road Toward Development: Growth and Ideology under Military Rule, David I. Steinberg

*Japan: Profile of a Postindustrial Power, Ardath W. Burks

Nepal: Profile of a Himalayan Kingdom, Leo E. Rose and John T. Scholz

Patterns of Change in the Nepal Himalaya, Mark Poffenberger

*Huadong: The Story of a Chinese People's Commune, Gordon Bennett

*The Chinese Agricultural Economy, edited by Randolph Barker and Radha P. Sinha

Mongolia's Culture and Society, Sechin Jagchid and Paul Hyer

Village Viability in Contemporary Society, edited by Priscilla Copeland Reining and Barbara Lenkerd

*Available in hardcover and paperback.

Westview Special Studies on Women in Contemporary Society

The Women of Rural Asia
Robert Orr Whyte and Pauline Whyte

Many studies of rural areas have ignored half the population of
those areas--the women who play vital roles in family economies, and
thus in national economies, throughout the world. This study looks
at the social and economic status, family and workforce roles, and
quality of life of women in the rural sectors of monsoonal and equatorial Asia, from Pakistan to Japan, where life often is characterized by unemployment, underemployment, and poverty.

The Whytes note that it has become increasingly necessary for
rural women in this region to contribute to family budgets in ways
beyond their traditional roles in crop production and animal husbandry. Many women are responding by taking part in rural industries, yet the considerable disadvantages under which they labor--
less opportunity for education, lower pay, and poor access to
resources and high-status jobs--render them much less effective than
they could be in their efforts to increase production and reduce
poverty.

Drawing on the more than 500 books, articles, and reports that
are listed in the bibliography, as well as on their own field observations, the Whytes provide a descriptive analysis of the historical,
cultural, and environmental causes of women's current status in rural
Asia, an analysis requisite to improving the quality of these women's
lives and enabling them to contribute to the economy without excessive disruption of family life and the social structure of the rural
communities. The Whytes also review the activities of national and
international agencies in relation to the status of women, outline
major needs, and point to current indicators of change.

Dr. Robert Orr Whyte is an honorary research fellow at the
Centre of Asian Studies, University of Hong Kong, where Pauline Whyte
is his research assistant. Since 1965 they have concentrated on
the study of applied ecology--plant, animal, and human--in monsoonal
and equatorial Asia. Among their numerous publications are Crop
Production and Environment (1962) and Land, Livestock, and Human Nutrition in India (1968).

The Women of Rural Asia

Robert Orr Whyte
and Pauline Whyte

Westview Press / Boulder, Colorado

Westview Special Studies on Women in Contemporary Society

Published in 1982 in the United States of America by

Westview Press, Inc.
5500 Central Avenue
Boulder, Colorado 80301
Frederick A. Praeger, President and Publisher

Library of Congress Catalog Card Number: 82-70031
ISBN: 0-86531-278-8
ISBN: 0-86531-337-7 (pbk.)

Composition for this book was provided by the authors
Printed and bound in the United States of America

In memory of
Elspeth McGregor Kraicsovits

Contents

14   HELP FOR WORKING WOMEN 193
15   CONCLUSIONS. 203
     Sub-regional Variation in the Status of Women. 203
     Some Measures of Improvement 206
     Major Future Needs 208
     Plans and Activities: National. 212
     International Activities 215
     Changing Attitudes 218

Bibliography. 221
Glossary of Terms and Abbreviations 251
Index of Geographical Terms 255
Subject Index 257

Tables and Figures

xiv

Acknowledgments

This study was made while the authors were working at the Institute of Southeast Asian Studies, Singapore. They would like to thank the Institute, particularly the staff of the Library, for valuable help given. The authors are also indebted to the many people who have carried out research throughout Asia for their generous assistance in providing unpublished papers, comments and advice.

Robert Orr Whyte
Pauline Whyte

What though I was born a woman,
    comrades, count it not for blame
If I bring the wiser counsels.

The Lysistrata, Aristophanes

1
Scope and Objectives

Over the past decade women from most parts of the world have
begun to question the value their societies attribute to women's role
and the way in which this affects their status. Western women have
sought explanations for their subordinate position in the evolution
and history of human societies by comparing the position of women in
pre-industrial cultures or those which have developed along different
lines. Knowledge of the daily lives of women in the developing
world, however, is still fragmentary. Too little is known of the way
in which historical processes, religious and mythological beliefs and
the structure of societies have contributed to the status of women
today and still define the roles they perform, while modern economic
pressures increasingly modify the traditional picture.

Our aim here, however, has not been primarily to explain the
reasons for female subordination, though historical causes for sub-
regional differences are discussed. Rather we consider how available
knowledge of women's role and status in Asia is relevant to rural
development generally. What do national governments and other agencies need to know in planning the social and technical improvements
that are likely to benefit third world women and their societies? We
try here to depict some of the forces that have shaped the lives of
women in the different countries of Asia. Evidence shows the vital
role they play in family and, therefore, in national economies, and
how this role is being affected by changes brought about by the
modernization of technology and the incessant and increasing pressure
of population on the land.

The objective of this study is to review the information available on the social and economic status of rural women in the home and
the village and their role in the processes involved in the production, harvesting and processing of food and other commodities from
the land. It is hoped that this overall review and the conclusions
reached will be of value not only to sociologists and anthropologists
concerned with women, but also to the much larger group of specialists working or about to work in diverse disciplines within the scope
of what has come to be called rural modernization. In particular, we
hope the study will be of value to the many workers within Asia who
have inadequate access to published material and are not fully
informed of conditions in neighbouring countries.

1

2

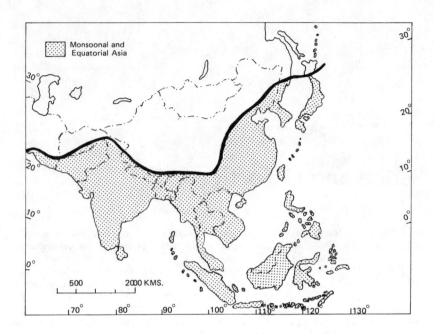

FIGURE 1.1   Monsoonal and equatorial Asia

Attempts to understand the current status of women in western[*]
society are often based on comparisons with that of women in innumerable other cultures. Here we concentrate on monsoonal and equatorial
Asia (Figure 1.1). The distinctions between monsoonal and equatorial
Asia on the one hand, and Africa, Latin America and southwest Asia on
the other in ecology, biogeography, land use, culture and history are
far greater than the differences to be found between the relatively
discrete parts of the Asian region itself. These latter differences
relate primarily to the geographical distribution and monsoonal
variations in climate: eastern monsoon Asia, where the cold non-
monsoon season has a continental to an arctic climate; western and
particularly northwestern monsoon Asia, where droughts of variable
frequency and intensity are an anticipated feature of life, settlement and the patterns of crop and animal husbandry; all the intermediate types between these extremes; and the humid tropical to equatorial bioclimates in southeast Asia and parts of south Asia.
    The region has many features in common: the monsoon winds them-
selves, which require that ways of life be intimately bound into the
seasonal swing from drought to rains; the staple crops, grown in
similar manner; the interplay of the great civilizations and

_____
    [*]Western" in this study refers to the United States, Canada,
Australasia and western Europe.

religions of India and China--the acceptance of some of their features and the struggle for freedom from their dominance by the countries of southeast Asia; the profound effect that colonialism has had
on the national economies and rural occupations of most Asian countries and the shared experience of the struggle to win freedom from
this last domination from outside. And it is in this region that
sheer pressure of numbers on the land has caused some of the most
fundamental changes in the way of life of women.

Restriction to one region is thus considered justified because
the cultures of societies in different continents diverge so widely
that there is little common ground on which to base useful conclusions on the evolution of women's status. The history, available
historical record, environment, degree and duration of influence by
other societies, access to education, health care and new technology
and innumerable cultural factors vary so greatly between, say, the
Iroquois, the Australian Aborigine, the Maring of New Guinea, the
Bedouin woman, the Tokyo housewife, the Rajput landowner's wife, the
Tamil landless labourer and the commune worker in Asian Communist
countries that cross-cultural comparisons can arrive only at a level
of generalization which has little significance. Although women in
the developing world can understand their problems better than can
women from the developed world, it is nevertheless difficult to
evolve broad cross-cultural theories which might be applicable within
the third world itself, as between Africa and Latin America, for
example (Lancaster, 1976, 1977; Sacks, 1976; Thompson, 1977).

This study does not claim to be a complete survey of the position in Asia today, nor to have covered all the relevant work which
is currently in progress. We have tried to present a cross-section
of the material available to us on the life of Asian women--to give a
picture of the immense diversity to be found in the most populous
countries on earth--against a background of some of the ecological
and cultural determinants which are shared by the different sub-
regions of Asia as a whole.

Some will say that this emphasis on one section of the community,
the women, gives a distorted or unbalanced picture of the needs of
the whole population of a region and its component parts, the villages and rural towns. It may be said that the problem of massive
male unemployment is so great that there can be little justification
for this emphasis on women. Children also contribute an important
part to the economic activities and survival of their families, to
the lasting detriment of their education. Why then, does the present
study focus on women?

Current attempts to evaluate the role of women throughout the
world have shown the degree to which male ethnographers have ignored
or been unable to obtain accurate information on the activities of
women in the home, in production and in community and religious life.
The United Nations Centre for Social Development and Humanitarian
Affairs points out that to most economists, third world women are
invisible. In this Asia is no exception. It is only now beginning
to be possible to appreciate the essential functions that women play
in the economic wellbeing of the family across Asia. Statistical
data on unemployment and underemployment mask the fact that Asian
women work long, hard hours at any task which will bring a return,

however meagre--and it is often very meagre. Underemployment and
unemployment do not mean idleness. Even in societies where women are
secluded, their vital role in processing agricultural products is now
coming to be recognized.

Those who support the goals of the women's movement in the west
may deplore the low proportion of Asian women in community and
national life. It must, however, be recognized that most Asian women
do not see representation in power forums as among their most pressing requirements. Nor are they yet ready to support the feminist
contention that marriage and child-raising are not necessarily the
ideal aim for the majority of women; there are few alternative
careers in rural Asia.

It will be evident that in areas which have traditionally interested anthropologists, such as marriage customs and social structure,
a good deal of information on women is already available. A large
body of studies on family planning activities deal with demographic
aspects of population growth and the methodology of control. Far
less material is available on the complex role of motivation of both
parents and on how limitation of family size affects the position of
women (see Chapter 9). In those fields of special interest to
planners of development and improvement of rural life for women and
their families, the picture is equally limited. Precise and qualitatively significant information is fragmentary or non-existent on
division of labour, the number of hours spent by women on different
tasks, the relation between the age and number of children and
women's participation in the labour force, the distance a woman will
travel to work if she has young children and the effect upon the
running of the household and the nutritional welfare, health and
development of children of the mother's prolonged daily absence. Yet
it is only upon representative samples of precise information of this
kind that realistic plans for development of rural areas in general,
and for the improvement of women's lives in particular, can be drawn
up.

2
Approaches to the Study of Women

The western scientific tradition, which seeks to categorize and
systematize information as a starting point for understanding rural
societies, may miss much of the infinite, elusive and rapidly changing diversity which characterizes the lives of women throughout Asia.
Attempts have been made to examine the status of third world women
against different classical theoretical frameworks. Statements about
the universal subordination of women to men are familiar from a wide
range of disciplines.

An evolutionary view of the development of society proposes that
throughout much of history, defence, subsistence and reproduction
were necessary for survival. Women naturally devoted most of their
time to reproduction, participating in subsistence when men were
engaged in warfare, or in favourable conditions, such as exist in
swidden or horticulture ecosystems (Sanday, 1974). Men's domination
of women everywhere was based on male control of strategic resources.

It has generally been held that women were precluded from participating in prestigious hunting activities and that this also
contributed to early male dominance. A need to maintain a suitable
balance between hunting males and gathering/childbearing females led
to female infanticide and exogamy (Washburn and Lancaster, 1968).
The family among hunter-gatherers "is based on a strong sexual com-
plementarity, men being primarily hunters and women being carriers of
wood and water, seed collectors, camp keepers and child tenders.
Unproductive as hunting may be in certain areas, it none the less
gives men a distinctive and important subsistence role and was presumably the principal factor that created the nuclear family"
(Steward, 1968). Evidence now shows that these conclusions may be
more an expression of modern cultural bias than of primitive reality.
Mesolithic cave paintings in central India[*] include a number of

---

[*]Throughout this study the designation India or Indian will be
used to refer to the south Asian subcontinent and its inhabitants
before independence in 1947, and thereafter to modern India and its
people. Bengal or Bengali refers to an inhabitant of West Bengal
State, India, and its people. Between 1947-1971, Pakistan refers to
West and East Pakistan; thereafter the latter becomes Bangladesh.

scenes depicting women hunters (Mathpal, 1978); anthropologists
working among the Agta Negritos of eastern Luzon have found that
hunting is an important activity for some women (Estioko-Griffin and
Griffin, in press). The low status of women throughout the world
has, however, been explained on the grounds that the dangers of hunting and the physical strength required meant that men always performed this essential activity; women's primary responsibility has
always been producing and raising children. "This has led to a
differentiation of the domestic and public spheres of activity that
can, I think, be shown to shape a number of relevant aspects of human
social structure and psychology" (Rosaldo, 1974).

Emphasis on the role of hunting in the formation of the nuclear
family and on the division of labour between active males and more
sedentary females restricted to childbearing and childrearing is
considered unjustified (Tanner and Zihlman, 1976; Zihlman, 1978a).
The place of plant life in the diet of early hominids has been overlooked, and the importance of meat exaggerated, because the former
leaves few traces, while bones have remained in the archaeological
record. Indeed, some have suggested that the abundance of bone
remains is the result of animal kills or of fluviatile action. The
dentition of early hominids who lived from 2 to 4 million years ago
in the savanna environments of east Africa shows that they were
omnivorous, with coarse plant foods a major component of the diet.
There is no evidence of camp bases where women were confined to care
for the young. Rather it is assumed that small bands of kin, composed of a mother, her siblings and children, including some protective males, roamed in search of food. Females chose their mates from
a larger group, probably based on a common watercourse. The reduction in size of male canines seems to indicate selective factors;
females preferred less aggressive, more supportive males, but these
were probably not enduring ties.

These hypotheses are based both upon evidence from hominid
dental and bone morphology and from studies of the social behaviour
of the primates most closely related to man, the chimpanzees. Only
many millennia later, when Homo sapiens domesticated plants and
animals, permitting settlement, is it believed that women's role
became more restricted and the division of labour more established
(Tanner and Zihlman, 1976; Zihlman, A., 1978a and 1978b; Zihlman and
Tanner, 1978).

The structural/functional outlook which stresses the importance
of the structure of society in governing economic relations and roles
between men and women sees the status of women as being low in pre-
industrial society and improving in post-industrial society (Tiffany,
1978). The historical dialectical approach proposed by Engels views
the status of women as high in pre-industrial societies, deteriorat-
ing with the introduction of class- and capital-based societies. To
those familiar with Asia, the suggestion that egalitarian relations
between men and women characteristic of tribal groups disappear with
the introduction of stratification (Leacock, 1978) conflicts with the
varied reality of female autonomy throughout the region.

Analysis based solely on economic considerations, in which
women's role in production dominates, fails to take fully into
account important structural variables which affect women's control

over their production and income. It is less likely that women will
have power over the products of their work in patrilineal than in
bilateral societies, and matrilineal societies give women this power
only if organization is matriarchal. Matrifocal groups, which may
occur with any kinship structure, attribute major importance to the
mother role and give women some power over economic resources and
kin-related decision-making, as pointed out by Tanner (1974).
 A measure of women's status as indicated by female participation
in politics—even when that term is stretched to include the influencing of family behaviour towards kin or co-villagers (Tiffany,
1978)—gives only a partial indication of women's status in relation
to their husbands. Considerable familiarity with any given society
is necessary before this aspect can be understood. Women may exercise considerable power in patriarchal societies, even in purdah
communities, in arranging their children's marriages. This in turn
can have important economic implications for their families. Such
power is not an indicaton of female power in male society. An
approach combining evolutionary, structural, cultural and economic
factors seems essential for a clear understanding of women's position
in Asia.

THE WOMEN'S MOVEMENT: WESTERN AND THIRD WORLD ATTITUDES

 The concept of women's liberation underlies most western thinking about the modern role and status of women. Women seek freedom
from family responsibilities to achieve intellectual and emotional
satisfaction from creative or professional activities; women claim
the right to freedom as individuals, not because of or in spite of
the fact that they are women.
 One of the best-known examples of the spirit of the crusade for
freedom for women was provided by Virginia Woolf when, in 1928, she
addressed students at Girton and Newnham Colleges, Cambridge:

 For genius like Shakespeare's is not born among labouring,
 uneducated, servile people. . . . How, then, could it have been
 born among women whose work began . . . almost before they were
 out of the nursery, who were forced to it by their parents and
 held to it by all the power of law and custom? (Woolf, 1945).

How far this is from the women in Bihar, India, who visit the village
midwife, touching her feet and begging for a medicine which will stop
them from having more children (Stokes, 1975). Yet both are an
expression of the need for the liberation of women from oppression.
 During International Women's Year, 1975, there was a feeling of
fellowship among women, the awareness that they shared common problems and that their problems were beginning to receive recognition
from women—and men—all over the world. Together it would be possible to work to bring about change. Since the meeting in Mexico that
year, however, there has been some disenchantment, not so much at the
limited results of international meetings, a fact which is by now
well known, but with the sense of fellowship itself. A participant
in the Conference on Women in International Development, convened by

the Center for Research on Women at Wellesley College, Massachusetts, in June, 1976, wrote afterwards:

> One thing that became clear at the Conference on Women and Development in Wellesley, as well as the other activities that marked the International Women's Year in Mexico, is that many of our assumptions about the universality of female interests and objectives are questionable. Apart from the distinctions of class, occupation, environment, etc., the position of women differs nationally, and, even more significantly, from Third World to developed countries. The problems of women, therefore, have to be examined within many contexts and with an awareness of differences (Awe, 1977).

A participant from India reached a similar conclusion:

> Some of the younger American women who came looking for sisterhood across the ocean were, I believe, equally dis-appointed. I have no doubt that many of them found Third World women lacking in feminist energy and too identified with their existing social establishments (Mazumdar, 1977).

This signifies, perhaps, a greater awareness of reality, of the enormous gulf which separates the background to life and national concerns of women in developing and developed countries. The Wing-spread Workshop, which immediately followed the Wellesley Conference, was attended by only 63 people, the majority from third world countries who themselves played a major part in the running of the workshop, its organization and the content of the various working groups. All participants from both the developed and developing worlds found this a rewarding experience (Casal et al, 1976).

Asian women are less inclined to see themselves oppressed as women than as members of a socio-economic group. "For most Third World women, class barriers are equally if not more important obstacles to genuine equality than sexual oppression" (Safa, 1977). The amenities to which a Japanese wife is accustomed are, making allowance for different cultural requirements, not so very different from those enjoyed by a farm wife in America, and the household appliances used by a Tokyo housewife are similar to those used in New York even if population density gives the urban Japanese a far more restricted living space. It is perhaps significant that so far only in Japan has the women's movement acquired the aspects of confrontation which are familiar in the west. Levels of female education are comparable to those in the United States and exceed those in Europe. Elsewhere in Asia, where the average standard of living is far lower than in Japan, the women's movement is submerged in the aim of improving the livelihood of society in general, even though it has been demonstrated that raising the standard of living does not automatically improve the quality of life for women.

The different focus of those campaigning for greater equality for women in Asia and the west is illustrated by the following quotations. The first is from the concluding address to the Seminar on the Changing Role of Women in Rural Societies at the Fourth World

Congress for Rural Sociology in 1976, by the Filipino sociologist,
Gelia Castillo:

> What happens to men, family and children and to society in
> general, when traditional roles of wife, mother and family
> member are altered, reduced or even eliminated? To minimize
> role conflict, a woman can forego being a mother; she does not
> even have to become a wife. What is the impact of this on the
> women themselves?
>
> To an incurable romantic (and one hopes that romance has
> not gone completely out of style) it is small comfort to a woman
> to be economically independent, gainfully employed, fully inte-
> grated, equal and liberated, if in the middle of the night, she
> wakes up cold and alone.

The second quotation comes from Simone de Beauvoir (1949):

> Le besoin biologique--désir sexuel et désir d'une
> posterité--qui met le mâle sous la dépendance de la femelle n'a
> pas affranchi socialement la femme. Le maître et l'esclave
> aussi sont unis par un besoin économique réciproque qui ne
> libère pas l'esclave . . . Or la femme a toujours été, sinon
> l'esclave de l'homme, du moins sa vassale; les deux sexes ne se
> sont jamais partagé le monde à égalité.
>
> Ce qui est certain, c'est qu'aujourd'hui il est trés
> difficile aux femmes d'assumer à la fois leur condition
> d'individu autonome et leur destin féminin; c'est là la source
> de ces maladresses, de ces malaises qui les font parfois
> considérer comme "un sexe perdu". Et sans doute il est plus
> confortable de subir un aveugle esclavage que de travailler à
> s'affranchir; les morts aussi sont mieux adaptés à la terre que
> les vivants.

> Biological need--the sexual urge and desire for offspring—
> which makes men dependent on women has not liberated women
> socially. Master and slave are also united by reciprocal eco-
> nomic need, which does not free the slave. . . . Woman has
> always been, if not the slave of man, at least his vassal. The
> two sexes have never shared the world in an egalitarian way.
>
> What is certain is that today it is very difficult for
> women to manifest at the same time their autonomous individual-
> ity and their feminine destiny; in this lies the source of
> their awkwardness, their discomfort, which sometimes causes
> them to be considered a "lost sex." And without doubt it is
> more comfortable to submit to a blind slavery than to work to
> free oneself. The dead, too, are better adapted to the earth
> than are the living.

The western woman seeks liberation as an individual, while the
Asian woman seeks greater satisfaction by the improvement of her
family's economic situation and of her status within the family.
Few Asian women, even today, would support the concept expressed in
the early part of this century by Arishima Takeo's Yoko Satsuki,

when she reflected, "He had never made the smallest effort to realize, it seemed to her, how closely for a woman the whole question of marriage is linked to that of livelihood, how much a woman suffers under the constraints this link implies (Arishima, 1919).

IMPLICATIONS OF SOCIOBIOLOGY

Strathern (1978) has remarked that "anthropologists are increasingly being called upon to explain the subordination of women to men as a cultural rather than a natural fact, giving hope that women can work to change this cultural bias." But some specialists oppose a cultural explanation of women's status. Profound controversy has been caused by the more extreme proponents of sociobiology who seek to show that much of human behaviour can be explained in terms of physiology. More precisely, behaviour is considered to be directed towards maximizing one's genetic representation in the next generation, a concept often contracted to the term "inclusive fitness." This implies that "altruism" is devoted primarily to those who share some of one's genes--nuclear family and kin.

This theory implies that the traditional role of women has been and is determined above all by the biological imperative of bearing and rearing children. The supporters of this school have been labelled biological reductionists by their opponents, the cultural determinists. The latter, spearheaded by leaders of the women's movement of different academic specializations, believe that the fundamental inequalities of society are wholly cultural in origin and have been determined from time immemorial by those in control of society: men. This controversy has been admirably analyzed by 2 sociologists interested in biology:

> Some of the tenacity with which extreme cultural relativists cling to their position may come from a misunderstanding of biological method and prediction. The assumption that biology determines behaviour, especially in complex species, is wrong. At its strongest, biology predisposes animals to act in certain ways; at its weakest, it is but one influence among many. Biology is not destiny, it is statistical probability. . . . Appreciating the reciprocity between what the individual brings to his social situation and how the situation affects him avoids the sterile, obsolete contest between nature and nurture. It then becomes possible to scientifically enquire into both the conditions and preconditions of social life. . . . There are probably no direct physiological causes for most social behaviour. The strength and appeal of this argument lies in its attention to human variability and flexibility, and in not raising the unappealing specter of determined limits on human freedom (Tiger and Shepher, 1977).

Investigations of working patterns and daily life over three generations in a number of Israeli kibbutzim showed that whereas during the difficult early years women performed many "male" tasks, younger generations have increasingly gravitated towards "female"

tasks. In the early years there was minimal distinction between male
and female clothing; today some kibbutzim have beauty parlours and
clothing is chosen individually. Originally children were raised and
slept in children's houses; over the years women have won more time
with their children and the nuclear family has gained in importance,
with some kibbutzim permitting children to sleep at home. Despite
every encouragement to take part in leadership roles, women are less
active than men and younger women less active than those of middle
age (Tiger and Shepher, 1977). The original idealism which aimed at
eliminating sex inequalities has been diluted by the women whose lot
it hoped to improve.

This supports the view of the more moderate sociobiologists who
acknowledge that behaviour is not tightly linked to genetics but that
all behaviour requires interaction with the environment and that
humans adapt to environment in terms of a socially transmitted system
of behaviour and meanings called culture, which is itself evolving.
Thus, "the link between the genetic substrate and most human behaviour is probabilistic rather than deterministic. . . . Sociobiology
will never find that women are innately superior or inferior to men,
but it may be that women on the whole are more likely than are men to
find some tasks pleasurable and, therefore, to learn them more
easily" (Barkow, 1978). In the light of the Israeli evidence, it is
clear that many women do not enjoy being too rigidly cut off from
raising their own children. But the sociobiologists do not insist
that all women are best left to run their own homes and raise their
children, while men are to be confined to productive occupations
outside the home.

The cultural pressures of socialization alone cannot adequately
account for the finding from studies of young children that there is
a greater tendency for girls to be nurturant and integrative, and
boys more aggressive and self-reliant (Parker and Parker, 1979).
Similar results from investigations of the development of behaviour
in infants have been linked to superior auditory-perceptual and
linguistic abilities in females and visual-spatial advantages for
males. Studies of non-human primates also demonstrate greater
aggression and tendency to explore in males, and higher levels of
sociability and nurturant behaviour in females, characteristics which
are linked to the primary roles of defence for males and of child-
raising for females. However, while granting an extra-cultural basis
for some of the behavioural differences between males and females,
Parker and Parker (loc. cit.) reject these as being sufficient explanation for the prevalence of the myth of male superiority, since
women's contribution to subsistence has often been quantitatively and
qualitatively as important as that of men. Rather they believe that
male activities have been more demanding and difficult than those of
women, and that the myth of male superiority has been functionally
adaptive as a spur to male achievement in the face of danger or
difficulty.

PRIMARY OBJECTIVES OF ASIAN WOMEN

Virginia Woolf was talking to the Cambridge students about creative talent and the impossibility of its ever being expressed when
women were financially dependent on their parents or husbands, when
all their time was devoted to domestic activities and when they
totally lacked privacy. Not many western women lay claim to genius;
they simply ask for the same freedom to achieve mental growth in any
activity, however mundane, which gives them financial independence
and takes them temporarily away from their homes.

Few Asian women, even in countries with a long history of female
literacy and higher education as in Japan, work to achieve purely
personal goals, though some among the educated professional élite of
capital cities are beginning to support concepts of personal intellectual satisfaction in work. A 25-year-old graduate in Ibaraki
Prefecture, Japan, married with one son, was given a questionnaire on
attitudes towards female independence (which theoretically she
strongly supported) by her sister, a student in sociology. Her
responses were so home-oriented that the student finally commented
sharply, "Now that you are married you are just another woman, aren't
you?" (Japan Times Weekly, Feb. 18, 1978).

Marriage in Korea is the strongest influence on withdrawal from
the labour force, showing that for most women the traditional role of
wife and mother is more important than considerations of self-
fulfilment or of economic requirements (Lee and Cho, 1976). This is
hardly surprising when parents often give "getting a good husband" as
the chief reason for educating their daughters. "Colleges and universities provide respectable waiting places for girls who wish to
get married" (Srinivas, 1977). For the vast majority of Asian women
who work, both in rural and urban areas, the reasons are economic and
almost all but the most highly educated and career-oriented would
prefer to stay at home and look after their children.

Asian women see themselves and are seen by their societies as
one component of a family, and often of an extended group related by
birth and marriage. The concept of individuality, still less individual freedom, is alien. It has been suggested that the widespread
practice of childrearing by siblings only a few years older may
inhibit individual differentiation of personality, thus preparing
children for societies in which personal achievement and independence
are not common options (Weisner and Gallimore, 1977). Friendships
for Asian women tend largely to be among kin and neighbourhoods,
making unlikely the enlarging of mental horizons and fostering of a
sense of separateness. Rural schools are attended by children of
relatively homogeneous backgrounds. In India, men make friends with
those from their own jati, often more commonly within the same jati
division, and this applies even more strongly to women (Mandelbaum,
1972). Close friendships between men across caste lines do sometimes
occur, though never when ritual distance is very great (Minturn and
Hitchcock, 1966). These friendships begin in school and are maintained thereafter, so the tendency may be increasing, at least for
boys.

The aspirations of Asian women are directed towards their
families; they seek enhanced status for the family and, above all,

better family economic wellbeing: a bigger, better house, more and better quality land, financial security, freedom from worry. Individual goals are rarely mentioned. In the Philippines, not only low-income but also career wives give financial reasons as the chief motivation for work; self-satisfaction and professional growth are secondary. Psychological and social motivations are important only among those with higher levels of education (Gonzalez and Hollnsteiner, 1976).

Middle-class women pride themselves on being "housewives only," while their western counterparts seek to break out of the monotony and solitude of housework for paid employment, provided they can find suitable child care facilities and job security during pregnancy. As pressure of population on scarce land resources diminishes the size of the family plot in Asia with each succeeding generation, Asian women must increasingly seek every possible alternative source of income. Government support is minimal; the family members must meet her needs for child and home care, and she must reduce the time taken off for childbirth and nursing to a minimum.

Only in the cities have small numbers of women graduates continued to work after marriage, although this tendency is likely to increase as standards of living rise more swiftly than the income of the principal breadwinner. These women are beginning to face the same problems of suitable child care facilities as are western women and those in eastern Europe, since city families are predominantly nuclear and older family members may not be at hand to help out. The problem is already acute in Japan. Educated city women are likely to experience the same crisis in middle life as are western women when, having raised their children, they find themselves with inadequate occupation. It has been noted in Korea that there is a growing multiplicity of possible goals, due to changes in society's expectations of women, accompanied by slower development of social institutions through which women can achieve such new goals (Koh, 1978). The urban poor everywhere are under the same economic pressures to work as are the rural poor.

Some aspects of improving life for women are universal, particularly those relating to inequality of pay. In 1977, a group of housewives demonstrated in London for the payment of housework, a call echoed by Japanese liberationists (Lebra, 1976). Factual support for the Japanese claim comes from the estimate that the total value of household labour was equivalent in 1976 to 37.3 per cent of total national income. The Leisure Development Center calculates that the general housework performed by the average Japanese woman—cooking, childrearing, etc.—is worth 63,000 yen per month, while home tasks performed by her husband—carpentry, gardening, repairs—are worth only 17,000 yen (Japan Times Weekly, May 6, 1978).

In 1978, the Osaka District Court ruled that a woman injured in a traffic accident should be compensated for loss of earnings both as office worker and as housewife, provided the total remained within the average national wage for women of her age (Japan Times Weekly, Feb. 11, 1978). This was hardly a signal victory in a country where women's wages are often half those of men, except during the early years of employment. Chinese women usually receive fewer work points in the communes, since part of their time is devoted to housework

which does not receive work points. A production brigade in Anhwei
established that women were transplanting more seedlings than men,
but ranked lower in the work point scale (David Bonavia, Far Eastern
Economic Review, April 14, 1978).

MULTIPLE ROLES

In most parts of the world the working woman is virtually performing two jobs, that of homemaker/child raiser and that of professional or employed worker. There has recently been considerable
discussion of the capacity of Communist governments to achieve the
Marxist goal of equality between the sexes (Jancar, 1976). This
debate has concentrated chiefly on eastern Europe, but conclusions
may apply in Asia. It is perhaps unduly western in orientation to
reproach Communist policies for aiming at the service of both sexes
to the state rather than at the "self-realization" of women--or men.
But the official view that only Communism can liberate--indeed has
liberated--women, is contested by the facts so far. Employment has
indeed risen in all countries, but the concept of the nuclear family,
which continues everywhere, has maintained traditional sex roles,
especially for women, so that today "women are performing four
roles--wife, housekeeper, child-rearer and mother--and no Communist
state has yet succeeded in creating an infrastructure of social
services necessary to reduce this load" (Jancar, loc. cit.). Women
account for over half the total Soviet labour force, with 92 per cent
of all women of working age either working or studying. Shopping and
housework take between 4 to 6 hours daily, leaving women inadequate
time for child care and none for themselves (The Economist, June 23,
1979). In January, 1981, new regulations banned the use of women in
over 400 occupations which are considered too demanding or unsuitable. This has been done despite a critical shortage of manpower
because the sharp fall in the birth rate, which has continued since
the 1960's, has led the authorities to realize that women exhausted
by a heavy workload produce smaller families. The average Russian
family in 1980 had only one child (The Times, Dec. 30, 1980). In
theory, the new regulations are a reversal of the Communist ideology
of liberating women from housework.
    Jancar (1976) proposes a universally applicable theoretical
framework for the attainment of equality and Table 2.1 illustrates
historical evolution under different regimes.
    It is proposed that an inadequate economic base has retarded
progress towards equality in China. Women's battles up to the 1950's
were merely to be recognized as thinking beings, and only subsequently have they given more attention to equal pay, opportunities
for political participation and freedom from housework (Chan, 1974).
    Whatever system prevails, the physical burden of these multiple
roles falls particularly heavily on a poor rural Asian woman who is
almost certainly inadequately nourished (Whyte, 1974), who has never
dreamed of the household gadgets which lighten labour elsewhere, for
whom even piped water is a rarity, and who has to toil long hours in
high temperatures on the backbreaking tasks involved in the agricultural cycle in the tropics and subtropics.

TABLE 2.1
Systems, Sexual Equality and Modernization

Regime Type	Early Phase of Modernization	Late Phase of Modernization
High authoritarian	Progressive with respect to sexual equality: high mobilization	Regressive with respect to equality
Pluralistic	Regressive with respect to sexual equality: low mobilization	Progressive with respect to sexual equality

Source: Jancar, 1976.

3
Status in Different Communities

It might be assumed that in traditional societies the status of women as seen by their communities and the way in which they view themselves largely coincide. One does not expect the degree of conflict between society's expectations of women and young women's own aspirations, which is fairly common in modern society. It must be admitted, however, that while a good deal is known about the status of women in Asia, very little is known of the ambitions or frustrations of women themselves. An anthropologist in Bangladesh had the utmost difficulty in eliciting opinions from women, so unaccustomed were they to being asked for their views (Ellickson, 1976).

DEFINITION OF STATUS

The term status has been discarded by some analysts as being too general; it is used here to convey its customary meaning both of standing and of ascribed respect, essentially abstract concepts understood in all communities. Role, by contrast, implies concrete activities. Status is also held to signify the degree to which women have authority or power in the domestic and/or public domain (Sanday, 1974). Authority usually implies the right to control the use of joint resources and the lives of others, while power is defined as the ability to influence decisions made by those with authority. The status of women in Asia is more closely linked to their exercise of power than to their much rarer exercise of authority. Stoler (1977) prefers the more specific terms female autonomy and social power to status. She defines female autonomy as the extent to which women exercise control over their own lives and returns from their labour vis-à-vis men. Social power signifies the extent to which women exercise control over the lives of others outside the domestic sphere.

In considering status in its broadest sense, one has to beware of the discrepancy between the élite model for behaviour and custom which tradition holds and actual behaviour which, especially for lower socio-economic groups, may diverge considerably from the ideal, usually for economic reasons. In northern Taiwan, for example, in the traditional and most valued form of marriage a mature girl comes

17

to the home of her affines as a bride. In the minor and formerly
more common form of marriage, a young girl is brought up with her
future spouse by her affines and married at maturity (Wolf, A.,
1975).

It is not always easy for an outsider to discern the real, as
opposed to the traditional and formal, status of a woman in her own
family and community. A woman may and often does have a prominent
position within her own family but a very minor one in her community.
In Korea, women are officially and formally denigrated, but are in
fact often self-assertive and highly valued (Brandt, 1971). Formal
indicators point to complete male dominance. It is unseemly, border-
ing on indecent, for open affection to be shown by husband to wife in
public; to support one's wife in a dispute with one's mother is
impious. Men are supposed to, and usually do, control finances, make
important decisions and represent the family in all official con-
texts. Women have no formal role in administrative or political
matters and do not attend village meetings, even as spectators. In
reality, however, an atmosphere of harmony is discernible in many
homes, and male superiority is asserted in proportion to the formal-
ity of the occasion. In one village studied, several women are more
competent than their husbands. Village women do not have subservient
personalities (Brandt, loc. cit.). It is easy for the casual
observer to be deceived by stereotyped behaviour. A husband known as
a cuckold throughout the village was none the less followed at a
respectful distance by his errant wife on the way to their field, and
she carried the heavier load.

Even an anthropologist thoroughly versed in the culture of the
group he is studying, well acquainted with individuals over a number
of years, may still find it difficult to ascertain correctly whether
a given form of behaviour is determined by cultural norms or by
individual personality (Jacobson, 1978). In the Mysore village
studied by Srinivas (1976), dominance of one spouse over the other
varied according to the strength of personality of the partners, a
finding with which most anthropologists would agree.

ECONOMIC CONTRIBUTION AND STATUS

Many studies have drawn correlations between the function or
role of women in production and their status in society. In China,
"forced seclusion, imposed ignorance, lack of educational opportunities, discrimination against working women and repressive marriage
customs inevitably resulted in women's economic dependence in traditional society" (Yang, 1959). Economic dependence implied inferior
status. Now the rural New Territories of Hong Kong show consistently
rising status for young women, based on the availability of jobs,
especially in city factories, and an independent income (Baker,
1968).

In a pioneer study on women in development, Boserup (1970) con-
cludes that where population is sparse and swidden (shifting cultivation) the basis of the economy, women perform most of the work;
with greater density of population and plough agriculture, men do
more work than women, and where land is irrigated and intensively

farmed, both put in a great deal of hard work. Boserup associates the first and last categories with higher status for women than the second. How far can these conclusions be applied to Asia? On the whole they can. In tribal societies, women are esteemed members of their hunting/collecting or swidden communities. In the former, the roots and other forest produce gathered by women provide the regular staple food of the community, but the supply of meat from the hunting of men is sporadic. In family decisions, women have an equal say with their husbands, and often a considerable role in community affairs, especially in those groups where men are customarily absent for weeks or even months, formerly headhunting, more recently on expeditions for collecting jungle produce for sale. In both such groups, women's contribution to subsistence is essential.

Women in early India supervised agriculture, animal husbandry and vegetable gardens. In modern Asia, however, women do not generally enjoy high status in regions of settled, dryland cultivation, thus conforming to Boserup's second category where men do more work than women.

Women enjoyed relatively high status in early China when it has been assumed that they were food-gatherers (Lang, 1968) and in the early stages of agriculture and pottery-making before the invention of the plough and the potter's wheel gave these tasks to men. Indeed, burial patterns during the Neolithic Ch'ing-lian-kiang culture (the earliest in the lower Yangtze in Kiangsu, Anhwei and Chekiang) seem to indicate that society was organized in clans, was possibly matriarchal and there was no sexual division of labour (Shih, 1974). To the north the slightly later Liu-lin culture of southern Shantung and north Kiangsu, however, appeared to be patriarchal and family-based. The Biographies of Women, ranging from peasant women to the wives of emperors and covering the legendary period to the late Han in the first century B.C., indicate that women had greater freedom of movement and participated more in work outside the home in the earlier period than subsequently (O'Hara, 1971).

The position of women deteriorated under the feudalism of Chou times among the nobility, but peasant women were still comparatively free. As feudal structure came to be replaced by centralized bureaucracy under the empire and family structure increasingly followed the upper-class patriarchal model which was enshrined in the teachings of Confucius, the poor and middle classes observed as best they could the manners of the upper classes; women became wholly subservient to their fathers, their husbands and subsequently in theory to their sons.* Since the poor were unable to afford the cost of divorce and a second marriage, their wives received more considerate treatment than those of the wealthier. Women achieved more freedom

---

*Women were not wholly without sympathy in their circumscribed lives. Li Ju-chen's traveller, Lin Chih-yang, reached the Land of Women, where traditional sex roles were reversed. He had to undergo the agony of ear-piercing and foot-binding, and was meticulously prepared to await the pleasure of the female ruler of the country (from the Ching-hua Yuan, written in the mid-Ch'ing dynasty). (Quoted by Brandauer, 1977.)

in Kwangtung, Kwangsi and Fukien than in the north and participated
more regularly in field work (Lang, 1968).

In the rice-dominated economy of Japan, rural women have enjoyed
greater freedom in the past, particularly in the southwest where
village structure was of a more egalitarian type, ruled by consensus.
The position of the bride was more secure and the status of women in
general higher than in the northeast, where the vertically oriented
dozoku structure predominated (Johnson, 1967). A more egalitarian
marital relationship characterized the southwest, particularly the
fishing villages where men were absent at sea and women assumed day-
to-day authority; they maintained relations with their own parents,
resulting in a greater tendency towards bilateral kinship structure.
With the onset of modernization at the beginning of the Meiji period
(1868) the status of women in rural areas became progressively lower
since samurai (Confucian) norms spread to other groups. This was
reinforced by the new uniformity of behaviour which resulted from
service in the army and from compulsory education which stressed
traditional values. None the less, fishing villages were too poor to
attempt to improve their status by the adoption of upper-class ways
(de Vos and Wagatsuma, 1973b).

Women have always played an important role in production on
Japanese farms. The difference in status between farming and fishing
villages relates not so much to function as to the authority which
fishermen's wives must exercise during the increasingly long absences
of their husbands. The farmer's wife can communicate with her husband in the city, but the fisherman's wife cannot reach her husband
at sea.

When one comes to consider Boserup's third category, that of
irrigated land where women are as much involved as men and where
their status should be correspondingly high, the immense variety of
custom in Asia conflicts with her scheme. In southeast Asia women
work in padi cultivation as intensively as men, but not, if they can
afford it, in Bangladesh or Bengal. In lower socio-economic groups
in north India women must work in the fields; they predominate among
landless labourers in some areas of the south. Nowhere do they enjoy
the equality of women padi workers in southeast Asia. Women perform
70 per cent of all farm work in Japan, but nominally, at least, they
seek the decisions of their husbands, even when they are working in
distant cities. It has been cautiously concluded that female production is a necessary but not sufficient condition for the development
of female status (Sanday, 1973); there are no universals in society
and culture (Needham, 1973).

A study comparing pastoral and agricultural societies in the
Balkans reveals that pastoralism requires solidarity among male members of a co-operative kin group, while women have low status
(Denich, 1974). It would be interesting to compare the status of
women among nomadic and migratory groups in south Asia. In nomadic
groups, the whole family moves together; in migratory groups only the
men move. The health and levels of education of family members left
in the village must be higher than among nomads. How does the necessity of making decisions during the six-month absence of men affect
the position of women? Is there any difference today in the position
of women among China's pastoralists of minority groups and among

neighbouring Han practising settled agriculture?

Murdock (1949) believed that ownership of land enhanced female status, but even where land is inherited matrilineally, actual power may reside with men--with a woman's uncle or brother, rather than with her husband or herself. As matrilineal Nayar households in Kerala, India, which shared the proceeds from land owned and worked jointly, came to be divided and eventually replaced by nuclear households, there were changes in the status of women (Fuller, 1976). Women still have important rights over property, but men bequeath property to their own children, no longer to their sisters' children. "Today husbands dominate their wives in a way which was intrinsically impossible when they did not live together, but men also seem to have greater power over women than they used to" (Fuller, loc. cit.). Tambiah (1973) considers ownership of land by women conducive to bilateral kinship structure and ambilocality, both of which appear associated with higher status for women. Murdock's theory appears to hold for Asia. While women rarely held land in traditional China or today in Korea ("daughters inherit nothing but personal memories"-- Brandt, 1971) or the south Asian subcontinent, women often hold land in southeast Asia, where society is more egalitarian.

Access to opportunities for production has been shown to have bearing on the standing of women in society. In north India, many agricultural tasks are male preserves, while in Islamic communities in India and Bangladesh women do not generally work in the fields. In south India, however, female agricultural labour is common and indeed, dominant in the rice-producing region of Tanjore. Greater value is attributed to women in the south than in the north (Leonard and Leonard, 1981).

It has been suggested that women have lower status than men because their tasks are mainly subsistence-oriented, while men work on cash crops (Boserup, 1970). This appears to apply more to Africa than to Asia, where women have been associated with men in work on cash crops. Others believe that it is not so much subsistence tasks as lack of ownership of the means of production which brings lower status (Castillo, 1976a).

In Java, women gain autonomy and economic independence through the flexibility of the sources of income available to them. Here it is not just the type of production, but the productive relations involved which are important for social power (Stoler, 1977). Female autonomy and social power are functions of their access to strategic resources within the domestic and social sphere, but economic independence of the poor does not mean social power. It may be asked whether these aspects of status will not become increasingly important as size of plots become smaller and less able to meet the subsistence needs of families. However, access to these strategic resources is independent of sexual distinctions, despite the clear division of labour between the sexes in rural Java (Stoler, loc. cit.).

The relation between earning capacity, status and autonomy within the family in India depends to a great extent on the status of a woman's earning activity (Indian Council of Social Science Research [ICSSR], 1975). Women employed as wage labourers or unskilled and menial workers do not enjoy higher status, but women in high prestige jobs may. The value which society places on different tasks is important; many observers have noted that the agricultural tasks performed by women are invariably of lower status than those performed by men. Men usually plough and control draft animals, whereas women more often carry out operations by hand (Boserup, 1970).

In southeast Asia, women commonly participate in petty marketing, but enterprises involving the accumulation of capital, both financial and in equipment, are in the hands of men and their activities are more highly regarded. Middlewomen operating between a central Javanese village and Yogyakarta have considerable economic independence, but not economic power (Stoler, 1977). Among poor households, a woman's earnings provide her with an important position within the household economy; among wealthier households such earnings provide her with the material basis for social power (Stoler, loc. cit.). Similar conclusions could be reached in Malaysia, particularly in the northeast.

Some believe that women's role in production is less significant in determining her status than is kinship organization. Patrilineal, patriarchal groups invariably confer low actual (though, as in south Asia, sometimes high ideal) status on women, while in matrilineal, matriarchal groups, women are dominant. Bilateral societies range between these extremes. Tribal women in India, for example, are equally productive irrespective of the prevailing kinship pattern, but have authority only in matriarchal groups (Sachchidananda, 1978). Comparison of polyandrous groups in the Himalaya leads to the same conclusion (Nandi, 1977). However, it still seems possible to demonstrate that women in control of the economic returns from their production invariably have higher status than those who are not, irrespective of kinship mode.

PURDAH

Purdah has long been viewed as implying a much inferior status for women. This may perhaps represent a simplistic, western bias. It is true that seclusion automatically reduces a woman's freedom of movement and above all her opportunities for economic independence by means of paid work. In this sense, purdah has an effect similar to footbinding in traditional China. Undoubtedly, the social status of women is low in communities practising purdah. But can it also be concluded that a woman's status in her own home is any lower than that of unveiled women at either socio-economic extreme in her own society, or of women in a comparable socio-economic position in societies where seclusion is not the norm?

Opportunities for employment are severely restricted in Bangladesh, even at higher levels of education (Martius von Harder, 1977), and in Pakistan, by inadequate provision of separate facilities for women at their place of work. Opportunities for work for rural women in Bangladesh are limited by their inability to move beyond their baris (Martius von Harder, loc. cit.) although the availability of "portable seclusion" in the form of the burqa has offset these restrictions in Pakistan and Bangladesh (Papanek, 1971). The acquisition of knowledge of improved crop processing and household

techniques is limited by the fact that the information has to come
from men, with whom a village woman cannot have contact (Martius von
Harder, 1977). Yet a rural women in seclusion is as fully and use-
fully occupied as is a woman working in the fields (Khatun and Rani,
1977; Martius von Harder, 1977).

In a broad sense, the purdah system is related to status, since
the poor cannot afford to forego income or pay for the extra service
required. It is related also to social distance and the maintenance
of moral standards, expressed as "separate worlds" and "symbolic
shelter" (Papanek, 1971). "In a culture where male pride is a very
significant--and very fragile--element of identity and status, the
seclusion of women is an important aspect of male control" (Papanek,
loc. cit.). Muslim purdah does not apply within the immediate kin
group, only outside; Punjabi women do not wear the veil in their
villages, but only when they go to town. Hindu purdah is based on a
set of avoidance rules between a woman and her male affines. However, in an Indian Muslim village women observe purdah before their
father-in-law and older brothers-in-law exactly as does a Hindu
woman[*] (Vreede de Stuers, 1968). Seclusion of women arose in Islamic
society because of men's distrust of other men, while the Hindu woman
was secluded because of men's distrust of her purportedly licentious
nature. The Laws of Manu state: "If she be chaste, it is because
she has not found a proper man, place or opportunity" (Kapadia,
1966).

The "separate worlds" denote the strict division of labour, yet
a high degree of interdependence in purdah society. "Symbolic
shelter" is provided as protection against sexual desire and a potentially hostile world outside the home; dominance and dependency are
integral to its operation. Women so sheltered are important demon-
strators of status and their behaviour is important in terms of
honour and family pride, underlining the male ability to control his
environment. Emphasis on female purity stresses the role of procrea-
tion (Papanek, 1973).

Hindu avoidance patterns, represented by veiling the face,
reduce friction between members of extended families, since a junior
bride is invisible to her husband's older brothers, father and uncles
and is thus theoretically not sexually competitive with their wives.
Equally, since the veil further prevents easy interaction between
spouses before a woman's mother-in-law, this most frequent source of
conflict is somewhat reduced (Sharma, 1978). All male members of a
village in the hill tracts of northern India are considered courtesy
kin by women, who must veil themselves and behave circumspectly

---

[*]Hindu avoidance patterns may apply even to the young. When
Nirad Chaudhuri was taken to his ancestral village in former East
Bengal, "we could never find a house or place where there was not at
least one uncle, nephew or cousin. Furthermore at five years old I
was the uncle of half a dozen grown-ups. . . . Nothing disappointed
me more in 1907 at the age of nine than not to have been permitted to
go near a bride, in fact to have been turned out after having sneaked
into the room, because her status in relation to mine was that of
daughter-in-law" (Chaudhuri, 1951).

before all senior to her husband. The low status of a young bride is
thus compounded by her inability to approach any senior member of her
affinal village--for example a panchayat leader--who might be able to
redress her wrongs (Sharma, loc. cit.).

There was no purdah in pre-Muslim times in India, although the
defenceless (daughters and widows) might remain within the confines
of the home. The ruling classes preferred to veil their women from
common sight. Only after the advent of the Muslims, however, was
purdah adopted, in imitation of the conquerors, and only in the north
and in the Muslim community of Hyderabad, Andhra Pradesh (Altekar,
1959).

It is a matter for speculation why those who adopted Islam in
south Asia imposed seclusion on women, while in southeast Asia this
did not occur. Dube (1978a) has suggested that seclusion was less
likely to be enforced in matrilineal or bilateral societies than in
patrilineal groups which subscribed to the notion that women belonged
to men. It cannot be said, however, that the purdah ethic was absent
in southeast Asia in the past. Isabella Bird (1883), who travelled
in the Malay peninsula 100 years ago, wrote, "They seclude their
women to a great extent, and under ordinary circumstances the
slightest courtesy shown by a European man to a Malay woman would be
a deadly insult, and at the sight of a man in the distance the women
hastily cover their faces."

Emily Innes (1885), who lived in Malaya where her husband was a
government servant from 1876 until 1882, also wrote, "Another sarong
is then thrown over the head and shoulders by the common women as a
veil, and when in the presence of men, this is drawn up over the face
till only a narrow slit is left open for the eyes. Women of a
superior class generally wear veils of cambric, muslin or figured
net." Women veiled their faces before strangers until comparatively
recent decades (Datuk Haji Mohammed Yusof Bangs, personal communication, 1979). Should one assume that lower socio-economic groups had
greater liberty, since Sir Frank Swettenham noted the predominance of
women in the markets of Kelantan? Or was this due rather to the
pronounced independence of women in northeast Malaya, an area which
remained relatively isolated from the western coast until after the
Second World War? At the time Isabella Bird and Emily Innes were
writing, knowledge of Malay custom was confined to western and
southern Malaya; few Europeans had visited the east coast. The
(British) Adviser from the Kingdom of Siam to the Raja of Kelantan
during the first decade of the twentieth century noted that women
wore a shawl (kelumbong) over head and shoulders which was intended
to cover the face, but which was rarely so used. Kelantan women
followed the customs of Siamese, Burmese and Cambodians, moving about
"with perfect freedom, buying and selling in the markets and in the
shops, visiting their friends and assisting their husbands in their
agricultural pursuits" (Graham, 1908). Seclusion of women is unknown
in aboriginal communities in Malaysia.

The segregation of girls before marriage is more strict in
Islamic southeast Asia than in Thailand or the Philippines, and is
thus in keeping with the norms of seclusion. It seems likely that
the secularization of education following the independence of Malaya
in 1957 somewhat mitigated the seclusion of young teenage girls and

contributed to the discarding of the head shawl. This is used exten-
sively by girls attending religious schools. Women who belong to
Islamic revivalist movements, which have gained support in the late
1970's, wear a head scarf which leaves the face visible only between
eyebrows and chin.

In modern India, a study of purdah revealed a whole range of
attitudes, from women who retain the burqa as an article of faith,
despite modernizing pressures from their husbands, to the poor who
are unable to afford its protection, but observe all the tenets of
purdah behaviour as best they can and look forward to the day when
their husbands or their sons will be able to afford to keep them
secluded in their homes. There are also young women who study
unveiled at college, but who wear their burqas when they return home,
to avoid hurting family feelings. Mothers living a life of seclusion
said they did not want their daughters to follow their example.
Purdah, whether maintained from religious conviction, a desire to
purify Islamic practices, or as a form of social propriety, is thus
described as being a state of mind (Vreede de Stuers, 1968). Those
who work in the fields unveiled, but take care to avoid men to whom
theoretically they could be married, are observing "unmanifested"
purdah.

Baluchi women are able to remain secluded in their homes because
of the availability of labour from pastoral nomads. Purdah here is
seen as a highly ritualized expression of explicit values, usually
referred to as "honour" and "shame", which are directly concerned
with the status of women. Male honour is dependent upon the unsul-
lied honour of women who, having more inherent shame than men, must
be protected and secluded (Pastner, 1974).

The ending of purdah restrictions is seen as a prerequisite to
improving the position of women in those Islamic societies which
impose seclusion. Attempts at abolishing purdah in Pakistan, chiefly
in the cities, led initially to social ostracism (Alvi, 1977). The
wife of Abdul Wali Khan, the Pathan leader, has emerged as a politi-
cian in her own right; she believes that a more favourable position
can be attained in society without challenging some of its norms.
"It's the tradition, even if we try we can't go without purdah. It
doesn't harm a woman to cover her head or her arms, so I won't oppose
it" (Begum Nasim Wali Khan to Richard Wigg, The Times, Aug. 25,
1977). After a detailed study of the role of women in Comilla
District, Bangladesh, an anthropologist concluded that overcoming
seclusion was a precondition for the integration of women in the
economic life of the country, but any improvements must take local
values into account (Martius von Harder, 1977).

One direct consequence of the norms of decency imposed by purdah
has been the stigma attached to nursing as a profession in south
Asia. Greater respect for this calling has been growing in India and
nurses and other medical and health technicians are now 72.2 per cent
female (Rao, 1978). In Pakistan, however, there are only 6,725
registered nurses, 95 per cent of whom are female (Shah, 1978).
Before the separation of Bangladesh, in 1965 there was one nurse per
32,000 of population and one doctor per 7,000 (Papanek, 1971). In
East Pakistan in 1947 there were only 50 nurses. In Bangladesh
today, while 1,000 out of 8,000 doctors (of whom 5,047 are graduates)

are female, there are only 1,350 nurses, of whom 1,180 are female.
This signifies one doctor per 10,000 of population, and one nurse per
80,000 (Sattar, 1978). Middle-class males look on nursing with a
disfavour only exceeded by that accorded to acting as a profession
for women. Nursing is considered both a threat to morals and in conflict with purdah requirements (Jahan, 1975). Nurses are therefore
more than usually overworked and under-rewarded in Bangladesh. Some
suggestions have been made to improve their prospects (Alam, 1975).

INFLUENCE OF MAJOR RELIGIONS ON STATUS

We have considered the bearing which economic factors have on
women's status, since they are seen by most observers to be crucial.
There is, however, a fundamental influence exerted by tradition but
with relations to economics which are not always clear. The effect
of the major religions seems at first sight to be equally important,
particularly that of Hinduism. This has influenced Indian society so
fundamentally that its traditions have not been eliminated even among
those practising the other religions subsequently adopted.
The oldest sacred text in Hinduism, the Rigveda (middle of the
second millennium B.C.) calls upon the wife to rule supreme, and the
Mahabharata (400-200 B.C.) considers women worthy to worship; it
further claims that if women are unhappy in a society, that society
cannot be successful in any field. Sons at this time were required
to respect their mothers even more than their fathers. The
Upanishads (about 800 B.C.) tell of many women taking a leading role
in highly learned discussions. It was only later in the time of the
lawgivers that woman's position deteriorated (Sen, 1961).
In Vedic times, daughters could undertake studies of the scrip-
tures and sacrifice to the gods, but when ancestor worship increased
in importance, only sons could sacrifice (Altekar, 1959). As prepuberty marriage gained wide acceptance from the beginning of the
modern era and as sub-caste complexity made the choice of a partner
increasingly difficult, so the anxiety caused by daughters made them
progressively less welcome (Altekar, loc. cit.). Many Indian
scholars have associated women's low status with the mingling of
Aryan invaders with the original population, whose women they took as
wives. Automatically wives were of low caste status. By about 500
B.C. women had come to hold inferior status, were considered danger-
ously polluting, scheming temptresses who must be kept within care-
fully circumscribed limits to protect the ritual purity and wellbeing
of men (Dube, 1963). The sexual appetites of women were believed to
be greater than those of men. Yet at the same time, the goddesses of
the Hindu pantheon are models of exemplary behaviour compared with
their male counterparts. The education of girls received low priority from mediaeval to modern times, yet the deity of learning,
Saraswati, is a goddess.
The raising of the status of women in Islam faces the special
problem of the immutability of Koranic injunctions, received by the
Prophet from Allah. Sura 4:31 of the Koran says: "Men have authority over women because God has made the one superior to the other
and because they spend their wealth (to maintain them). So good

women are obedient, guarding the unseen (parts) because God has guarded (them). As for those from whom you fear disobedience, admonish them and banish them to beds apart and beat them; then if they obey you seek not occasion against them" (Guillaume, 1954). Injunctions and advice by later followers of Mohammed are susceptible to modification, the Koran is not. This led the modern Indian poet and philosopher, Iqbal, to write:

I, too, am most sorrowful at the oppression of women;
But the problem is intricate; no solution do I find possible.

The adoption of Confucian ideals came to restrict the hitherto comparatively free life of women, first of the upper classes and progressively of society in general, in those countries which adopted Chinese culture--Korea, Japan, and, to a lesser extent, Vietnam. The rigorously circumscribed lives and the leisure thus imposed led to a remarkable flowering of literary talent among the women of the Heian Court in tenth-century Japan; Lady Murasaki and Sei Shonagon are the best-known writers.

In Buddhism, women have been vilified thus: "Women are soon angered, Ananda, women are full of passion, Ananda, women are envious, Ananda, women are stupid. That is the reason, Ananda, that is the cause, why women have no place in public assemblies, do not carry on business, and do not earn their living by any professions" (Sullavaga X.1.6, quoted by Rudra, 1975).

Yet, in Thailand, no greater value is given to men than to women, as it is deemed that all will be reborn many times as either men or women (Hanks and Hanks, 1963). This equality is underlined in the marriage ceremonial: "Let the wife know how to please her husband, saying sweet words to him and admonishing him only in private, not before others. Let the husband perform his duty of loving and protecting his wife and never use harsh words to her." A less egalitarian relationship is, however, discerned in a study of a north Thai village, where male dominance is clearly accepted. Property is inherited in the matriline, but authority passes from father-in-law to son-in-law. A proverb states that men are superior to women as the front legs of an elephant are superior to the hind (Potter, 1977).

In Burma, men are universally acknowledged as superior to women spiritually and also widely considered as intellectually and morally superior (Spiro, 1977). There is none the less social and legal equality. If men manipulate the symbols and control the tokens of power (religion and politics), men are manipulated and controlled by women in the domain of real power (the family and household). They play an important role in production, the provision of family income and in family decisions, and their status is high, even though outwardly they are deferential. A common saying is: "Having a husband in the house is like having a nat around"--the nats being powerful spirits requiring deference and devotion (Nash, 1965).

Thus, there is a conflict between the scriptural stereotype and the actuality, for if women hold low symbolic positions in the Buddhist hierarchy, Burmese and Thai society is as egalitarian as is the predominantly Catholic Philippines or largely Islamic Indonesia.

The great religions, particularly the newer reforming religions of
Buddhism, Islam and Christianity, are not after all useful guides for
predicting social structure and the status of women. They have been
grafted on to older belief systems which had a profound influence on
the ordering of society long before they were adopted. The contrast
between the dominating Kelantanese market woman, overseeing her
stall, telling her husband (if he is visible at all) what to do,
driving a shrewd bargain while cracking jokes with all comers with
complete self-possession, and the Bangladeshi woman who retires from
view the moment a stranger appears at the entry to her compound,
never goes to market and is reluctant to express an opinion, even to
another woman when her confidence has been gained, is overwhelming.
Yet both are followers of Islam.*

STATUS AND PERFORMANCE OF RELIGIOUS DUTIES

A devout woman is respected by her family and community, but
this does not imply that she will be regarded as competent in secular
matters or will be accorded high status in village affairs. There
is, in the more primitive religions of the region, a division of
labour in ritual which reflects daily life, where women play an
important part. The great religions often severely limit the role of
women. The effect that this may have on women's public role was
shown in the 1978 elections to the State Legislature of Kelantan,
Malaysia, where no woman candidate was put forward by any party; each
knew the opposition would call on the populace to vote against her,
as "a woman could not lead prayers or recite the khutbah and neither
could they enter a mosque during their periods" (New Straits Times,
Feb. 25, 1978).
In India, festivals without "great tradition ties" are women's
festivals; women participate and even dominate life cycle rites.
Men's rites focus on a good crop, or ridding the village of disease.
Women are active practitioners but have little religious authority in
orthodox Hinduism (Wadley, 1977). Thus, the religious duties of
women are accorded a lower status than those of men. However, the
cook is crucial in maintaining the orthodoxy of the family (Khare,
1976); except where families are able to employ a Brahmin, the cook
is invariably one of the women, under the instruction of her mother-
in-law. Women ensure the ritual wellbeing of the family and derive a
sense of importance therefrom (Jacobson, 1977; Srinivas, 1976).
Production of food for the temple in a northern Thai village
gathers women together and gives some authority. Ancestral spirits
inhabit the oldest house in the family compound, which will be
inherited by the family's youngest daughter (Potter, 1977).
In traditional China, the ancestral hall was the locus of an
agnatic community, where women had no public place. This was in
sharp contrast with domestic ancestor worship, which was the sphere

_____

*It is not claimed that all Kelantanese or Bangladeshi women
conform to this picture, but these stereotypes are acknowledged as
such by their societies.

of women and in which they played a crucial part (Freedman, 1970b).
This still applies in Taiwan and to overseas communities of Chinese.
In Korea, while the most valued form of worship is the male rite
of ancestor worship, women may consult shamans (who are mostly
female) to counteract the inauspicious influence of restless ghosts
and ancestors. Male rites acknowledge only those "ancestors" who
produce sons and die within the patrilineal family. Women's rituals
acknowledge a broad bilateral kindred, including sisters and daughters who marry out of the family and the wife's own natal kin
(Kendall, 1979).

Islam also appears to confer lower status on women's sacral
duties. In the Prophet's time women attended public prayers in the
mosques, standing behind the men, "but there is a tradition that he
said it was better for women to pray at home and . . . they do not
attend public prayers" (Guillaume, 1954). In Malaysia it has been
said that "women do not go to mosque for worship on any occasion"
(Zainal Abidin, 1949). Women are, however, permitted to attend
Friday prayers, separated from the men by a curtain.

It seems that historic, probably prehistoric, societal norms
must be sought to explain the differences which prevail between the
patrilineal societies of south Asia and east Asia and the less
rigidly structured societies of southeast Asia where, no matter what
the major religion or form of economic production, women enjoy a
fairly egalitarian position vis-à-vis their husbands and in society.

STATUS AND THE LIFE CYCLE

Female status does not remain unchanged throughout the life
cycle. Inferiority is acknowledged at the moment of birth, when midwives commonly receive better payment, in cash or kind, for a boy
than for a girl; in a Pakistani village Rs. 10 are paid for a boy,
and Rs. 5 for a girl (Khan and Bilquees, 1976).

Preference has traditionally been expressed for male children.
In Pakistan, when asked how many daughters they had, men would answer
"God has been merciful" or just "thank God" to indicate they had
none (Saghir Ahmed, 1974). In the People's Republic of China, economic considerations make parents as anxious to have sons today as in
the past (Parish, 1975). In the rural New Territories of Hong Kong,
sons are preferred, daughters "goods on which one loses" (Potter,
1969). Another stricture in traditional China is: "A boy is born
facing in, a girl is born facing out" (Freedman, 1958). In Taiwan,
sons are crucial to the identity of a woman in the family and village
into which she has married and much affection is lavished on them;
close emotional bonds unite mothers and daughters, but a female child
has lower status than her brothers (Wolf, 1970).

Poverty at one end of the social scale in India and at the other
the practice of hypergamy, which automatically meant that there were
not enough high-status men for high-status girls to marry, have in
the past caused harsh treatment of girls. Even today poverty and the
reservation of scarce resources for boys means that girls are less
well treated. The Harvard School of Public Health, in collaboration
with the Governments of India and the State of Punjab, found during

the 1950's and 1960's that girls of less than 2 years of age had a
substantially smaller chance of survival than boys of the same age,
who were given better medical care and probably more supplementary
food (Wyon and Gordon, 1971). Mortality is higher in Bangladesh
among female infants, being 38 per cent for parities 0, 1 and 2, and
is similar for the 1 to 4 years age group (Mosley, 1979). The
mortality rate for girls under the age of 5 years is 30 to 50 per
cent higher than for boys (Jahan, 1975).

In modern Asia, infants of both sexes are generally the centre
of family affection, though discrimination starts early and girls are
soon made aware of their responsibilities in the care of younger
siblings and household tasks. Thailand seems to be an exception,
without a clear division of roles, even between adults. It is felt
there that women contribute more to the continuity of generations
than do men (Hanks and Hanks, 1963). Westernization has introduced
sharper distinctions between boys' and girls' dress, behaviour and
roles than was traditional.

In the traditional east Asian and south Asian worlds, a girl
learns quite early to keep what is today called a low profile; her
brother has greater freedom until he is of an age to assist in agricultural activities. Excellence in studies is no excuse for the
incompetence of an Indian girl in household affairs (ICSSR, 1975).
Girls learn early in life the need to be flexible and submissive;
they hesitate to develop strong opinions and commitments which they
may not be allowed to pursue after marriage. Among poorer people,
the education of girls is sacrificed in favour of boys, and there is
a lurking fear that education may alienate girls from their roles and
submissive behaviour (ICSSR, loc. cit.; see also Chapter 4: Attitudes Towards Education). In the People's Republic of China, girls
are withdrawn from school more readily than boys to help in household
tasks (Parish, 1975; Orleans, 1978). The same is true of Hong Kong
(Field and Baber, 1973). An adolescent boy in southeast Asia has
considerable independence and may work for a wage rather than help on
the family plot. A close link unites women with their parents for
life in this sub-region.

Girls on reaching puberty have their freedom greatly curtailed
and are often withdrawn from school to work within the home until a
suitable match is arranged. At this time in most settled communities, girls experience the ritual impurity associated with menstruation, an impurity which also occurs later at the birth of their
children. Males, by observing rules of distance from potentially
polluting women, need never experience this sense of inferiority.

In many Asian communities young women, like their husbands,
achieve adult status only with marriage, often only after the birth
of their first child. In Malay kampongs, children mix freely until
about the age of 13, when girls are segregated, supervised and
trained for marriage. In the past if married before puberty, a girl
stayed at home or with her affines but did not cohabit with her husband. If a child was born immediately after marriage at 13 or 14, a
girl was considered too young to look after it and her parents would
take charge, giving her extra training in the process (Hashimah
Roose, 1963). The young couple would be allowed to set up home only
when considered sufficiently mature and experienced. Even then they

were still under parental influence, especially regarding family life
and social obligations. Similarly, a Pakistani bride did not have
the right to bring up her children, who were under the jurisdiction
of her mother-in-law (Gani, 1963). A Bangladeshi daughter-in-law is
responsible for work, her mother-in-law having authority, even over
the young bride's husband, whom she instructs about marketing
(Abdulla, 1976). An educated Bengali wife in Calcutta finds her
relations with her husband improve only after she has borne a child;
he shows her more overt attention and affection as his child's
mother. Before then such attention was more properly directed to his
mother, sisters and the wives of his older brothers (Roy, 1975).

In Java, it is impressed upon a young couple that they should
provide for themselves (Jay, 1969); they are considered minors,
unable to contract social and economic debts, until they are economically independent. This can be achieved by the control of an
independently earned food store and maintenance of separate cooking
hearth, even though still within the home of one of their parents.

A Thai girl is considered an adult at the birth of her first
child, but her husband attains adult status only when his father-in-
law retires, if it is a joint family, or when he himself farms his
own land. Only then can he take part in village affairs (de Young,
1966).

In traditional China, the subservience of a woman's lineage to
her husband's was underlined by the fact that her family took no part
in the ceremonies of the marriage; the groom's lineage ancestors were
worshipped and homage paid to his parents, on whom the bride's economic dependence was absolute (Yang, 1959). At each stage of her
life, a woman was in an inferior position to male members of her
family of the same generation in vital matters, and to those of the
next generation in all matters (Yang, loc. cit.).

If it is only in the criteria for achieving adulthood that there
is no discrimination between male and female, the female in south and
east Asia traditionally holds a position of complete inferiority to
all family members older than herself and a fairly remote relation
with her husband. The southeast Asian bride is far more secure.

Some have suggested that teknonymy, the practice of addressing a
married woman as "mother of . . . " or "auntie of . . . ," leads to a
weakened sense of individuality in the adult woman, implying that her
status is achieved only in relation to some other, usually a male.
However, in societies where this is the norm, such as in south Asia,
it would be necessary to apply psychological tests and to compare the
results with societies where the practice was not prevalent. No such
investigations have been seen by the authors. Some evidence suggests
that, on the contrary, those excluded from the practice where it is
current suffer accordingly. Men who never have children in Bali and
who continue throughout their lives with their childhood name, while
their peers progressively become "father of . . . " and "grandfather
of . . . ," feel the shame deeply (Geertz and Geertz, 1975).

For both men and women age, particularly experience and success
in agricultural and domestic and childrearing undertakings, brings
greater respect from their society. Older women often exercise
considerable authority and, even in patriarchal societies, have an
important role in arranging their children's marriages. An older

woman may control the income of a number of daughters-in-law in India
(Dube, 1978a).

The effect of widowhood on status varies greatly throughout
Asia. In south Asia, widows often have to shave their heads, perform
menial work and observe enforced ritual and physical distance from
family and community events, so polluting and dangerous to others are
they. Remarriage remains almost totally unacceptable among castes
and communities which prohibited remarriage in the past, despite
higher levels of education and legislation (Leonard and Leonard,
1981). A traditional Chinese widow left in charge of family land
would leave its management to her sons, but would still enjoy considerable power within the family. Remarriage was not sanctioned,
however, and entailed loss of children and property. A Korean woman
can succeed temporarily to the household headship until her son (or
adopted son) is of age, but after the early Yi dynasty, she could not
become the ritual heir (Deuchler, 1977). A Vietnamese widow traditionally supervised land, but this was merely a continuation of the
high status she enjoyed throughout life. A southeast Asian widow has
traditionally held property and been free to remarry. The change in
Japan from the extended patrilocal to nuclear neolocal family pattern
has robbed the Japanese widow of the respect and security which she
formerly enjoyed (see Chapter 7 for a more detailed discussion of
widowhood).

Divorce has traditionally entailed little stigma in southeast
Asia, although this is changing among the more educated. In east and
south Asia, divorce has always been unacceptable, even among Islamic
communities in south Asia. The Shariat Act of 1936 safeguarded the
right of Muslim women to divorce, but social convention makes this
difficult even today (ICSSR, 1975)(see Chapter 7, Divorce).

MARRIAGE NEGOTIATIONS AND STATUS

It has been claimed that the status of women in any society can
be gauged by the form of negotiation involved in her marriage. The
institution of bride price, with its assumption of the value of the
girl and of her labour, reflects a higher conception of her position
than does that of dowry, with its undertone of "buying" a husband.
The prevalence of ruinous dowry payments makes the arrival of several
daughters a family disaster and soon makes a girl aware of her bur-
densomeness. It follows that the different systems are a function of
the division of labour--perhaps at some time in the past--in any
region.

Bride price is often common where women take an active part in
production, particularly in shifting forms of cultivation. In mainland and insular southeast Asia, bride price has, with few exceptions, been the custom in all societies, both settled and swidden.
If a groom was unable to obtain the bride price, he worked for a
varying number of years for his father-in-law until the sum was considered paid (Lebar, Hickey and Musgrave, 1964; Lebar, 1972; Lebar,
1975). Dowry is more commonly the norm where the role of women is
confined to "unproductive" household tasks and child-raising. In
south Asia dowry is associated with the transmission of property

through both males and females, as enshrined in classical treatises
such as the Dharmashastras, even if in India women's rights are confined to movables (Tambiah, 1973).
  There is often confusion regarding the significance of dowry,
dower and bridewealth. Dowry is always given by the bride's parents,
and dower by the groom's; both form part of the conjugal estate.
Bridewealth, however, is given by the groom's family to the bride's,
and clearly represents compensation for the loss of the girl. Controversy regarding the function of bride price goes back some decades
(Gluckman, 1953; Leach, 1953; Schneider, 1953) and continues today.
Some argue that bridewealth discourages the bride from seeking
divorce, since her parents would be obliged to return the sum. Under
Islam, however, bride price payment restrains the groom, since his
family pays only part of the sum at marriage, the remainder at
divorce. The Islamic dower given by the bridegroom is intended for
the bride herself and thus is not bride price. Canon law fixes the
amount of dower according to that received by the Prophet for his
daughter, Fatimah. In north India, however, a customary dower of
unrealistic amount is fixed in the marriage contract as a symbol of
status of the bride's family. Canon law dower was intended to protect the women against capricious divorce, but customary dower is so
high that it could never be paid, and is in any case usually
renounced by the wife. This is in her interest, for it enhances the
responsibility of her affines towards her if her husband dies (Vreede
de Stuers, 1968). A recent study of a Bedouin community sought to
show that bride price was above all a status symbol (Kressel, 1977),
but this aroused considerable disagreement; there is still no consensus on the true function of bride price (Current Anthropology, 18:
450-458).
  In rural Burma, dower is an essential component of marriage and
protects the girl against the insecurity of philandering, improvident
husbands, particularly since divorced women find it difficult to
remarry (Spiro, 1975). Dower is actually the groom's inheritance and
helps the couple to become established. It is argued that bridewealth in Thailand is actually dower, since residence is matrilocal
and girls expect to inherit, whereas conventional bridewealth stays
with the bride's parents.
  Status and family honour are also factors; a poor Burmese bride
commands a lower dower, and a poor Thai girl a lower bridewealth,
than the wealthy. Dowry may occur along with dower in rural Burma,
but dowry alone is paid among certain élite urban Burmese, associated
with hypergamous marriages between wealthy, low-status women and
impoverished, high-status men. As in India, dowry is a recent innovation, following the introduction of western education and the
availability to men of high-status jobs in the civil service.
  It is suggested that when neither side gains status or wealth
from a marriage there is no payment, but if the cost-benefit ratio is
unbalanced, marriage payment repairs the balance (Spiro, loc. cit.).
It is difficult to find a theory to meet all Asia's variations, for
the status of a Chinese girl for whom bridewealth had been paid was
comparable with an Indian girl who brings dowry.
  Bride price was common in south China and dowry, varying greatly
in amount, in the north (Smith, 1899/1970). In Taiwan, however, the

father of the bride gains face by the payment of dowry (Wolf, 1972).
Domestic services and fertility were the chief ritual attachments
transferred to a girl's agnatic family in marriage; this was vali-
dated by the payment of bride price (Freedman, 1958). Chinese bride
price was in fact indirect dowry, since cash payment by the groom's
family was used to dower the bride with furnishings and other neces-
sities (Goody and Tambiah, 1973). The bride's family in Taiwan is
expected to contribute as much again as the bride price in the form
of dowry (Diamond, 1969). The diminution or disappearance in the
People's Republic of China of dowry payments reflects the increased
economic value of women (Whyte, 1977; Parish and Whyte, 1978), while
bride price remains common. Today, however, only part of this is
used to dower the bride, most being saved and used later to marry off
a brother of the bride (Parish and Whyte, loc. cit.). These improvements in the status of women are still closely related to economic
sufficiency. The Chairwoman of the National Women's Union, K'ang
K'e-ch'ing (People's Daily, Nov. 27, 1978), discussing the economic
deterioration of the previous decade, stated "social morality (was)
also greatly corrupted to such an extent that there was restoration
of buying and selling of brides. (There are) great differences
between well-to-do villages and relatively poor villages. In places
where production levels and living standards are low, the buying and
selling of brides . . . are not easy to eliminate completely" (London
and London, 1979).

A Korean women receive dowry on marriage and have no further
economic claims on their natal lineage (Deuchler, 1977). Dowry does
not often come in the form of money or jewellery which gives a woman
security, but as household costs and clothing (Soon, 1977a).

A dowerless girl's lack of face in her new home may be aggravated by many reproaches; the custom is proving extremely difficult
to eradicate in modern India, despite much propaganda. Indeed, the
ensuring of good treatment for their daughters is one of the major
reasons fathers give for high dowry payments.

In early times bride price was the norm in India, and frequent
protests at the system are recorded throughout history; it increased
with child marriage (Altekar, 1959). The dowry system was connected
with the idea of marriage as a gift of a daughter, when a religious
gift in kind was normally accompanied by a small gift in cash or
ornaments. In mediaeval times it was only among the Rajputs, where
competition for high status grooms was intense, that the dowry system
assumed serious proportions. It became widespread only in the nineteenth century, assuming excessive proportions during the past 50 to
60 years with the advent of higher education for men (Altekar, loc.
cit.). Since the beginning of this century, men from higher castes
sought English education to obtain jobs in the bureaucracy and to
enter the professions. Such men were in great demand as grooms, and
over a period of time this stimulated the spread of the institution
of dowry. Previously in Bengal and throughout south India (with the
exception of Kerala) cash was paid to obtain a bride. Dowry began
among the upper levels of society and has now reached even the
sweepers of Calcutta (Srinivas, 1977). In Bangladesh bride price was
formerly provided by the groom's family, but today the family of an
educated groom will require dowry (Abdulla, 1976). The bride's

position may be improving slowly, however. Much of the dowry of a
new wife in a Rajput community, studied over a period of 20 years,
was formerly taken by her mother-in-law and placed in the dower of
her own daughter; today this is left in the control of the bride herself (Minturn, 1976).

An exchange between the parents of the bride and groom, such as
that described above for traditional China, is in fact common.
Marriage expenses paid by the Malay groom's father are often supplemented by the bride's father and the total often exceeded by the sum
the groom's family traditionally gives the bride as her own property
(Swift, 1963). Among the tribal Gonds of central India, marriage by
negotiation involving heavy expenditure by the groom's family is most
prized, but the alternatives, whereby a poor youth works for his
father-in-law for a stipulated number of years to earn his bride, or
capture (prearranged or otherwise), are more common (von Fürer-
Haimendorf, 1974). These practices are found among many tribal
peoples in southeast Asia.

STATUS AND PERSONALITY

The effect of status on the development of personality is
undoubtedly of great importance, but little work has been done in
this field in Asia.

An explanation of differences in male and female personality
which are considered almost universal has been based on psychoanalytic theory (Chodorow, 1974). Most traditional accounts of socialization stress early role training, but Chodorow considered unconscious
features of personality. After the age of 3, male and female development is radically different: a boy's gender development is based
on identification with the father who, Chodorow assumes, is generally
relatively inaccessible to his son. Identification with him is thus
more abstract, and conception of the masculine role based on fantasy
rather than observation. Gender identification for boys is also
achieved at the expense of devaluing what is feminine in the world
around him. A girl's relation with her mother, on the other hand, is
unbroken, her identification with her personal, and she is likely to
participate in an intergenerational female world, while her brother
will associate chiefly with his peers.

Current patterns of socialization lead Chodorow to conclude that
while men feel "sociocultural superiority", they are also "psychologically defensive and insecure. Women by contrast, although always
of secondary social and cultural status, may in favourable circumstances gain psychological security and a firm sense of worth and
importance, in spite of this."

As Chodorow admits, psychoanalytical theory is based largely on
western culture. Asia would seem to provide a promising testing
ground for theories of the effect of patterns of socialization upon
the development of personality. Fathers tend to become more remote
to sons at the age generally associated with the development of
"reason," around the age of 6 to 8, when discipline becomes more
strict (Nydegger and Nydegger, 1966; Jocano, 1969; Minturn and
Hitchcock, 1966; Wolf, 1972). Asian boys around the age of 3 are not

36

cut off from their father or other adult males, and small children of
both sexes grow up in close interaction with a number of relatives
and children of different ages. In the extended family an aged
grandparent or a young uncle may be a regular companion. Fairly
close participation of men in the socialization of boys seems to be
characteristic of much of rural Asia, with the exception of Japan,
and girls rarely grow up in close interaction only with their mother.
Chodorow considers these characteristics make for the development of
strong individuality and are a means of bringing about greater
equality between adult men and women.

A study of childhood in India, however, shows that while the
father is present, his son is unable to identify with him as is
required for the development of autonomy, since tradition requires
the father to remain distant, treating all children in an extended
family with impartiality. A boy is separated from his mother
abruptly at the fourth or fifth year, when absolute obedience and
conformity to familial standards may be imposed upon him. "The slow
detachment from the mother considered essential to the development of
a strong independent ego is not a feature of early Indian childhood;"
consequently "the mental processes characteristic of the symbiosis of
infancy play a relatively greater role in adult personality" (Kakar,
1978). This prepares the individual for participation in a world
requiring strict observance of a traditionally elaborated hierarchi-
cal social order and the subordination of individual preferences and
ambitions to the welfare of the extended family and jati communities.

This pattern of child-raising has fundamental consequences for
the future relationship between husband and wife. The extreme
dependence of the son on his mother is allied to fear (Kakar, loc.
cit.). "Underlying the conscious ideals of womanly purity, innocence
and fidelity and interwoven with the unconscious belief in a safe-
guarding maternal beneficence is a secret conviction among many
Hindu men that the feminine principle is really the opposite--
treacherous, lustful and rampant with an insatiable, contaminating
sexuality." This leads to "avoidance behaviour in sexual relations,
which in turn causes women to extend a provocative sexual presence
towards their sons, which eventually produces adult men who fear the
sexuality of mature women. . . . Taken into the child's ego, the
good mother's maternal tolerance, emotional vitality, protectiveness
and nurturing become the core of every Indian's positive identity.
Alongside this positive identity, however, and normally repressed, is
its counterpart; the negative identity that originates in experiences
with the demanding, sometimes stifling, all too present mother."

A further contributory factor to this pattern is derived from
the early age of marriage. The process of adolescent development is
normally incomplete at the time of marriage when a girl is transplanted into an unfamiliar, possibly hostile environment, a "traumatic transition which an Indian girl undergoes at precisely the most
sensitive and vulnerable period of her development." Her position
becomes tolerable when she bears a child. It is thus comprehensible
that the great emotional investment she places in her infant, especially if it is a son, prolongs and intensifies the mother-son
relationship.

Socialization in Asia usually shows favouritism to boys and

stresses that girls must defer to their brothers. What effect does
this have on personality development? Psychoanalytic theory would
lead to the expectation that the cultural devaluation of girls would
heighten female hostility and envy towards males, producing strong
antagonism between the sexes. Kakar (loc. cit.) finds little evidence of this in India. There is, however, evidence that women turn
aggression against themselves, transforming cultural devaluation into
feelings of worthlessness and inferiority. This may be offset by the
strength of wellbeing and self-esteem generated by a strong mother-
daughter bond which sustains a girl through the realization during
late childhood of her cultural inferiority; she comes to accept that
submission and docility are inseparable from her role. Conformity to
expectation is reinforced by the Hindu concept of dharma (roughly
translated as right-living), which implies that behaviour is good if
it conforms to the traditional pattern of kinship and caste groups.
This leads to suspicion of innovation and unconscious avoidance of
unconventional activities by both men and women. The fact that older
women gain power to make vital decisions affecting the family further
contributes towards conservatism, since older women wish to be able
to control their daughters-in-law as they themselves were controlled.

In Japan, girls learn that men and boys have fragile egos which
women and girls must build up and protect. A girl must develop an
amiable, flexible, nurturant personality, but the emotional support
she later gives her husband is overwhelmingly one-sided. Women may
gain their own support from mothers or sisters, but increasingly
these live too far away for frequent contact. Inevitably such comfort comes from her children, in the past chiefly from her sons, but
in modern times more from her daughters (Vogel, 1978).

In the Philippines, despite the widespread acceptance of woman's
role in economic activities, whether it be as a professional in the
cities or tending a small rural sundry store, the primary role
remains that of mother, and children are her greatest emotional
satisfaction. "A person grows up in the Filipino culture with one
paramount assumption; that he belongs to someone" (Lapuz, 1973). He
belongs to the family as a whole as well as to its members, especially to his parents and principally to his mother, "partly because
of biological circumstances, but also because of the intense emotional nurturing received from her." Women remain very close to
their mothers, even after marriage (Lapuz, loc. cit.). The successful carrying out of the role of mother is more important than individual achievement as a woman.

It has been suggested that patterns of socialization in Thailand, whereby the affection showered on the youngest is withdrawn
when the child is supplanted by another infant, leaves a boy without
a real role until adolescence, whereas a girl is soon given tasks
around the home. This may account for female dominance in Thailand
and to the weak ego of men (Piker, 1975), or--since similar patterns
occur in Java--to "the most henpecked men on earth" (Jay, 1969).
Daughters in Thailand are reared as mothers, wives and caretakers of
the elderly; men's roles are far more diffuse. Moreover, emotional
support is gained more from mothers than from husbands (Muecke,
1974), further strengthening female solidarity. Thai boys are traditionally taught to receive things and attention in the home. They

are treated with greater consideration, made to feel that they are of first importance and can have what they want, while girls give in to them and please them. This differential pattern is the basis for an evaluation of Thai men as immature and narcissistic, while girls have stronger characters. But women are less secure and self-confident than men as a result of this training (Boonsanong, 1971).

It is believed that the need of Burmese men for dependence on their wives, despite the formal role of female subservience, results from their early relationships with their mothers in which they are "spoiled" and strongly dependent on them. Thus the domination by women of their husbands may be viewed rather as the dependence of the men (Spiro, 1977).

A clear understanding of cultural values is as essential for understanding adult personality in Asia as is knowledge of child socialization. Western stress on economic and occupational achievement, and derogation of the maternal role, overlooks the fact that in many cultures achievement motivation is towards the maternal role, seen as a specialized counterpart to that of men. The relative lack of discord in Japanese marriages is partly due to the degree to which women derive personal satisfaction from being competent in their roles, rather than from having a mate who meets their personal needs (de Vos and Wagatsuma, 1973a). It should not be supposed that the acceptance of the maternal, home-making, nurturant role signifies a more submissive character. Overt behaviour masks the frequent operation of actual control of the family by women; no significant differences are found between men and women in the incidence or distribution of structural traits of personality--basic active or passive attitudes, dominant or submissive needs. The personal self has been de-emphasized in Japanese culture, and traditional self-awareness is fused with some conception of expected role behaviour; the Japanese person is uncomfortable thinking of the self as separable from the role (de Vos and Wagatsuma, loc. cit.).

An attempt to assess personality in central Thailand was based on a number of questionnaires, one such relating to aspirations. It was found that 40 per cent of all replies were related to status (Phillips, 1966). A woman respondent wished to be the mother of a doctor, district officer or governor, showing perhaps a realization that higher status was more likely to be achieved by reflected glory from a close-related male than by her own achievements. Twenty per cent of replies from both sexes showed that individuals wished to be good, respected and non-trouble-making. The "most important thing in life" for the majority, however, was earning a living, or food and money (Phillips, loc. cit.). The same emphasis on economic preoccupations and status is revealed in more recent studies of ten villages in north and ten in central Thailand. Thirty-six per cent of women wanted their daughters to be teachers and 23 per cent either nurse or doctor; 15 per cent hoped their daughters would take up dressmaking and only 11 per cent wanted them to work in agriculture, as did the mothers. Ninety-nine per cent of these women worried "a lot" about economic factors and, knowing the importance of woman's financial contribution to the family budget, only 3 per cent wanted their daughters to confine themselves to household activities (Nantanee et al, 1977).

    A survey of major life concerns of Filipino women stresses two
basic Filipino values: economic security (house and home; social
benefits and family health and the good provider factor); and social
acceptance (education, childrearing and marital relationship, housekeeping and social participation, status and esteem). "Being a woman
in Filipino society means that her prestige lies mainly in her
credible performance as a mother, wife and home manager. Although
she might be a success in her profession or career, her 'failure' as
mother or wife is given greater weight" (Illo, 1979).
    An anthropologist working on the life history of an elderly
woman in central India, whom she had known intimately for some years,
was struck by the clarity with which she remembered trivial details
from her early youth, compared with the confusion which appeared to
cloud her memory of the birth order of the 8 of her 12 children who
had died during childhood; this was recognized as a form of defence
mechanism against distress (Jacobson, 1978). May it be asked what is
the effect upon a woman's personality of the awareness of a constant
threat of disease to her family, of economic hardship of one kind or
another, of the difficulty of attaining education for her children
and concern at their future employment and marriage prospects? All
these preoccupations are more acute at lower socio-economic levels
throughout Asia.
    An apparent lack of introspection has been noted among lower
socio-economic groups in the Indian subcontinent by various workers
(Jacobson, loc. cit.). This echoes the findings of Lewis in a
Mexican community (1951), who wrote:

Like many peasant peoples, Tepoxtecans are not introspective.
They have little insight in understanding their own character
and even less of others. There is little interest in or need
for self-revelation, mutual confidences, confession, or lengthy
conversation; imaginativeness, fantasy life, originality,
initiative, and individuality are either undeveloped or sup-
pressed. Always, the emphasis is upon conformity to traditional
ways.

    The science of psychological anthropology is still at its
beginnings in Asia. What do we know of the effect on personality and
development of an abrupt break from an affectionate family life to a
hostile environment in which a young bride's status is low? Surely
the confidence of a young bride, and consequently her self-esteem and
ability to assert herself and her ideas, must be far greater if she
can turn to her mother for support, advice and companionship, as in
southeast Asia, than in the isolation, the "psychological aloneness"
(Wolf, 1975) of east and south Asia. The psychological isolation
must have made for greater submissiveness and malleability, and perhaps difficulty in raising her status in her husband's eyes--
especially when he probably preferred a peaceful life wholly undis-
turbed by difference of opinion among the women of his family.
    Under the joint family system which prevails among higher status
Bengalis in India, considerable frustration is engendered by the gulf
between the romantic view of marriage envisioned by educated young
women, and the more prosaic actuality of their limited role:

Personality needs are generated, and then in part frustrated; but to achieve any level of gratification, the full array of joint-family roles is required. A system such as this must sacrifice the whole satisfaction of one individual, either on the structural or psychological level, so that other members in different roles may be at least partly satisfied (Roy, 1975).

Marriage for a young man does not involve separation from his mother, sisters and sisters-in-law, from all of whom he receives affection; he does not expect his wife to fulfil romantic needs, and sexual enjoyment is connected not with her, who will become another respected mother, but with women not to be respected. It is usually his mother who looks after his needs during the day (Roy, loc. cit.). The effect of this upon a young woman expecting love and fulfilment can be imagined. Emotional satisfaction with her own children is not permanent, since they too will eventually grow away from her. Many women in middle life find the emotional satisfaction and support they have missed in devotions to a guru (Roy, loc. cit.).

But we are dealing here with patterns which Roy has shown to be in part confined to Bengal and, moreover, to a highly favoured minority. Of the frustrations and satisfactions of the majority of poor Indian women, as of Asian women in general, we know remarkably little. More studies within the different cultures, preferably by specialists from the same culture, are needed before any clear con- clusions can be drawn on the effect of acculturation on personality development and on the status of Asian women. In particular, it needs to be demonstrated that there are differences in child-raising, not apparent from the literature, which explain the differences in public self-confidence between women in southeast Asia and those in west and east Asia. If no crucial differences are found, then different female experiences at other stages in the life cycle must be isolated. It seems to us that marriage (discussed in Chapter 5) is the most promising variable.

4
Women's Status in Public Life:
Indicators of Advancement

Legislation providing for the equitable treatment of women, the provision of adequate education facilities for girls, the acceptance of women's participation in political life and their representation in the professions and at management levels in commerce and industry can all be seen as public reflections of the status of women in their societies.

LEGAL PROTECTION

Legislation exists in most Asian countries to protect women both from the effects of disruption of her family and from exploitation of her labour (ILO, 1978). Protective labour laws are increasingly being viewed as obstacles to equality of opportunity in employment. An advisory organ to the Japanese Labour Ministry recommended (November 20, 1978) that the Labour Standards Law should be revised to abolish clauses prohibiting overtime and night work for women and requiring monthly menstruation leave. Laws intended to protect pregnant women merely end by discriminating against all married women in the labour-surplus markets of Asia, since employers will hire unmarried women or men, rather than bear the cost of paying absent workers. If tradition sanctions lower pay for women and women are anxious for work, then they will be employed in favour of men, irrespective of legislation decreeing equal pay. In both the Communist and non-Communist worlds the freedom of women, their right to productive employment and income are not the result of legislation, but of the availability of employment.

There is still considerable discrimination against women, even on the statute books (Chung and Ng, 1977; Buxbaum, 1977; Hering, 1976; Sarkar, 1977; Soewondo, 1977; Cortes, 1977; Mosqueda, 1977; Malaysia FFPA, 1976). It is not our intention to give details here, since this would require a separate study. Moreover, however well-intentioned some modern provisions may be, they are nullified by the weight of tradition and indeed ignorance of their existence in rural areas (Mukherjee, 1974). The Law Reform Act in Malaysia for non-Muslims was gazetted in 1976 and was expected to usher in "a social revolution of great significance" (New Straits Times, Aug. 11, 1978).

The Act has not yet been implemented, due to "lack of machinery."
The principal aim of the Act is to ensure that marriage for non-
Muslims is monogamous, to give official status to religious ceremonies and to give women, as well as men, access to divorce.
Attempts at reforming Muslim family law by enforcing nationwide uniformity and making divorce more difficult for men still await
approval and enactment; subsequent implementation will face the same
difficulties as that encountered by legislation relating to non-
Muslims.

Legislation initiated "from above" has not drastically altered
women's status in Japan (Bernstein, 1976). As rights of inheritance
are often waived in return for promise of care by the heir, primogeniture is still customary. Divorce or remarriage is still considered to be morally wrong. There are disparities in the Korean
Civil Code between constitutional rights accorded women and the
provisions regarding family law which still reflect traditional
attitudes. Individual freedom and sexual equality were provided in
the Constitution of 1948, but not fully implemented in the Civil Code
of 1960 (Deuchler, 1977). Sixty-one women's organizations have
combined to promote the passage of a Bill to give a widow legal
seniority over her son so that she may become head of the family and
be given joint ownership of family property. Leading the opposition
was the Association of Confucian Scholars who foresaw a threat to the
traditional family system (Asiaweek, Dec. 2, 1977). The revised
Family Law of 1977 met some women's requirements: a widow's share of
her husband's property has been raised from one-third that left to
her oldest son to an equal amount.

Legislation restricting the payment or amount of dowry, prohibiting child marriage, setting a minimum age for marriage, permitting
remarriage of widows where this is proscribed by tradition, establishing the right to own property and land where this is not the
norm, as well as the right to equal pay, is difficult to apply without the support of society. Article 53 of the Constitution of the
People's Republic of China, adopted on March 5, 1978 by the Fifth
National People's Congress, states

> Women enjoy equal rights with men in all spheres of political,
> economic, cultural, social and family life.
>
> Men and women enjoy equal pay for equal work.
>
> Men and women shall marry of their own free will. The State
> protects marriage, the family and the mother and child.
>
> The State advocates and encourages family planning (New China
> News Agency, March 7, 1978).

As will be shown, Chinese women have attained some of the rights
enshrined in the Constitution, but others are still a distant goal.
Abusive practices in Hong Kong have been removed over time not by
legislation but by economic forces (Wong, 1973). This confirms the
view of Asian reformers of every political belief, from Gandhi to
Mao, that the position of women will improve only with the improvement of life for the entire society.

LITERACY

The degree of literacy among women is an important factor in
their appreciation of their legal rights and in widening the range of
possibilities for employment. Female literacy in Japan is the highest in Asia; increasingly in the People's Republic of China, Korea
and Taiwan, female literacy is catching up with that of men. In the
Philippines, girls outnumber boys from elementary to post-graduate
levels (Monteil and Hollnsteiner, 1976). In most of Asia, however,
women, particularly those above the age of 30, have a far lower level
of literacy than men. In Buddhist countries, especially in rural
areas, literacy has been associated with the period young boys spend
in monasteries, from which girls are automatically excluded. In
1971, 39.5 per cent of men in India were literate and 18.4 per cent
of women, with only 13.2 per cent literacy among rural women (ICSSR,
1975). Some 92.1 per cent of the rural female workforce is illiter-
ate (Indian National Commission for Co-operation with UNESCO [INCCU],
1977). Twelve out of nineteen districts in Bangladesh have female
literacy rates below 13.7 per cent. In 1974, only 10.9 per cent of
rural women were literate, with those over 25 years of age most disadvantaged. Male literacy varies from 21-39 per cent (Islam, 1977b).
In many villages no females are literate. Attempts to raise the
literacy of adult women are often defeated by high drop-out rates
because of conflict with family roles. In Pakistan the most recent
figures relate to 1961, when 23.9 per cent of men and 7.4 per cent of
women were literate. A lively oral tradition in south Asia, to some
extent, compensates for these very low figures (Sebo, 1975).

The difference between male and female literacy in Malaysia is
great over the age of 25, less from 15-24 years; literacy is almost
equal from 10-14 years (Figure 4.1) (Malaysia, FFPA, 1976). In a
village near Muar, Johor State, 70 per cent of men above 21 years
were literate, but only 21 per cent of women; of these the majority
could read Jawi but not romanized Malay (Rogers, 1977). The proportion of boys to girls in Indonesian primary schools in 1971 was
59:41, but only 23 per cent of students at higher institutions of
learning were girls (Ihromi, 1973). It must be remembered, moreover,
that levels of literacy are not in themselves an indicator of the
amount or content of reading of individual women. Reading is also
restricted by lack of material, time and cost.

Certain of the high expectations of literacy are not always ful-
filled. It has been assumed that literacy will automatically lead to
a reduction in the number of children. In the Philippines, only when
women have graduated from at least Grade 6 or 7 of high school do
they limit the size of their family (see Chapter 9). The acquisition
of literacy may actually diminish the opportunity of rural women to
work since higher status confines her to the home. One sympathetic
observer reported the practice of educating up to the level of a job
but not above it, in the People's Republic of China, in order to
avoid boredom with a repetitive task (Sidel, 1972).

44

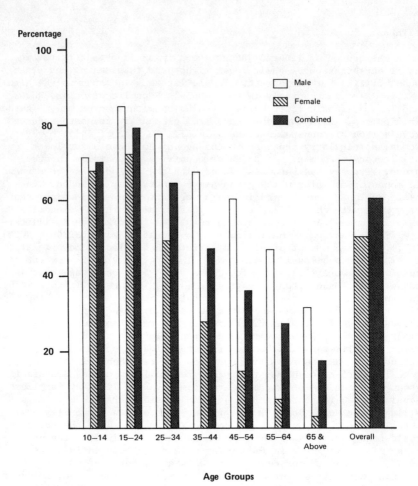

FIGURE 4.1 Malaysia: Percentage of literate population by specific age group by sex in peninsular Malaysia, 1970 (Malaysia, FFPA, 1976).

ATTITUDES TOWARDS EDUCATION

It is perhaps above all in access to education that Asian women have suffered most discrimination, although in early Hindu times women were considered worthy of education and Islam records many renowned women scholars. In China only in exceptional cases did women receive instruction. In one south China village in 1950, 65 per cent of the men and only 8 per cent of females over 10 years were literate. In Szechuan in 1942-43, 48 per cent of the men and 19 per cent of the women were literate (Yang, 1959). In a Hong Kong rural lineage renowned for the number of its scholars, few females were educated until after World War II (Baker, 1968).

Japanese women have long enjoyed equality of opportunity for education. In 1904, 90 per cent of girls attended primary schools; since 1969 the percentage of girls attending senior high school has exceeded that of boys and women represented 31 per cent of all students in higher education in 1973 (Japan, Prime Minister's Secretariat, 1976a). Traditional attitudes still prevail, however. In 1976, a survey by NHK (the national radio and television company) showed that parents of sons hoped they would acquire professional skills; they hoped their daughters would become "happy family women" (Bando, 1977). (How many western parents would answer differently?) Despite the high level of educational attainment, the concentration by women upon a limited number of "female" subjects restricts their choice of opportunities for employment (Japan, Prime Minister's Secretariat, 1976b). This applies to women who have reached higher education throughout Asia.

In Sri Lanka, education was centred on the temple and thus traditionally confined to men. The growth of missionary education was followed in 1945 by the introduction of universal free education from kindergarten to university, giving Sri Lanka exceptionally high rates of female literacy. At the University of Ceylon in 1966, nearly half the students were girls. Forty-four per cent of those with primary, 43 per cent of those with secondary and 37 per cent of those with higher education are women. More surprisingly, of urban G.C.E. (General Certificate of Education) holders 45 per cent are female, while in the rural areas 49 per cent are female; 29 per cent of those with higher education in urban areas are female and 42 per cent of those in rural areas, a ratio which is unique for Asia. However, lack of facilities in rural areas means a heavy concentration on arts subjects; science university students are predominantly urban and male (Kannangara, 1966). These high levels of education present great difficulties in finding suitable employment.

Access to education in recent decades and the levels achieved are changing the status of young women, making them less ready to accept subservient roles in joint families or minor roles in relation to their husbands and the upbringing of their children. Education is not, however, universally available, particularly in societies where female seclusion prevails.

South Asian education reformers wished both to improve the miserable plight of widows and to bridge the gap between the educated husband and his ignorant wife. It must be remembered that 9 years of Vedic and literary education was given to girls up until about the third century B.C. as a prerequisite for marriage (Altekar, 1959), and marriage took place at about 16 years. Women were accepted in Buddhist orders, and consequently educated, until the same period. By the beginning of this century, however, the situation had deteriorated to the point where in 1919, 0.9 per cent of the female Hindu population and 1.1 per cent of Muslim females were in school (Progress of Education in India, 1917-1922). There were innumerable sterile debates about the propriety of educating females; the consensus was that education for women broke down the ideals and instincts of Indian womanhood.

In traditional Bengal, women were educated only if a male family member was a teacher. Today most girls in Bangladesh at least start primary school, the reasons being given by their parents as "to obtain a good husband," "to perform religious duties better," "to enable her to work should necessity arise," "to enable her to understand what educated people say." The reasons for not educating girls are "no schools nearby," "unable to afford it," "she must help her mother," "too many siblings to look after" and "education is not valued for females" (Abdulla, 1976). In the past only high-status females were given religious education, but this is now much more general. However, "at most one-third of primary school attendants are female" (Germain, 1976), and they drop out earlier than boys. Enrolment at primary school has risen from 19.8 per cent of total enrolment in 1951 to 36.75 per cent, but of 6.9 million school-age girls, 64 per cent were out of school in 1975; in rural areas 73 per cent of girls, compared with 34 per cent of boys, were out of school. The proportion varies widely from district to district, and the dropout rate ranges from 57 to 73 per cent from Classes I and II. There is some indication that family economic circumstances are more important than distance from school in determining attendance, but the topic has been little studied.

During the period 1964-1974, female teachers were 5.17 per cent of the total and only 10.66 per cent of rural primary schools had a female teacher. The disparity between availability of secondary education for boys and girls is great, the average coverage of a boys' school being 6.54 square miles and that of a girls' school 50.27 square miles, again with wide regional differences. Eighty-four per cent of secondary-school-age girls and 56 per cent of boys are out of school, the drop-out rate for girls being nearly double that for boys, accelerating with each higher class (Islam, 1977b). A detailed survey of female education in Bangladesh has concluded that there is a serious imbalance between sexes in enrolment and drop-out rate; between rural and urban areas; in curriculum and in age-group. No agriculture is taught to girls, despite their important role in production from the land. Vocational training needs to be more realistically attuned to women's needs and potentialities, and overall needs are so great that increased recourse to non-formal education at all levels is considered essential (Islam, loc. cit.).

A survey of school textbooks in Bangladesh revealed both the low representation of women in stories and their characterization as passive, resistant to change, unintelligent and intellectually inferior to men (Krippendorff, 1977). This attitude further contributes to diminishing the importance of education for girls and reinforces the inferior content of the curriculum considered suitable for them, as well as perpetuating a poor adult image of women and their own low view of their abilities.

In India, there is a similar imbalance in female education, despite the increase in proportion of girls from 28.1 per cent of total primary school children in 1950-1951 to 38.3 per cent in 1974. There is great variation, however, between states and within states, especially in relation to socio-economic status. Special programmes to encourage female education started in 1957 and have continued with

varying measures of support. A review by the Planning Commission was
initiated in 1971, showing that free tuition and stipends and the
provision of free textbooks encouraged female enrolment, as did mid-
day meals and the provision of school mothers and sanitary facilities
for girls. Few schools, however, were able to provide these facilities (India, Planning Commission, 1978b). Parents of school-going
girls thought their daughters would manage homes and care for their
children better than those who were uneducated, could find work in an
emergency and would marry more advantageously. The major reasons for
preventing girls from enrolling or withdrawing them from school were
economic, stressing the help they gave in the home and caring for
siblings, as well as their ability to work for a wage.

In 1973-1974, 3 out of 10 girls in Class I reached Class V, one
from Class V reached Class VII and one of 12.5 girls passed the
secondary leaving examination. A girl should not be more highly
educated than her husband and she should marry within her jati; her
level of education is therefore directly related to the level of
education of males within that jati and is thus one of the reasons
for the high drop-out rate of girls (Srinivas, 1977). "The pressure
to get women educated is part of the process of securing good husbands for them." Secondary education and above is confined mostly to
the urban middle-class and élite groups, but there are now more women
post-graduate students than men in India and the figure is increasing
(Rao, 1978).

Pakistani villagers do not consider education of value for
women. In a west Punjabi village, literacy at the time of the 1961
Census was 4.8 per cent for both men and women, with religious education being more important for women. Forty-three per cent of women
interviewed in 1975 saw no need for their daughters to receive primary education, although poverty and the lack of separate facilities
for girls in the village were also factors. Wealthier families would
not educate their girls for prestige reasons--"they will not need to
earn a living." But among those who wish to educate their daughters,
enhanced status is clearly perceived as a benefit by many--"she will
become wise with education and will command respect from her
husband"; "her husband will regard her as his equal." Only 4 women,
themselves literate, wanted their daughters to complete secondary
education: one woman lived in a nearby town so that her girls might
attend school while her mother-in-law looked after the village home.
However, 84 per cent of villagers think that the concept of equal
educational opportunities for girls and boys is absurd. Boys have to
gain their livelihood, and their education is an investment. Girls
themselves believe that boys are cleverer than they, and so have the
right to more education. One educated girl in the village wanted to
teach, but her family would not permit her to do so--"there are no
blessings in a woman's earnings." Women are more anxious to learn
skills which will bring them income than to become literate (Khan and
Bilquees, 1976).

The requirements of purdah are a major obstacle to the education
of girls from around the age of 12; separate schools in rural areas
are few, and few educated women teachers are willing to live in villages. Even in cities, questions of sexual propriety are inextrica-
bly linked with the pursuit of higher education for girls, as the

following report from the <u>Khyber Mail</u> of March 29, 1977, shows:

> A young woman in Peshawar attempted suicide on being
> refused permission to enter a medical institution "because her
> parents feared that she would become involved in a love affair".
> The orthodox consider co-education leads to corruption and moral
> laxity, and "fail to understand how the boys find it convenient
> to attend to their lessons in the classrooms when the girls are
> so near and when exotic perfumes, wafted by the wind, fill their
> nostrils". Girls who thus keep company with boys "become
> dewomanized and emerge bolder and immodest and eventually begin
> to hate and neglect their household chores".

It will take some time before the editorial writer's plea that "when
there is free and indiscriminate mingling of girls with boys, sex-
consciousness will be least aroused" is generally accepted.

Only 20 per cent of girls of primary school age are enrolled in
Nepal and, by 1975, only 5 per cent of the female population was
literate (Rana, 1978). A study in a Nepali village showed that while
boys aged 6 to 9 years devoted 13 per cent of their time to school
activities, girls spent only 2 per cent of their time in school.
From 12-14 years, boys spent 18 per cent of their time in school,
while girls at this age were fully occupied in household activities
and spent only 3 per cent of their time at school (Nag, White and
Creighton Peet, 1978).

The lack of interest in female education attributed to Confucius
has had far-reaching consequences in east Asia. In the first century
A.D., the exceptional Han woman scholar, Pan Chao, in her <u>Lessons for
Women</u>, which served generations of women up to modern times, maintained that women should be educated:

> Now examine the gentlemen of the present age. They only know
> that wives must be controlled, and that the husband's rules of
> conduct manifesting his authority must be established. They
> therefore teach their boys to read books and [study] histories.
> But they do not in the least understand that husbands and
> masters must [also] be served, and that the proper relationship
> and the rites should be maintained. Yet only to teach men and
> not to teach women--is that not ignoring the essential relation
> between them? According to the "Rites" it is the rule to begin
> to teach children at the age of eight years and by the age of
> fifteen years they ought then to be ready for cultural training.
> Only why should it not be [that girls' education as well as
> boys' be] according to this principle? (translated, Swann, 1932).

Yet this education was in no way aimed at the self-realization of
women as individuals. "The way of respect and acquiescence is
woman's most important principle of conduct." Women should have 4
qualifications: (1) womanly virtue; (2) womanly words; (3) womanly
bearing; and (4) womanly work. Chastity, appropriate and sparing
language, personal cleanliness, industriousness, hospitable behaviour
and avoidance of gossip and silly laughter were all involved in these
4 qualifications, as was obedience to her mother-in-law and harmony

with brothers- and sisters-in-law. Education was proposed only for
girls of the upper classes, not for women in general (Swann, loc.
cit.). These aims were supported centuries later, by Li Ju-chen's
Ching-hua Yuan, written in the mid-Ch'ing dynasty (Brandauer, 1977).
Even today, the boy/girl ratio in rural primary schools in China
averages 60:40 (Orleans, 1978). In Taiwan more males than females
are enrolled at every level of education, but there has been a
gradual change. From 1964 to 1973, the percentage of females in high
schools has risen from 37 to 43 per cent; in colleges and universities from 29 to 37 per cent, and in national universities from 28 to
40 per cent. In 1965 fewer than 3,200 women graduated from colleges
and universities; in 1972 there were 17,800 female graduates (Appleton, 1979).

The traditional Chinese view of suitable education for women
came to be widely adopted into the samurai way of life in Tokugawa
Japan* (from the late sixteenth century). Samurai women were educated in the home, though some lower-class girls did attend school
with boys. The Onna Daigaku, the manual of education by Ekiken
Kaibara (1630-1714), stressed the self-abnegating obedience to
father, husband and son which was the Confucian ideal, with some
flavour of aggressiveness in the defence of her honour and of her
husband which was characteristic of Chinese heroines (Dore, 1965).
Literary attainment was permitted, but was to be limited to Japanese
classics; Chinese classics were reserved for men, a division of culture which went back to Heian times (794-1185 A.D.). Moreover, a
woman must keep her learning a profound secret, since it would be
viewed with disfavour by men (Dore, loc. cit.).

A survey of attitudes towards education in 4 Thai and 2 Malay
villages made by members of the Center of South East Asian Studies,
Kyoto, unfortunately paid little attention to sex differences
(Murata, 1978). In particular, one would like to have seen a break-
down of enrolment at different levels of education between boys and
girls, specific reasons for keeping girls at home and reasons for
different educational aspirations for sons and daughters. Compara-
bility of the results is further vitiated by the fact that while 2 of
the Thai villages are in poor areas practising traditional rice technology and 2 in irrigated double-crop areas, both the Malay villages
are situated within irrigation schemes. Average Malay income in the
study is thus considerably higher than average Thai income. In Thailand, 40 per cent of children aged 7 to 18 were not enrolled in
school; 30.7 per cent of those 11-13 years, 68.3 per cent of those
14-16 and 73 per cent of those 17-18 years were not enrolled. Under
10 per cent of Malay children aged 6-11 years were not enrolled, 22.7
per cent of those 12-14 years and 45.2 per cent of those 15-18 years.
In both countries, economic and personal factors account for children
not being enrolled in primary schools; at higher levels, economic

---

*The ancient Chinese Shu Chin (Book of Government) says "The hen
rules in the morning--the hen crows louder than the cock; the wife
wears the breeches." Japanese sages expressed this sentiment as
"When women are learned and clever in their speech, it is a sign that
civil disturbance is not far off."

reasons predominate, particularly the need for older children to help
in work.

Parents in both countries value education as a means of attaining better jobs, an easier life and a higher standard of living and
overwhelmingly prefer white collar jobs for their children. Malays
favour the civil service and teaching for both sons and daughters and
nursing for daughters, while Thais favour teaching for sons and
daughters, the civil service above all for sons and nursing for
girls. More Thais than Malays are prepared for their children to
become cultivators. Forty-seven and a half per cent of Thai and 78
per cent of Malay teachers in the survey would prefer working at
urban schools. Thais consider higher education more important for
sons than daughters, though some thought it equally important for
both. Malay parents regard religious and moral education as more
important for boys and girls than learning to read and write and
practical training. Thais stress reading and writing and practical
training in farming, daily life, health and rural development
(Murata, loc. cit.).

Attitudes towards the education of children are modified by
improvements in the standard of living following the introduction of
irrigation, improved infrastructure and higher incomes. There has
been an increasing interest in higher education in a village which
came within the Muda irrigation scheme of Kedah, northwest Malaysia
in 1973. In 1968 there were only 3 middle school students in Form 6,
while in 1976 2 had graduated from university and another 2 were
attending university. Even the poorest villagers wished to educate
their children to the highest level. Special facilities for higher
education to promising Malay children have also raised villagers'
aspirations (Kuchiba, 1978).

The traditional low importance given to education for girls in
Malaysia is revealed by the fact that 75 per cent of those without
formal education are women, mostly above the age of 25. Even today,
with each successive year of school, there are increasing numbers of
drop-outs, particularly of girls; while the proportion of women
undergraduates was 25 per cent in 1962, in 1976 when the number of
undergraduates had increased tenfold, the proportion of women was
still only 30 percent. The Ministry of Education has observed that
the sex-typing of roles does not encourage girls to pursue their
education (Malaysia, FFPA, 1976). (See Figure 4.2, p. 61.)
Increased enrolment has been accompanied by different emphasis on
educational content, the primary aim for girls being to produce good
mothers and future employment in roles subordinate or nurturant to
males--as secretaries, teachers, social workers and nurses
(Manderson, 1978a).

A report released by UNESCO in 1979 showed that while overall
expansion of primary education in Asia had increased greatly up until
1965, the rate since then has declined steadily. Korea, Malaysia,
the Philippines, Singapore and Thailand are approaching universal
enrolment. Burma, Indonesia and Sri Lanka have made slightly less
progress; over 50 per cent of girls of primary-school age in India
are enrolled in school, while less than 50 per cent of eligible girls
attend primary school in Bangladesh, Nepal and Pakistan (UNESCO,

TABLE 4.1
Percentage Enrolment of Girls in Primary School

	1960	1965	1970	1975	(Projections) 1980	1985
Bangladesh	27	28	28	30	30	31
Burma	47	47	47	48	49	49
Indonesia	45	46	47	46	47	47
Pakistan	21	23	26	30	32	35
Nepal	13	16	16	18	23	26
Sri Lanka	45	48	48	51	(not available)	
Thailand	48	48	48	48	49	49

Source: UNESCO, 1979.

1979).[*] Table 4.1 shows the percentage of girls enrolled in school
at different periods, together with future projections, for some of
the countries in UNESCO's Asian region.

There are wide regional disparities in the rate of female enrolment within these countries. However, countries with a high gross
enrolment of girls (over 75 per cent) show small disparities by sex,
while those with low total participation of girls also show wide gaps
in enrolment between the sexes (UNESCO, 1978b). Girls represented by
far the highest proportion of the out-of-school population in 1975
and the proportion, as well as total numbers, are expected to grow in
the future. The drop-out rate for girls is consistently higher than
that for boys. In 12 countries in UNESCO's Asian region, boys in the
last grade of primary school represent 31 per cent of those in the
first grade, while girls in the last grade are only 27.5 per cent of
those in the first. Korea has a female drop-out rate of 5 per cent,
Malaysia 20 per cent, the Philippines and Sri Lanka 45 per cent and
other Asian countries have drop-out rates for girls exceeding 70 per
percent (UNESCO, 1978a). Only three-fifths of girls enrolled continue beyond the first year of primary school.

POLITICAL PARTICIPATION

Despite the early momentum gained in independence movements in
Asia, when women participated in large numbers, the proportion of
women in the political life of their countries is low. Politics is

---

[*]Figures provided at international meetings must be regarded
with caution for various reasons: for example, geographical access
to remote areas may be difficult, necessitating rough estimates, and
statistical expertise may not be adequate.

still seen as a male preserve, and this applies from the national
level down to the village. While women vote in great numbers, few
hold high political office, either in the Communist or non-Communist
countries, a fact often overlooked because of the prominence of
Indian Prime Minister Indira Gandhi and Madame Nguyen Thi Binh, first
Education Minister of unified Vietnam. Many outstanding women poli-
ticians in Asia are daughters, wives or sisters of men who have themselves taken a leading role and who have encouraged them to enter
politics.

Roles which are granted during independence movements and times
of war are later withdrawn and goals set almost exclusively in areas
of social welfare and education. There is "a general trend of
socialization towards passivity in the public sphere" (Jaquette,
1977). This makes the task of would-be reformers especially difficult, since they need to arouse women as well as men to an awareness
of women's public rights and duties; this imposes a greater aggressiveness than many cultures permit women. The rout of the feminist
party of Misako Enoki, in the elections of July, 1977, was an expression of the distaste of both men and women at an outspokenness and
behaviour not tolerated from women in Japan.

The numbers of women in office have not risen with the spread of
literacy and increased job opportunities for women, as was expected.
Twelve women, including Chiang Ching, were dropped from the Central
Committee during the Eleventh Party Congress of the People's Republic
of China in August, 1977, including the only 2 women in the Polit-
buro. Only 4 were added to the Central Committee. Chien Cheng-ying,
Minister of Water Conservancy and Power, appointed to the Central
Committee in 1973, retained her position. At the National People's
Congress which met in March, 1981, Chen Mu-hua, the only woman Deputy
Prime Minister, was appointed Minister in charge of the State Family
Planning Commission; she was already Minister of Economic Relations
with Foreign Countries. The Central Committee of 201 full members
has only 14 women, and there are only 24 women out of 132 alternate
members (David Bonavia, Far Eastern Economic Review, Oct. 7, 1977).
There is still a disproportionately low number of female cadres
(Croll, 1976). An article in the People's Daily for July 1, 1973,
reported that out of 6,000,000 new members of the Communist Party
enrolled between 1966-1973, only 27 per cent were women, though
higher proportions of women are active in the Young Communist League
(Croll, 1979).

While press accounts claim 25 per cent or more of rural cadres
in model areas in Kwangtung are female, the average appears much
lower. In 1973-1974 most teams and brigades had at least one female
cadre, and a few 2 or 3. Usually a brigade women's federation chief
served among 6 to 11 male cadres, and one woman served as women's
team head at production team level (Parish and Whyte, 1978).
Increase in women's representation is a result of political pressure
from above, rather than a result of women's increased role in production. Team and brigade female cadres concentrate on female-centred
activities, such as field work and birth control, rather than
serving as general leaders. The team head, who is almost always
male, is responsible for assigning field tasks (Parish and Whyte,
loc. cit.).

It has been suggested that the durability of village cohesion in the form of production teams reinforces the patriarchal stress in Chinese society: political advancement is discouraged because women marry out of their natal villages (Diamond, 1975). Reluctance of women to take on additional roles may be a reason for inadequate representation of women at lower levels of politics, but their very low representation at the higher levels of the party is not to be attributed to them. When the Women's Federation was founded in 1949, Teng Ying-chao accused women of narrow-mindedness, frailty, a sense of reliance on others, susceptibility to sentiment, vagueness in political conceptions and lack of principles (Croll, 1974), failings which have not been altogether removed.

The Women's Federation played an important part in involving women in production and making them aware of their new rights. Representation from brigade level through commune and provincial levels to the National Committee enabled women to influence policies affecting women. During the Cultural Revolution, however, the Women's Federation was suspended, since it was considered that women were actively participating and represented in overall commune activities. Over recent years women's solidarity groups have again received attention, as it came to be conceded that their specific interests were being neglected (Croll, 1979). In 1978 the reconstituted Women's Federation had 42 members (New China News Agency, Feb. 25, 1978/SWB Feb. 28, 1978). In his report to the Fifth Chinese National People's Congress, Chairman Hua Kuo-feng stressed the need to elevate the status of women and to promote outstanding women and young people to positions of leadership at all levels (NCNA June 25, 1979/SWB June 28, 1979).

It is difficult to escape the conclusion that the principal reason for the lack of participation in politics by Chinese women today is the heavy double burden of field work followed by housework and care of children in the home. For this reason, also, it is believed that women play little role in informal village affairs, which are discussed mainly by older men sitting together in the evenings, while women are busy at home (Parish and Whyte, 1978).

In Vietnam, higher proportions of women take part in politics, perhaps reflecting the rule that women are more visible in public life in the early years of independence. One hundred and thirty-two women were elected to the National Assembly in 1976, making them 26 per cent of the total (Gough, 1977). Women are said to be strongly represented in party committees and in provincial and district government. However, Madame Nguyen Thi Binh, in an interview in 1980, said there were few women holding major political positions. There were 10 female deputy ministers, and none of the 17 Politburo members were women. Women constitute about 30 per cent of the National Assembly members, but only 6 of the 131 members of the Central Committee are women (Far Eastern Economic Review, June 20, 1980).

The institution of purdah severely restricts female participation in leadership in Pakistan, and women are nominated to reserved seats, not elected. Recent developments have, however, brought the wife and daughter of former Prime Minister Bhutto into prominence. In Bangladesh women are nominated to 15 reserved seats (Jahan, 1975).

Women political leaders all belong to the middle classes or élite, all have been educated to university level or above, all are married with children and have domestic help. Many have male relations who have been, or are, active in politics (Jalal, 1975). It is believed that while nomination to reserved seats may diminish chances of direct election, it is unlikely as many as 15 women would receive seats unless so nominated.

In Korea, "leadership from parliament to village level is male" (Soon, 1977a). In recent years the number of women elected from regional constituencies to the Korean National Assembly has been 3 or less, the same proportion as 28 years ago. The total number of candidates has decreased. In 1973, out of a total of 219 seats, 146 were elected, including 2 women, and 73 appointed, including 8 women. In 1976 one woman was elected and 7 appointed.

In 1979, 9 women were elected to the Thai House of Representatives, out of a total of 310 seats, and 3 women were nominated to the Senate, out of a total of 225 seats. The Deputy Minister of Education is a woman. It has been claimed that women have some voice in village government, since they may represent their husbands while they are away (de Young, 1966). However, women are not well-represented in community, district, province or national decision-making arenas. Rural women feel competent to hold political or village leadership office and able to solve community problems, feel that they are as "smart" as men, but also that men should lead and women follow (Nantanee et al, 1977).

Manderson (1977c) warns against evaluating the role of women in politics without at the same time studying changes in overall political participation. In Malaysia, participation in national politics is a postwar phenomenon for both men and women. None the less, the role granted women is far more limited than that accorded men. Women are allowed only 1 per cent of seats on the supreme decision-making body of the United Malays National Organization (UMNO), though they represent about 50 per cent of total membership. During the period 1955-1969, 9 women were nominated as election candidates and 8 elected to the Federal Parliament, out of a total of 362 seats. In the State Assemblies, 34 women were nominated and 24 actually elected out of a total of 851 seats. In local council elections in 1962, 6 of 7 nominated ruling party candidates were elected out of a total of 2,436 seats on 287 councils (Manderson, loc. cit.). No party in the traditional state of Kelantan put up a woman candidate for the crucial (on a national scale) elections of 1978. None would risk losing the vote on the grounds that women could not take a leading role in Islamic worship and were therefore ineligible for election. In 1978, out of 154 members of Parliament, 6 were women, and 5 of 58 senators were women. One woman in 730,000 is elected to Parliament, but one man in 30,000 men (Malaysia, FFPA, 1976).

Women leaders in the women's branch of UMNO holding key positions are members of the élite, while those at division and branch levels are educated, married and usually able to afford domestic help. Members, however, are predominantly rural, middle-aged and uneducated, though the spread of education is beginning to attract younger, more educated women (Manderson, 1977a).

While women branch members of UMNO involved themselves in social, educational, economic and political work, this did not represent a departure from their traditional role; they were subordinate to the party and to its male leaders (Manderson, 1977c).

In a village near Muar, Johor State, 84 per cent of women were only passively involved in politics, while 16 per cent were marginally involved. Kampong leaders did not try to persuade women to join the women's branch of UMNO because it was considered that politics was not their proper concern; they were confident that women would vote as instructed by their husbands and socially prominent villagers (Rogers, 1977).

In Indonesia, 7 per cent of members of parliament and 10 per cent of members of the provincial legislatures are women (Noor, 1976). A junior minister for women's affairs was appointed in April, 1978.

In Japan, the female voting rate since 1968 has exceeded that of men, with a higher proportion of women in their fifties, rather than twenties and thirties, voting (Japan, Prime Minister's Secretariat, 1976a). In the 1976 elections to the Lower House, however, women were only 7 out of 511 elected; this figure rose to 11 in the 1979 elections. Eighteen women were elected out of 250 senators in the Upper House in 1977. In Prefectural Assemblies they were 32 out of 2,796, and in town and village assemblies, 217 out of 48,003. However, women are active in a large number of women's organizations and in trade unions (Bando, 1977). Two-thirds of all adult women belong to local or national associations covering a wide variety of activities, from defence of the peace constitution, nuclear disarmament, consumer rights, pollution control, confrontation on education policies, child care facilities for employed mothers, etc. In 1967, only 13.5 per cent of women were so affiliated (UNESCO, 1976). Yet only 16 per cent of women in a recent survey said they were positively interested in politics; 54 per cent said they were "somewhat interested." Women are not politically doctrinaire or socially utopian and, hence, focus on the specific issues dealt with by a specific association. Social scientists have pointed out the difficulty women encounter in obtaining their husbands' consent to political participation. Even in the Citizen's Movement, they talk of the "4:30 lady," who, no matter how involved, must return home to be ready for her husband (Jones, 1976).

A major explanation for the low proportion of women holding political office must undoubtedly come from their perception of the most valuable use of their time. Benefits from time devoted to home and child care, from the income gained in employment and victories which may result from participation in citizen's movements are immediately perceptible. The concept of benefits to women or society as a whole as a result of individual efforts in the political arena remains nebulous to all but a small proportion of the educated urban élite. In India, "the benefits which women as a group derive from the prominence of a few women in leadership positions are not substantial" (Katzenstein, 1978). Asian women active in politics tend already to have raised families and, consequently, to have more time for other pursuits. Table 4.2 shows the age and background of women in both houses of parliament in Japan in 1978.

TABLE 4.2
Japan: Women in Government (1978)

Name	Home	Party	Function	Educational Attainment	Age	Times Elected	Short Career
Members of the House of Representatives:							
Mitsu KANEKO	Tokyo	Socialist	Member, Council of Social Welfare	Toronto University	62	2	Assistant Professor, Tokyo University
Masako KOBAYASHI	Tokyo	Communist	Member, Council for Transport	Left Nihon University before graduation	52	3	Leader, Women's Branch of Communist Party; Primary School teacher; Member, Tokyo Municipal Assembly
Michiko TANAKA	Aichi	Socialist	Member, Council for Society and Labour	University	54	2	Assistant Professor, University for Social Welfare
Chiyose CHIBA	Chiba	Socialist	Member, Council for Education	Art College	69	1	Consultant to Chiba municipal office; Member, House of Counsellors
Takako DOI	Hyogo	Socialist	Member, Council for Foreign Affairs	Doshisha University	48	3	Chief, Pollution Control Office of Socialist Party; Lecturer, Doshisha University
Hiroko FUJIHARA	Kyoto	Communist		High School	50	1	Member, Kyoto City Assembly; Primary School teacher
Shizue YAMAGUCHI	Tokyo	Socialist	Member of Council	High School	59	12	
Members of the House of Counsellors:							
Chiyose CHIBA	Chiba	Socialist	(see above)	Art College	69		Head, Council for Society and Labour

Name	Prefecture	Party	Council	Education	Age	No.	Background
Shigeru ISHIMOTO	Ishikawa	LDP	Member, Council for Labour and Accounts	Short-course School for Efficiency	63	3	Parliamentary Under-secretary for Social Welfare
Fusae ICHIKAWA	Aichi	Second Club	Member, Council for Finance	Normal School	84	4	President, League of Women Voters
Taeko IWAGAMI	Ibaraki	LDP	Member, Council for Agriculture	Medical School	49	1	Consultant, League of Politicians for Promotion of Agriculture of Ibaraki Prefecture
Sadako OGASAHARA	Hokkaido	Communist	Member, Council for Labour	High School	57	2	Chief, Hokkaido Branch of Communist Party; Vice-President, Japan Women's Federation
Toshiko OTAKA		LDP	Member, Council for Foreign Affairs	High School	57	1	Deputy Head, International Branch of LDP; Film actress; Adviser, Animal Welfare Association
Yasu KASHIWARA	Nagano	Socialist	Member, Council for Education	Normal School	60	4	Chief, Special Committee for Science and Technology; Leader, LDP Women's Branch
Terumi KASUYA	Niigata	Socialist	Member, Council for Education	Normal School	53	1	Deputy Head, Japan Teachers' Union Women's Branch; Primary and Secondary School teacher
Takeko KUTSUNUGI	Osaka	Communist	Member, Council for Post and Accounts	Medical College	55	2	Member Standing Committee, Japan New Women's Association; Hospital matron
Akiko SANTO	Tokyo	LDP	Member, Council for Education	Art College	35	1	Literary critic; Film actress; Radio/television personality

TABLE 4.2 (cont'd)

Members of the House of Counsellors: (cont'd)

Name	Home	Party	Function	Educational Attainment	Age	Times Elected	Short Career
Aiko SHIMURA	Tokyo	LDP	Member, Council for Post	National High School for Music	60	2	Parliamentary Under-secretary, Hokkaido Reclamation Agency
Kyoko SHIMODA	Fukushima	Communist	Member, Council for Agriculture	Fukushima University	37	1	Middle School teacher; Member, Town Assembly
Sumiko TANAKA	Hyogo	Socialist	Member, Council for Finance	University	67	3	Former Chief, Women's Section Ministry of Labour
Hiroko HAYASHI	Tokyo	LDP	Member, Council for International Affairs	Takarazuka School of Music	44	1	Actress
Hiroko YASUTAKE	Kobe	Communist	Member, Council for Commerce and Accounts	High School	48	1	Women's Leader, Hyogo Prefecture Union
Michiko WATANABE	Hyogo	Komei	Member, Council for Labour	Waseda University	45	1	Member, House of Representatives
Ikuko YAMANAKA	Tokyo	Communist	Member, Council for International Affairs	Waseda University	45	1	Standing Committee, Nippon Union of Telegraph and Telephone Corporation

Source: The authors are indebted to Professor M. Kanematsu, former Dean, Shinshu University, for the information in this table.

It is not easy for women to regard politics as an acceptable arena for their self-expression. Most positions of power in all major societies are held by men; in many countries, as in Japan, women were prevented by law from attending political meetings (Pharr, 1981). Women who participate in political activities in Japan drop out during the years of "marriage crisis" from 23 to 26 years. The wife-mother role is seen as excluding political life. Popular definitions of woman's proper role in most societies continue to pro-scribe power-seeking behaviour as legitimate for women. The struggle to achieve acceptance by society of a political role, however, is greater than that involved in changing her own outlook. Family background, the presence of someone who has served as a model, family situations favouring a woman's independent choice of action or access to politically-inspiring literature have been shown to be important in a woman's decision to enter politics (Pharr, loc. cit.).

The number of women in both central and state governments in India has fluctuated around 5 per cent since independence—still higher than in some western countries. However, in the 1977 elections the figure declined to 3.6 per cent (Katzenstein, 1978). The average age of women in government has risen from 48.6 years in 1952 to 54 in 1972. Women's attitudes towards politics range from those who consider politics "too complicated an activity" and "would like to leave it to my husband," through those who would wish to vote differently from their husbands but refrain out of deference; those who take no part; and those who exercise their rights independently. There is little encouragement for women to participate. Once elected, they are unable to act without seeking help from a man with an established sphere of influence, particularly as most women do not remain long in office. When elected to party or legislative positions women do not find it easy to concentrate on women's special concerns (Imtiaz, 1975). A survey of successful candidates in the 1971 elections to parliament and of successful and defeated candidates in the 1972 state assembly elections showed that the majority did not take special interest in women's affairs, nor did they read their party's women's journal. Furthermore, 38 per cent of members of parliament and 48 per cent of state assemblywomen had not read their own party manifesto; higher proportions had not read those of opposition parties. On perception of their political role, only 26 per cent received high scores; 54 per cent were average and the remainder were completely ignorant of their duties and functions as members of the legislature. (It would be instructive to see a similar survey of male legislators.) Despite this, many were aware of important current issues and had useful suggestions for their solution (Mehta and Billimoria, 1977). The Congress Party had intended reserving 15 per cent of total seats for women, though they achieved only 12 per cent, while the Socialist Party did not achieve its target of 10 per cent. There was little hostility by voters to women candidates, but influence with the party bosses was found to be a major qualification for nomination. Parties did not educate candidates in party structure and constitution, nor did they maintain discipline. The costs of electioneering and the pressure of domestic duties, coupled with the traditional dominance of men in politics were all seen as obstacles to the active participation of women in

politics. Mehta and Billimoria propose a minimum allocation of 25
per cent of seats in the legislature to women, and better education
of both voters and candidates.

On the whole, Indian women are characterized by passive political orientation based on the traditional division of labour and
authority. "Naturally, with few models of 'independent' women to
emulate, only a small percentage of women are willing to risk failure
in the female world of marriage and motherhood in order to prove
their worth in the male world of politics" (Imtiaz, 1975).

ACCESS TO HIGHER POSITIONS IN THE
PROFESSIONS AND MANAGEMENT

The overriding factor governing women's public role, whether it
be in modern metropolitan cities or distant villages, remains custom,
what society expects of them. At least 83 per cent of all women
professionals in southeast Asia are either nurses/midwives or teachers, showing the continuing close links with women's traditional,
supportive and nurturing roles of wife and mother (Manderson, 1978b).

Concern is expressed at the very small number of women in the
higher echelons of the professions in Singapore, where promotion is
found to be increasingly difficult in competition with men further up
the scale (Cheng, 1977; Wong, 1975; Aline Wong in Straits Times,
Sept. 16, 1977). Few are yet prepared to grant women significant
long-term roles outside their homes.

According to the 1976 Report of the Philippine National Commission on the Role of Women, there are 4 women ambassadors, 6 women
provincial governors, 3 Justices of the Court of Appeals and one
Supreme Court Justice. The Secretary, Department of Social Service
and Development is a woman. Discrimination against women is greatest
at middle levels of management; a training course for high level
government executives has had a low proportion of female participants, while half the junior executives have been women.

The current situation in Malaysia is shown in Figure 4.2, where
it is seen that only 3 per cent of administrative and managerial
workers are women (Malaysia, FFPA, 1976).

In Japan, 7.3 per cent of male workers are in managerial posts,
and only 1 per cent of women; only 5.8 per cent of all administrative
and managerial posts are held by women (Willing, 1978) (Figure 4.3
and Table 4.3). Fifty per cent of elementary school teachers are
women, and only 1.4 per cent of these are principals. Women form 20
per cent of the civil service; only 0.9 per cent of managerial posts
are held by them (Bando, 1977). A survey made July, 1977 by the
Labour Ministry noted that opportunities for self-fulfilment in
career-oriented jobs are exceedingly rare for women; job dissatisfaction among women increases with age, being much higher in the 35-44
age group than among young women. The Ministry considers reform
necessary to rectify the situation (Japan Times Weekly, April 8,
1978). Prejudice remains entrenched; only 6.7 per cent of management
staff support the concept of equality of opportunity for promotion
for men and women (UNESCO, 1976). A Labour White Paper (July 14,
1978) confirms that significant structural changes have occurred in

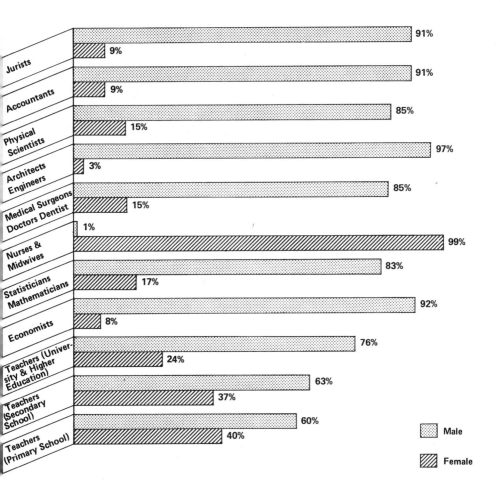

FIGURE 4.2   Malaysia: Percentage of male and female participation in selected professions, 1970 (Malaysia, FFPA, 1976).

Source: Department of Statistics

62

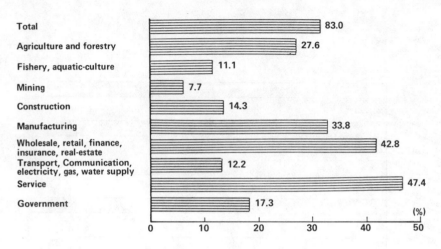

Source: "Labor Force Survey," Statistics Bureau, Office of the Prime Minister.

FIGURE 4.3   Japan: Women employees as percentage of all employees, by industry, 1973 (Japan, Prime Minister's Secretariat, 1976a).

Source: "Labor Force Survey," Statistics Bureau, Office of the Prime Minister.

the labour market since 1973.   Employment has increased only in the services sector, which employs temporary, mostly female workers. Temporary workers receive unfavourable terms in respect to wage rate, bonus, stability of work and fringe benefits (Japan Times Weekly, July 29, 1978).
    Women hold only 1.8 per cent of professional, administrative and managerial posts in Korea (Lee and Kim, 1976).   In government administrative (including schools) and judicial branches, only 15 per cent of the total employed are women (Lee and Cho, 1976).   Highly skilled women technicians account for less than 1 per cent of the total number of technicians, while only 5 per cent of women are doing professional, technical or administrative work (Lee, B., 1977).   A similar picture of the difficulty women encounter in attaining job satisfaction, particularly promotion in jobs involving direction of others, especially men, can be found throughout Asia.   One striking exception occurs in India, where in the prestigious Indian Administrative Service, Indian Foreign Service and Indian Political Service, the ratio of women to men has risen from 1:65 in 1960 to 1:7.6 in 1972. However, only 6 per cent of female employees in the central government earn over Rs. 600 per month (Katzenstein, 1978).   Women are only

TABLE 4.3
Japan: Women in Selected Occupations

Selected Occupations	Number (Persons)		As Percent of Total Employed	
	1965	1970	1965	1970
Technicians	2,700	9,795	0.6%	1.4%
Teachers	304,100	379,375	35.5	37.9
Physicians	10,500	11,245	9.9	9.5
Pharmacists	15,300	24,170	60.9	48.2
Nurses	230,500	306,780	98.3	97.6
Artists	37,000	30,445	35.5	25.7
Scientists	4,900	5,160	7.0	5.2
Judges, Prosecutors, Lawyers	200	300	0.5	2.4
Nursery nurses	64,800	95,845	100.0	100.0
Social workers	8,600	16,140	39.5	44.8
Managerial workers	79,200	97,590	5.6	4.8
Clerks	1,666,100	2,240,265	39.4	45.2
Stenographers, Typists	85,200	86,930	96.6	96.9
Operatives (electric machinery)	228,900	488,740	42.1	52.2
Operatives (yarn, thread and fabric mills)	858,200	788,745	71.9	71.0
Service workers (except household)	1,814,600	1,877,665	67.8	66.8
Household workers	185,500	138,810	100.0	98.3
Civil servants in managerial posts	900	1,060	1.1	1.0
Telephone operatives	161,400	145,110	96.6	97.0
Farmers	5,790,000	5,078,185	54.4	56.1

Source: Population Census; Japan, Prime Minister's Secretariat,
1976a.

17 per cent of all professional and technical workers and, of these,
over three-quarters are teachers (INCCU, 1977).
    In rural areas men's jobs are almost universally more highly
valued by society than are women's and are consequently better paid.
"The overriding impression is that while men bring in the greatest
tangible benefits, women work the longest hours for less or no
remuneration" (Papanek, 1977).
    It has been suggested that legislation, education, political
participation and level of employment opportunities are public indicators of women's status. Protective legislation has been enacted in
most Asian countries, but social and economic conditions prevent its
application. The need for primary education for girls increasingly
finds widespread acceptance, but economic and cultural constraints

limit enrolment and lead to high levels of drop-outs in later years.
The range of subjects considered suitable for girls who do
attend secondary school and college makes it difficult for them to
enter professional fields and employment which have traditionally
been considered "men's jobs." Reluctance to appoint women in positions of management is compounded by male unwillingness to take
directions from women. This is changing in metropolitan cities, but
these changes are not yet affecting the lives or prospects of rural
women.

Asian women participate in elections, but are reluctant to
compete with men for public office. This is especially true of Japan
where, despite decades of universal secondary female education, women
are only a small proportion of the members of parliament. Women are
readier to join action groups composed chiefly of women to campaign
on issues relating to social welfare. May one expect that as more
women educated to secondary level and above in southeast Asia reach
adulthood and have raised their own families, there will be more
women seeking office in a region more accustomed to seeing women take
initiative in economic matters than in east Asia?

5
Marriage

Anthropologists have suggested that marriage systems are basic-
ally communication systems, and geographers have attempted to relate
marriage patterns to an evolving market system. It is believed that
in a traditional area with undeveloped communication systems, there
is likely to be a high degree of peasant endogamy within the standard
market community. As transportation improves, villages focus more on
the intermediate marketing area, the next stage up in the market
hierarchy, and the marriage network is extended correspondingly.
With still greater improvement in communications, the central market
area is expected to be the endogamous community (Adams and Kasakoff,
1976b). The work of Skinner on China (1964/1965) and Knapp (1971)
and Crissman (1976) on Taiwan has been placed within this theoretical
framework. It is found, however, despite modernization in Taiwan,
the intermediate market town still maintains a 60 per cent rate of
endogamy. Temple sites and the locus of daily shopping also have 35
per cent endogamy. Even in traditional systems, élite groups linked
standard marketing communities (Skinner, 1964/1965) while the
marriage strategies of farmers, craftsmen and labourers living in the
more rural part of towns in Taiwan appear to differ from those of
shopkeepers and businessmen in the commercial part; the former may
make most marriages within the hinterland of the intermediate market
town or towns, while the commercial families make very few. Skinner
(1971) proposed that the degree of openness of communities was cycli-
cal, reaching a peak during periods of economic expansion.

Those who have worked with village communities in Asia are
likely to find these analyses too mechanical; it is, in fact, concluded that marketing alone does not structure marriage patterns.
There is probably no society in which proximity alone determines
marriage choice, as different segments of local groups make different
choices and thus belong to different endogamous enclaves. Some
societies make a conscious attempt to avoid making choices on the
basis of proximity in order to spread marriage ties more evenly
throughout a larger area. The size of such endogamous groups is
related to population density, the most highly endogamous groups
being those with lowest population densities and most likely to have
preferences for kin (Adams and Kasakoff, 1976a).

Marriage in Asia involves 2 groups, sometimes, especially in

66

bilateral societies, 2 nuclear families, but more commonly (in south
Asia, among traditional Chinese communities, Korea and still to some
extent in Japan), lineages or clans, resulting in relations with and
obligations to a large number of people. Relations within kin groups
are more a matter for individual decision in southeast Asia; which
members become trusted familiars in Thailand, for example, depends
entirely on the choice of the individual concerned and may be ter-
minated by either (Hanks and Hanks, 1963). Throughout the region
interchange between parents and other kin of the couple may cease
with the celebration of the marriage, following a number of visits
mediated by a go-between who bears a heavy responsibility for a
satisfactory agreement upon terms. Whether the marriage is between a
couple belonging to groups of equal status or between a woman of
lower and a man of higher status groups (hypergamy), an elaborate
code governs the behaviour of all participants.

In the past in China and often in India, the partners had not
usually set eyes on one another. The lengths to which a family would
go to prevent their daughter from being seen by any member of her
future husband's family have been described by Smith (1899/1970),
although in Taiwan there has been a trend over recent decades towards
a formal meeting prior to engagement (Diamond, 1969). In Japan, the
formal meeting or miai* at least ensured that if there was overriding
antipathy on either side and the candidate had enough courage to
express this, the marriage would not go ahead, though no knowledge of
compatibility could be expected from such a stilted occasion, in
which the chief protagonists would usually be too shy to utter a
word. Similarly, a young Indian might catch a brief glimpse of a
possible bride during a formal visit to her home in the company of
his parents and the go-between. In southeast Asia the couple may
know one another, often because they are related (in Malaysia,
Thailand and Indonesia). Increasingly the wishes of the young people
are considered (Ihromi, 1973). However, a trend towards free choice
in pre-Independence India has since largely been replaced by the
traditional pattern of parental choice (ICSSR, 1975).

RESPONSIBILITY AND CRITERIA FOR CHOICE OF PARTNER

Marriage is undoubtedly the most significant event in the life
of a rural girl and affects her wellbeing for the greater part of her
existence, particularly in east and south Asia. Here we attempt to
show to what extent a girl has any say in the selection of her mate
and how far interests other than her individual happiness may intervene.

A survey of the ethnographic material organized by Lebar, Hickey
and Musgrave (1964; Lebar, 1972; Lebar, 1975) reveals that, for the
majority of the tribal peoples of southeast Asia, marriage is based
on free choice; premarital sex is not usually frowned upon. Some

---

*The complexity of behaviour expected of participants in miai is
described in Tanizaki's The Makioka Sisters (translated by Edward
Seidensticker, Tuttle, Tokyo. 510 pp.).

groups which have come under Chinese influence may arrange their
children's marriages; this is especially so for the élite among them.
Some Philippine communities have practised infant betrothal. On the
whole, however, abundant opportunities are provided for young people
to meet and various forms of courtship, such as antiphonal singing,
are traditional.

It seems safe to conclude that the swidden base of culture in
most of southeast Asia, and among tribal peoples in India, has been
associated with lack of restriction upon young people. Free choice
and romantic love have been an accepted prelude to marriage, modified
only in the case of élite, property-owning groups and under the
influence of the great traditions imported into the region from both
east and west, which have not, however, completely obliterated the
freedom which prevailed before their adoption.

In Burma, young men initiate courtship, and none occurs without
a minimum of romantic love. The boy then informs his parents or,
more rarely, the girl does so. Burmese marriage takes place between
near equals, held together initially by physical attraction, tempera-
mental compatibility and joint decision-making (Nash, 1965). A
common Cambodian saying, "il faut cultiver le riz quand la terre est
chaude, et courtiser la fille quand l'amour s'anime"/"Rice should be
cultivated when the earth is warm, and a girl courted when love is
awakened" (Delvert, 1961), shows that romantic love was a normal
preliminary to marriage. At wat festivals in Laos young marriageable
girls used to set up small tables in the compound where they sold
fruit, sweets and soft drinks to young men, providing an excellent
opportunity for courtship (Halpern, 1964).

This would seem to contradict the views of Sanday (1974) who
believes that where mutual dependence for subsistence is an important
factor in marital stability, romantic love is uncommon as a basis for
marriage. It may be that mutual dependence is more crucial in
settled forms of land use where community labour is infrequent or
non-existent, but membership in a swidden group is based chiefly on a
number of active couples, who are thus also mutually dependent.

In patrilineal societies where inheritance of property, particularly land, is an important issue, marriage is expected to be enduring and the views of the partners have consequently been of lesser
concern. It has followed that virginity gained in importance, since
it was essential that a son should inherit his true father's share.
This was less important in matrilineal societies, where a child's
relation to the mother was crucial. Even here women have not invariably been free to choose their partner. Among the Nayar during the
traditional period (up to the end of the ninteenth century and early
in the twentieth) the approval of the male head of the matrilineage
was required before a relationship could be initiated (Fuller, 1976).
In patrilineal societies, however, the purity of women became linked
to the transmission of property (Goody, 1976) and the requirement of
virginity became a constraint upon the freedom of movement of women
(Dube, 1978a).

Today young men all over Asia may now request their parents to
initiate proceedings with the family of the girl of their choice;
53.7 per cent of young Thai men in one study made their own decision
on their partner (Luechai, 1975). However, parental approval and

traditional arrangements are still held to be essential. If subsequent difficulties arise, there is a whole circle of family members on both sides to advise, conciliate and do everything possible to save the loss of face to a group and economic hardship to a girl that rupture still entails in south and east Asia, or to bring public opinion to bear when a daughter is being ill-treated. In southeast Asia, however, and particularly in the Islamic societies of parts of Indonesia and in Malaysia, divorce has been so thoroughly institutionalized that, after some attempt at reconciliation, the alliance is dissolved. Relations between the 2 kin groups may then cease, particularly if there are no children. In these societies the obligation to arrange for the marriage of daughters as soon as possible outweighs any consideration of the likely stability of the union, although increasing levels of education are in some areas reducing the high rate of divorce. In east Java, relatives do not generate strong mutual interest in maintaining a marriage; there is usually no contractual or emotional bond of importance and strain between the couple is immediately reflected by strain between their families (Jay, 1969).

Throughout Asia, for those following the great traditions, the religious and social obligation of seeing one's daughters married as advantageously as possible, as early as possible in the interests of family honour, overshadows consideration of their probable happiness, even though it must not be assumed that such considerations are altogether absent. Love between spouses is not a precondition of marriage, nor is it formally expected to occur after marriage, practical considerations predominating. None the less, even if spouses do not show affection publicly, it is obvious that it often exists, reflecting reality rather than the convention (Swift, 1963).

Arrangement of marriage by parents does not appear always to have been the practice. At least some young couples in India seem to have exercised free choice until about 500 B.C., and educated girls had a say in the choice of their husbands (Dube, 1963); this persisted among some Khsatriya groups (Altekar, 1959). In rural Japan before Tokugawa times, marriage within the hamlet was a matter of choice by the partners. As the samurai code came to be widely adopted, so marriage came to be negotiated between families (Befu, 1971). In more remote areas, arranged marriage was not adopted until the turn of the present century and women enjoyed greater sexual freedom; fertility, not virginity, was the chief criterion in the selection of a bride (de Vos and Wagatsuma, 1973b). In modern Japan, social and financial security is an important consideration in the choice of a marriage partner. One-third to one-half of middle-class marriages are still arranged. Romantic love is a valued ingredient of a good match, but security is considered more important (Vogel, 1978). In rural Hong Kong modern marriages are based on free choice (Potter, 1969).

In Malaysia, segregation of girls has made parental choice almost inevitable, though boys may try to steal a look at the girl and parents say you cannot force a boy to marry against his will (Swift, 1963). Girls are increasingly having a say, however (Hashimah Roose, 1963). Changes over a 10 year period in Trengganu village have shown that advanced education and economic independence

are giving young people decision-making power (Strange, 1976a).
Moreoever, the traditional segregation of girls is being offset by
the increasing necessity for them to work. A study of a village in
Johor showed that the proportion of women working outside the home
was much higher than before the war, when higher yields were obtained
from larger family holdings and the desire for consumer goods was
more limited (Rogers, 1977). Wealth, the status of the spouse's
family, economic prospects and educational level of the partner are
all factors in the choice of a child's spouse, cousins being nominally preferred (Swift, 1963), though cousin marriage does not predominate (Husin Ali, 1975). Girls from Kedah, Pahang and Johor
usually marry outside their villages but within the same area; half
marry first, second or third cousins. In one Trengganu village,
first-cousin marriages were disapproved of (Strange, 1971), but were
common in a poor fishing village in the same state (Wilson, 1970).

Fragmentation of land in a Melaka village has produced a trend
away from kin marriages to marriage with non-kin, as new alliances
are more likely to lead to opportunities for employment elsewhere
(Maeda, 1978). None the less, 30 per cent of all marriages were with
first or second cousins, particularly first marriages; 73.9 per cent
of all marriages were endogamous, within the different hamlets which
make up the village, and 91.6 per cent of all partners had come from
within 10 miles of the village. Some favoured kin-marriage as a
means of cementing relations, while others feared the disruption of
kin-relations which might follow divorce (Maeda, loc. cit.). The
aboriginal Senoi of northern Malaysia marry anyone not brought up in
the same household (Carey, 1976).

Among the matrilineal Minangkabau of Sumatra, Indonesia and
Negri Sembilan, Malaysia, the most desirable form is cross-cousin
marriage (Swift, 1963). Young women in central Java show a greater
tendency to select their own husband, but even within this age group,
over 60 per cent of marriages were arranged (Singarimbun and Manning,
1974). Parents generally choose their child's first spouse in the
traditional manner, but subsequent mates are selected by the partners
(Jay, 1969). In Bali, commoners seek to marry partners of the same
or equivalent title and failure to do so brings tensions which are
often dissipated only with the birth of the first child. Such marriages are often by capture. A marriage is usually arranged by
parents, who may have been discussing the probability since the
partners were children. The couple is certainly acquainted and they
often sleep together before the simple ritual which is all that the
Balinese secular view of marriage requires. Marriage with the
father's brother's daughter is the ideal form; failing this, a wife
is best chosen from the group of relatives in the household cluster,
or at least from within the village. Gentry marriages are between
people of comparable rank, or with a commoner wife who also brings
the allegiance of her own group, as well as land to which she retains
rights, taking it back if divorced. Balinese marriages are generally
stable and divorce is rare (Geertz and Geertz, 1975).

In the Philippines, young couples whose parents object to their
alliance have always had recourse to elopement, though once the fait
accompli has been accepted by their families, the marriage is formal-
ized with as good grace as possible. It has been suggested that

shortage of land, which reduces the bargaining ability of parents, has tended to increase the number of elopements (Murray, 1971). In southwest Nueva Ecija Province, kin exogamy is the norm; in addition, a girl may not marry her neighbour's children nor those of the fictive kin of her parents.

In Thailand, parents with wealth which children will inherit arrange their marriages. Money and property are settled on the new couple before witnesses on the day of the wedding, but title to land is never conferred until the stability of the marriage is assured. Indigent young people frequently elope and may be encouraged by parents to do so in the interests of economy. They are later received back into their families (Hanks and Hanks, 1963). Marriages should be outside the hearth group, but marriage to first cousins is encouraged to keep property intact. Another account states that marriage to kin is not favoured, but is forbidden only within second cousin range (Piker, 1975). Today the majority of Thais in rural areas will choose their own spouse; 76 per cent of women considered this a right (Nantanee et al, 1977), though ethnic Chinese have a greater tendency to select their children's spouses.

First-cousin marriage is disliked in Burma, but village endogamy is preferred and was as high as 93 per cent in one village studied (Nash, 1965). Free choice is almost universal (Spiro, 1977).

Among the Limbu of Nepal, marriage is usually arranged by parents with children's consent and cousin marriage is forbidden (Caplan, 1974). There are often love marriages, based on acquaintance at the institutionalized courtship dances (Jones and Jones, 1976).

In Pakistan Punjab, men preferentially marry their father's brother's daughter and practise endogamy within the birdari or patrilineage. This is underlined by the belief that a child is seen as taking its qualities exclusively from its father, a woman's role being merely nurture. "If you sow barley, you cannot expect to harvest wheat, regardless of where you sow it" (Saghir Ahmad, 1974). Out of 287 marriages in a Rajput birdari, 234 were within the birdari, 209 being households in the same village. Marriages outside the birdari are regarded as hypergamous, with zat or caste being irrelevant (Saghir Ahmad, loc. cit.).

Cross- and parallel-cousin marriage sanctioned by Islam is subordinated in Bangladesh to the concept of adding new and potentially useful members to the kin-group, assisted by matrilateral and affinal kin who, by definition, reside elsewhere (Bertocci, 1974). Forty per cent of marriages took place between people residing within the same market area, the rest within the thana, up to 107 miles. The Hindus, being fewer in number, sought their spouses from greater distances. Among élite, educated, urban groups, many women choose their husband themselves (Islam, 1975).

In north India, marriage should not ideally take place with those related within 7 generations on the father's and 5 generations on the mother's side, though this is more commonly reduced to 5 and 3 generations respectively (Altekar, 1959). Intercaste marriage, especially hypergamous marriage, remained acceptable until about the tenth century. Clan exogamy is the norm in the north and a new alliance is created with each marriage. In south India, marriage to

cross-cousins is preferred and village endogamy may result (Mandelbaum, 1972). The girl is likely to know at least some members of her
new family.

Among the élite Ashraf (high-born of foreign descent) of north
India, group endogamy, with cross- and parallel-cousin marriage,
according to Islamic norms, is preferred. Marriage with patrilateral
cross-cousins is favoured, since theoretically this keeps property
intact. However, daughters rarely receive the land to which they are
entitled and, indeed, land holdings themselves have declined in
importance, as many have been broken up. Following Partition in 1947
and the departure of many unmarried young men for Pakistan, standards
for the status of daughters' spouses have had to be lowered, though
attempts are always made to find a groom within the biahdiari or
endogamous circle. Cousin marriage is abhorred by the non-Ashraf
Muslims who are descended from Hindu converts (Vreede de Stuers,
1968).

In north central Sri Lanka, 70 per cent of all marriage partners
among the Sinhalese come from within 3 miles of the village. In
kindred groups short of resources, men marry endogamously, keeping
both men and property in the group. "Respectable" people are most
likely to find a partner living near the village and to marry first,
second or third cousins. There is a tendency for uxorilocal marriages to occur with "overprivileged females"--those without brothers
who stand to inherit a large share of property, or "underprivileged
males"--without property or the likelihood of inheriting any (Leach,
1961). Parents choose their children's spouses only in formal marriages which occur between higher-status, influential, potentially
hostile groups. The majority of alliances are informal and are contracted casually by the partners themselves (Leach, 1960). A woman
who cooks for a man is considered his wife, such relationships being
as easily entered upon as they are broken (Leach, 1961).

In Korea, lineage exogamy became mandatory with the adoption of
Confucian values during the fifteenth century (Deuchler, 1977) and
women in recent times have campaigned for the right to marry someone
of the same surname (Lee and Cho, 1976); this was granted in the
revised Family Law of 1977. Children are segregated at the age of 7,
and women are secluded in the house or with other women. It is
improper for a girl to look at a man who is neither kin nor neighbour
(Brandt, 1971). In fact, ways of meeting are devised among young
people, and premarital intercourse may take place between the ages of
17-19. Thereafter more serious thought is given to reputation and
marriage. Villagers reported that such laxness had arisen only
during the past decade. Parents still choose their children's
spouses, but increasingly the wishes of the young are being consulted. Neighbourhood exogamy is still fairly strict, but marriages
resulting from pregnancies after illicit meetings within the village
do occur. The formal proscription is only on marriage within the
lineage. Prejudice against village endogamy arises from the fear of
conflict, expressed in the proverb "The toilet and the in-laws should
be far from the house" (Brandt, loc. cit.).

Marriage within the Japanese lineage has traditionally been
allowed and, in fact, preferred (Taeuber, 1970a). The former taboo
against marriage of 2 people from the same lineage or the same

TABLE 5.1
People's Republic of China: Change Over Time in Closeness of
Marriage Partners (in percentages)[a]

	Pre-1949	1950-1958	1959-1967	1968-1974
Community of Origin:				
Same village	3	21	30	23
Same commune,[b]				
different village	47	33	38	42
Outside commune[b]	50	46	32	35
Total	100	100	100	100
Total number:	34	48	53	158
Surnames of Couple:				
Same surname	0	38	44	22
Different surname	100	62	56	78
Total	100	100	100	100
Total number:	5	8	16	55

[a]Rounded to nearest per cent.
[b]Or same area as the commune, in the cases of the pre-1949 and
1950-1958 period.

Source: Whyte, M. K., 1977.

village, even if of different lineage, is beginning to break down in
south China, although there are still no marriages between members of
the same lineage branch (Table 5.1) (Whyte, 1977; Parish and Whyte,
1978). Village endogamy had occurred among one-quarter of the women
in a Taiwan fishing village and most wives had come from within 10
miles (Diamond, 1969). Another Taiwan village preferred exogamy to
avoid conflict within the village, but some thought more mutual help
resulted from village endogamy, as reflected in the earthy proverb
"While relatives through the penis may have their differences, relatives through the vagina tend to get on smoothly" (Pasternak, 1972).
Cousin marriage, especially patrilineally, is disfavoured.
     The conditions of poor farmers and labourers in Kiangsi inspired
Mao Tse-tung to promulgate an amendment (1934) to the Marriage Law of
1931 guaranteeing free marriage in the Kiangsi Soviet, under which a
couple was considered married if they had set up household together,
even if not registered (Hu, 1974). Mao had found that a middle
peasant in Kiangsi who wanted to marry had to spend a sum equivalent
to the overall value of his total assets, while among the poor only
10 per cent, and among hired farm hands only 1 per cent, were
married. The promulgation of a decree in 1930 giving men and women

liberty to marry led, within a few months, to nearly all the unwed being married, and a period of social anarchy was followed by the legislative text of 1931. A peasant's son in villages near Canton in 1949 needed 35 piculs of rice to get married, more than the net income for a year for the poor (Yang, 1959).

An initial difficulty in the marriage reform act was in gaining acceptance for the concept that marriage was a government-controlled and not a socially-controlled event; opposition to free choice came even from some cadres (Yang, loc. cit.). While free choice is guaranteed under law, parents still have a good deal of control (Whyte, 1977), initiative varying greatly from case to case (Salaff, 1973). One study showed that more than half rural and all urban marriages since 1958 had been between well-acquainted partners. However, marriage in which the couple meets and decides to marry is still confined to the "political élite, the geographically mobile, those in urban areas, and among the highly educated." Old types of marriage and the customs accompanying them are more common in the countryside (Salaff, loc. cit.).

If parents have started proceedings, the couple must give their consent and a meeting between both families, often in a teahouse in a market town, is arranged. If either party does not wish to proceed, the matter is dropped. If either young person takes the initiative but the couple is not acquainted, the same ritual meeting takes place, but if they know one another, the marriage negotiations proceed; pairing off for courtship before formal engagement is frowned upon as immoral behaviour (Whyte, 1977).

All marriages in rural areas of China involve substantial financial transactions. Clothing, food items and cash are listed as required bride price. The groom's family examines the list, presents a somewhat reduced counterlist of what they will provide, or calls off negotiations. The sums involved range from 100 to 1,000 yuan, estimated as being no lower than during the 1930's. Parents of boys have to save long in advance and still often have to borrow to meet the bride price and the feast they are expected to give to welcome the bride; the poorer have great difficulty in meeting these costs. In this respect, therefore, the 1950 Marriage Act has not yet been successful, either in doing away with bride price or eliminating marriage feasts. Dowry, however, is minimal. Bride price is used for the marriage feast in the bride's village and contributes to a brother's bride price (Whyte, loc. cit.; Parish and Whyte, 1978).

AGE OF MARRIAGE

National planners in Asian countries have all come to accept, at different times and within the constraints of religious and ideological beliefs, that limitation of population growth is essential. Education of girls is seen as contributing towards this aim both directly, since family planning may be taught in schools, and indirectly, since girls who pursue education beyond primary levels inevitably marry later. Raising the age of marriage has been seen as another means of limiting population growth, since it reduces the number of years in which women bear children. The advocation of

secondary education for girls and later marriage have both met with
resistance in rural Asia, for cultural and economic reasons, though
the adverse effects of childbearing before physiological maturity
have been well documented (Whyte, 1974).

A girl's virginity is considered a crucial factor in making a
good marriage among most settled peoples in rural Asia. Thus,
marriage has been early and, despite legislation, child marriage is
still not uncommon. This has not always been so. In early India,
girls received formal education before marriage, which necessarily
took place later. From about 300 B.C., the age of marriage declined,
until it took place at about 8 or 9 years for a girl[*] (Altekar,
1959). In modern times, education is affecting the age of marriage
in cities, but in the countryside it is rising only very slowly,
postponement being perhaps due as much to poverty as to rising
literacy (Dixon, 1971). Primary education for a girl is considered
adequate qualification for marriage to a college or university student in Bangladesh (Ellickson, 1976).

Supervision of Thai girls after puberty is not sufficiently
rigorous to prevent their meeting young men, particularly during
harvest or other co-operative work parties. If a child is born,
efforts are made to arrange a marriage (Hanks and Hanks, 1963).
Marriage for most women in central and north Thailand had taken place
between 15 to 19 years, though a slowly rising trend was discernible,
and 68 per cent of mothers preferred that their daughters marry
between 20 and 24 years (Nantanee et al, 1977). Burmese brides are
usually virgins, or have had sexual experience only with their future
husbands (Nash, 1965). Sexual relations during engagement, though
not openly sanctioned, are not morally censured in fishing villages
in southern Taiwan (Diamond, 1969) and marriage following betrothal
tends to be expedited for this reason.

There is no minimum age for a Muslim or Customary (Chinese or
Hindu) marriage in Malaysia; in civil and Christian marriages the
minimum ages were 14 for a girl and 16 for her groom until 1972, when
18 years was fixed for both. Parental consent is necessary for those
under 21 years (Malaysia, FFPA, 1976). It was observed in Kelantan
that there was little place for the unattached dependent young person, either socially or economically and this made for early marriage
(Firth, 1966). This position has changed radically with the introduction of tobacco cultivation, giving young girls employment as
graders. The age of marriage has risen from 12 years to about 23
years (Narendran, 1975).

In Indonesia, the Co-ordinating Body for Welfare of the Family

---

[*]The traditional attitude is well illustrated in the story
Vidya-Sundara, written in the eighteenth century by the Bengali
Bharatchandra Ray but based upon a much older version. Vidya,
daughter of King Visasimha of Burdwan, had vowed to wed only one who
could conquer her in learned argument and had beaten all princely
comers, so that her father began to despair, though she was only 15
or 16 (from The Thief of Love, ed. and translated by E. C. Dimock,
University of Chicago Press, 1963). This story exemplifies many of
the traditional Hindu attitudes towards women.

and Children recommended in 1970 that girls and boys should not marry before 18 and 20 years respectively, but recognized that this was difficult to achieve; it was hoped that ages would be at least 16 and 18 years (Ihromi, 1973). In east Java, marriage ideally occurs before the first menstruation (Singarimbun and Manning, 1974). Consummation of marriage is delayed or never occurs with 24 per cent of first marriages, making the first exposure for women with no education at an average of 17.8 years; for those with primary educa- tion, 18.9 years, and for those who have graduated from primary school or above, 19.5 years (Hull, 1976b).

In Bangladesh, girls marry between the ages of 8 to 16, and the presence of an unmarried girl over the age of 16 is often a sign of poverty (Ellickson, 1976). Another observer places marriage for girls between 12 and 16 years, with restriction on her movement from the age of 10. There is less urgency in marrying off a daughter who is attending school (Abdulla, 1976). Most Pakistani girls are married a few months after the first menstruation and poverty is the chief reason for delay (Khan and Bilquees, 1976). The legal age is 19 for girls and 25 for boys.

In much of rural India prepuberty marriage is the ideal (Dube, 1963). Between 1901-1911 the average age at marriage for boys was 20.2 and 13.3 for girls; from 1961-1972 it rose to 22.2 and 17.2 respectively, but for girls in rural areas it is 16.7 years. In the northern belt of Himachal Pradesh, Bihar, Rajasthan and Uttar Pradesh, the average in 1961-1972 was below 15 (ICSSR, 1976). Tribal marriages, however, take place after puberty (Elwin, 1958/1975). Among the Gonds, for example, this has been the norm, though some are adopting Hindu customs; marriage rites may be conducted during child- hood, but both partners stay in their respective homes until maturity (von Fürer-Haimendorf, 1974). Virginity is not important, but a pregnant girl must name her lover, who must marry her or pay a heavy fine.

In Korea, in 1925 less than 30 per cent of teenage girls were unmarried, whereas in 1970 99 per cent were unmarried. Three per cent of those between 20 and 24 years were single in 1925, compared with 85 per cent in 1970, although the proportion is lower in rural areas (Kim, 1974).

In China, the minimum age for marriage was set in Sung times at 16 for men and 14 for girls; these ages were adhered to in subsequent dynasties (Lang, 1946/1968). A revised Marriage Law presented to the Fifth National People's Congress in 1980 raises the lowest permissi- ble age for men from 20 to 22, and for women from 18 to 20. The offically sanctioned ages are 24 to 26 for women, and 26 to 29 for men, but there is evidence that marriage still takes place much earlier (Parish, 1975). The average age of marriage is 21 for girls and 25 for men. These have changed little since the 1960's, despite official pressure to raise the women's age to 23 (Whyte, 1977; Parish and Whyte, 1978). Local zeal may bring pressure to bear, however; the 26-year-old brother of a family whose other members, known to the writers, are living in Hong Kong, has been told that he may not marry until he is 28. Forty to sixty per cent of males and 60-80 per cent of females interviewed had married before 23 and 25 respectively (Whyte, 1977). This is achieved by help from

TABLE 5.2
Average Age of Girls at Marriage

Pakistan	16.5	South Korea	21.3 (in 1970, 23.2
India	16.8		to 24.18--Lee
Malaysia	19.3		and Cho, 1976).
(peninsular)		Thailand	21.9
Sabah	19.4	Sri Lanka	22.0
Sarawak	19.8	Hong Kong	22.3
Singapore	20.5 (in 1970,	Philippines	22.3
	24.3--	Japan	24.7 (in 1973, 24.3--
	Cheng,		Prime Minis-
	1977).		ter's Secre-
Taiwan	21.0		tariat, 1976a).

Source: Dixon, 1971.

complaisant brigade cadres (often kin), and by holding a family
ceremony and waiting until the partners are of age before registering
the marriage. Illegitimate children have all the rights of children
born in wedlock.

It has been noted that there is a tendency for the age of
marriage to rise in densely populated areas, both rural and urban
(Flieger and Smith, 1975).

POLYGYNY

Polygyny was adopted for political and status reasons by the
wealthy of ancient India and by others to obtain sons (Altekar,
1959). It ensured continuity of lineage in traditional China and was
institutionalized approval for a varied sex life among the wealthy.
Polygyny also brought the economic asset of more sons (Yang, 1959).
Islam permits polygyny only if the wives are treated equally
(Schieffelin, 1967), an injunction even more difficult to follow
psychologically than financially. Indeed, reformers have questioned
the Koranic sanction of polygyny. Sayyid Amir Ali, a Shi'ite of
India, in his Spirit of Islam condemns polygamy; since the Koran
ordered a man to take up to 4 wives only if he could treat them
equitably and "as absolute justice in matters of feeling is impossible, the Koranic prescription amounted in reality to prohibition"
(Guillaume, 1954). It is becoming more uncommon, largely for economic reasons, but also because of resistance from women's groups.
Draft legislation in Malaysia, if approved, will make polygyny
difficult.

In Thailand, there are occasionally additional wives, though
this is not legally sanctioned. A young girl of poor family may
become a secondary wife in a wealthy family as a means of securing
her future (Hanks and Hanks, 1963).

In 1953, a survey among educated Indian men revealed that fewer than 10 per cent considered bigamy incompatible with justice or derogatory to the status of women; more were concerned at the adverse economic effects for men (Kapadia, 1966).

Undoubtedly, the first wife, forced to accept a younger woman into the home to produce the sons she herself has been unable to bear, the second wife, who is always conscious of her inferior status, and the concubine, who raises her own children only to call the chief wife "mother," have all suffered emotionally. So too, has a second wife, common-law wife, or mistress in an independently established household who knowingly or unknowingly shares the attention and income of her children's father with another family elsewhere.

It is not possible to obtain an accurate picture of the proportion of polygamous to monogamous marriages in southeast Asia. Support for the institution of polygyny remains strong among the orthodox (see, for example, the report of the seminar on Kedah's Administration of Criminal and Family Laws, New Sunday Times [Malaysia], May 14, 1978). In 1967, a bill was introduced into the Indonesian National Assembly aiming at a uniform marriage law for the whole country which would make polygamy illegal. A bill was finally passed in 1974, with numerous amendments which made polygamous marriage acceptable if the wife was physically unable to perform a wife's functions or bear children, and provided she agreed to subsequent marriages; even here, some exceptions were permitted (Utsumi, 1978; Katz and Katz, 1975).

Looking to the future, it may perhaps be assumed that polygyny will diminish in importance among the difficulties which Asian women have to face. The possession of sufficient income implies that children will receive education and, among the educated, polygamy is becoming socially unacceptable. At the lower end of the social scale, economic hardship makes polygyny increasingly rare.

POLYANDRY

The Himalayan area has a number of communities in which polyandry has been one of the available forms of marriage. This is usually accounted for by the constraints of limited availability of land and the need to avoid division by inheritance of small plots. However, there are complex ecological and cultural differences in different areas and no single explanation satisfactorily accounts for the phenomenon (Goldstein, 1978). Among Tibetans until recent times, the reduction of fertility per generation which results from polyandry protects the inheritance; it also concentrates labour in an area where terrain, as well as poverty, make mechanization difficult and agriculture is consequently highly labour-intensive. The closing of the border with China has disrupted ancient trading patterns and there is increasing out-migration. The growth of a cash economy, providing opportunities for younger sons to obtain work and independence outside the region, as well as increasing exposure to other cultures which devalue polyandry, are fast eroding the practice among Tibetan groups (Goldstein, loc. cit.).

78

The relation between availability of land and availability of labour explains different forms of marriage among the Hindu Pahari of the western Himalaya (Berreman, 1977). It is calculated that every 2 acres of cultivable land demand one working adult and every consuming adult (3 children below 15 years represent one consuming adult) requires half an acre of land for support. The labour of men and women is equally valued and productive, only ploughing and harrowing being exclusively male tasks. Thus, the adult labour force can be maximized by marriage and the ratio of consumers to producers controlled; monogamy, polygyny, fraternal polyandry and fraternal polygynandry (several brothers sharing more than one wife) all present advantages in different circumstances. If bride price is high or land scarce, fraternal polyandry is chosen; if land resources are ample and labour scarce, monogamy is chosen by several brothers, while few brothers or a man with no brothers may form polygamous unions. Widow levirate retains a woman's labour within her affinal family and avoids separating her from her children. Uxorilocal marriage brings male labour into a family without sons. Polygynandry can encompass any number or ratio of family members and is unique to the western Pahari area (Berreman, loc. cit.).

In the Himalayan region, therefore, there is a close relation between polyandry and the availability of land and labour. Among the Nayar of Kerala, who practised polyandry until early in the present century, no such explanation can be proposed, since men assumed no economic responsibility for the maintenance of their wives and children and did not take up residence with them (Fuller, 1976).

Commentators in the past have spoken of the high status of women in polyandrous society, but women in polyandrous patrilineal groups, such as the Druk-pa-Bhotias of Sikkim and the Lahuli, have lower status than among matrilineal polyandrous groups such as the Tibetans, and even here men are dominant. Polyandry does not guarantee higher social status without economic independence (Nandi, 1977).

6
Quality of Marital Relationship

Traditionally for a man of south and east Asia, the marital bond is subordinate to the bond with his agnates, particularly his mother, while in rural southeast Asia, the bond between a woman and her children, especially her daughters, is of primary affective significance. It is, however, apparent that there were in east and south Asia, even in the past, clear distinctions between the élite model of society, characterized by extended families and sharp dichotomy between male and female roles, and the practical existence of the majority living in smaller families with few active adults, where both husband and wife were required to work together. A less formal, more companionable, more egalitarian relation must have existed between spouses.

In ancient India, a woman was expected to be a companion to a man as well as mother to his children. However, as marriages increasingly took place when women were younger, were deemed unworthy of education and their status was consequently lower, the companionship aspect of marriage became attenuated. Today the companionship model of marriage is increasingly becoming known from the popular press and fiction and is the ideal of the educated young in many parts of Asia (Jay, 1969; Lee and Cho, 1976; Robinson, Somboonsub and Suwannapirom, 1975). Yet investigations of a business community near Delhi showed that most men still said they were closer to their mothers than to their wives, though many, particularly when wives were educated, said they were equally close to both. The greatest change in attitude comes when a traditional occupation has been changed; more in this group said they were closer to their wives. A traditional occupation is strongly correlated with a traditional outlook. Among matriculated wives, 86 per cent believed their husbands were closer to them than to their mothers-in-law (Kapadia, 1966). Rural or urban upbringing is not as significant in change of attitudes towards family relations as are age and literacy. The younger generation seeks a new relationship in marriage in which each partner must be able to share aspirations and interests with the other.

Young Thai men regard marriage as giving them freedom from economic dependence. Both partners marry for the wealth or productive capacity of the spouse and may stay together if the economic disadvantage of splitting is too great, even if considerable

dissension arises. Both men and women said they married because
society expected it and their parents wished it. Both thought marriage provided someone to care for one if one were sick and made
merit for their parents in return for having been brought up by them
(Phillips, 1966). However, among middle-class educated Thai youth,
intelligence and education are the primary factors in choosing a
spouse. Harmony between the couple comes next in importance and then
love. Both men and women agreed that harmony between their families
was important. Thus, the transition from the traditional/biological
to the economic framework for marriage described for the western part
of Asia has occurred among the minority better-educated, middle-class
Thai (Robinson, Somboonsub and Suwannapirom, 1975). In traditional
Thailand, however, the emotional tie between a woman and her mother
is stronger than that with her husband (Muecke, 1974).

   In the Philippines, a woman's family of origin also comes first;
daughters are happiest when they can return their mother's great love
and endless sacrifices. Later, a woman belongs to her children. Her
husband does not attain the same degree of central importance in her
emotional life (Lapuz, 1973). Even in husband-wife relations,
"the Filipino woman's exquisite training for motherhood imperceptibly
but inevitably takes over her wifely or womanly intentions" (Lapuz,
1977) and she treats her husband like a son in many ways. This is
reinforced by the double standard of morality which allows men wide
latitude in sexual life, but not women, thus refusing "to acknowledge
the reality of her as a woman. On the other hand, it affords her
protection, security and status simply by awarding her the position
of wife" (Lapuz, loc. cit.). Thus, the dimension of 2 separate
adults relating in married life is difficult to achieve.

   In Burma, economic factors and closely related attitudes to work
are important qualities sought in one's marriage partner, though
personality and decorous behaviour are also considered (see Table
6.1). Love and affection are important emotional components of
marriage, but these are not often manifested in psychological inti-
macy or sharing of emotional burdens (Spiro, 1977).

   The strength of a woman's tie with her children in Taiwan has
led Wolf (1972) to stress the concept of the uterine family, seen as
a bulwark of female solidarity against the patriarchal system. However, there are signs that the companionship model of marriage is
beginning to take hold among the young, who are demanding some say in
the choice of their spouse, with a consequent trend towards marriage
based on mutual attraction. Men share their concerns with their
wives and rely upon them for recreation and companionship (Diamond,
1969; Appleton, 1979).

   In traditional China, solidarity between husband and wife was
greater among the poor—the wealthy tried to follow the Confucian
model (Freedman, 1958). Today only young peasant activists tend to
be concerned about common interests with their spouses. The majority
are more concerned with the traditional qualities of earning power in
the husband and submission and physical strength in wives (Salaff,
1973). The character for love, absent for 10 years in novels and
films, reappeared in The People's Daily in spring, 1978 (South China
Morning Post, May 3, 1978).

   The husband and wife tie is becoming the most important family

TABLE 6.1
Burma: Ideal Qualities of Marriage Partners

Ideal Husband (including duties to wife)	Ideal Wife (including duties to husband)
1. good provider	1. efficient performance of domestic duties, especially cooking, cleaning house, washing clothes
2. hard and dedicated worker	2. industrious, not given to idleness
3. leads "simple life"-- refrains from drinking, gambling, womanizing, squandering of savings	3. remains at home, does not "roam about" village
4. good-natured, easy tempered	4. good-natured, unquarrelsome
5. worldly wise	5. efficient manager of family finances
6. does not physically ill-treat wife	6. concerned with pleasing husband, respects and obeys him
	7. sexual fidelity

Source: Spiro, 1977.

tie in rural Hong Kong, where the educated wife may completely dominate her rural mother-in-law (Potter, 1969). The extended family pattern is retained out of necessity, however, and traditional separation of the male and female worlds persists, with husband and wife rarely going out together except for a family tea on Sunday.

In Korea, in the past great emphasis was laid on the Confucian requirements of deference and obligation. Today more consideration is being given to the quality of marriage, to mutual understanding. Young women concentrate more on being wives than daughters-in-law, and leisure time is often spent by the nuclear family together, a new phenomenon in Korea. And if the traditional role is still important, with families coming together for worship and ceremonies, women today are better able to maintain links with their natal families than in the past (Lee and Cho, 1976). Despite the improvement in marital relations, a survey of middle-class women in Seoul showed that the majority considered most fortunate a woman whose children had grown up and were successful; an amicable relationship with one's husband was of secondary importance (Koh, 1978).

In a central Javanese village there is more segregation of roles between husband and wife among poorer socio-economic groups than among the middle classes, and the bond is greater among the latter. Poorer women consider the forming of an economic partnership and having children to be the greatest benefits of marriage. Middle-class women stress having children, and some mention love and companionship (Hull, 1976a).

In ancient India, the companionship model of marriage pre-vailed.* The wife was expected to control the budget, supervise agriculture and cattle and the kitchen garden (Altekar, 1959). Today the companionship type of marriage is confined mainly to educated, young city couples (Dube, 1963).

Fifty per cent of Japanese marriages in 1966 were made for love, while by 1973 these had risen to 62.8 per cent (Bando, 1977). The arranged marriage became general in Japan only in fairly recent times and it appears that Chinese forms, in which romantic love and common-law marriage are inadmissible, were at variance with Japanese custom, in which freer choice was the right of the principals (Taeuber, 1970b). However, most Japanese housewives look upon marriage not as a romantic fulfilment, but as a lifetime career, requiring training, special skills and endless devotion, a job parallel and complementary to that of a salaried husband. The husband depends on his wife for physical, emotional and developmental needs of the family, and she on him to provide family income. She has considerable autonomy and independence, separate but equal. From a low-keyed and non-authoritarian position she manages her husband and children, gener-ally having them do what she thinks they should. Since her marriage is defined more by her role than by the emotional relation with her husband, a wife does not necessarily feel that her marriage is a failure if this relation is inadequate (Vogel, 1978). If marital harmony is disturbed by a husband transferring his sexual attentions outside the home, peace may be restored by the wife taking a maternal role in relation to her husband. "Given the desirability of depend-ency coupled with the idealized mother-child relationship, love or marriage involves maternal nurturance. . . . When sexual passion is replaced by maternal indulgence, the husband acquires more freedom but at the same time becomes more dependent upon his wife. Maternal love can be shown even when marriage has broken down" (Lebra, 1976).

A Survey by the Enquiry Council on Women's Problems in 1974 revealed that marriage was equated with women's happiness by only 40 per cent of women and 36 per cent of men, with even fewer of those under 40 years of age supporting the concept (Jones, 1976). Modern young couples want more love and companionship in marriage than did the older generation, and this is usually typical of the early years of marriage. Once children are born, however, the couple spends

---

*This is well expressed in an early mediaeval Sanskrit poem:

"Do not go", I could say; but this is inauspicious.
"All right, go" is a loveless thing to say.
"Stay with me" is imperious. "Do as you wish" suggests
Cold indifference. And if I say "I'll die
When you are gone", you might not believe me.
Teach me, my husband, what I ought to say
When you go away.

(Translated by John Brough, Poems from the Sanskrit, Penguin, 1968.)

progressively less time together, often inhabiting different worlds, the husband that of his company and the wife the world of her children (Vogel, 1978). A survey of attitudes towards marriage showed that 42 per cent of married women thought the home should be centred on the children, while only 34 per cent of married men were of this view. Among the unmarried, 33 per cent of women and 34 per cent of men thought marriage should centre on the husband/wife relation (UNESCO, 1976).

Thus, it can be seen that if among the minority educated, middle-class young people of Asia, particularly those in the towns, the modern ideal of marriage, based on mutual love and companionship in a self-supporting economic unit able to raise children without help from other family members, is becoming the norm, for the majority of rural Asian women the chief theoretical benefits of marriage remain economic security and the companionship of their children who promise security in old age. Social life for women in most of Asia is still based on interaction with other women, and emotional support is derived from their children.

It may be expected that in marriages in which the relation between the spouses is of major importance, there will be a higher degree of mutual consultation on all decisions, on the need for family planning (Chapter 9), on economic matters and the lives of their children. It will be seen in Chapter 10, however, that while a companionship model of marriage does guarantee participation in decision-making by women, this also occurs in some traditional marriages, particularly in bilateral and matrilineal societies.

UNHAPPY BRIDES

In the past, a young bride's wellbeing was far more dependent upon the personalities of her mother-in-law and sisters-in-law than upon that of her husband. The sense of isolation or "emotional aloneness" (Wolf, M., 1975) suffered by a new bride in south Asia is perhaps partly mitigated by the custom of home visits, whereby a young bride returns to her own family for fairly protracted periods. But whereas marital disharmony leads in southeast Asia to divorce, no such solution existed in south and east Asia. Something of the tensions suffered by young girls, uprooted from a loving family environment to one where, at best, they must be on their guard because their behaviour and performances of duties are being subjected to critical scrutiny by all those around them, is revealed in studies of suicide. A well-known Suicide Inquiry Committee found cases of female suicide in Saurashtra, northwest India, to be double those of men, 60 per cent being between the ages of 13 to 30 years. Some 44.7 per cent were attributed to family tensions, but the figure was certainly higher, since families gave investigators less blameworthy reasons. Sympathy by friends and neighbours might be expressed in ineffective critical remarks: a relative wishing to prosecute for ill-treatment is strongly dissuaded (Kapadia, 1966). It is significant that a survey among educated women found 75 per cent opposed to the joint family.

Disappointed expectations regarding the amount of dowry a bride brings with her is a common cause of resentful behaviour by her affines. An extreme form was found formerly among the Kulin Brahmins of Uttar Pradesh, whose strict orthodoxy required that food be cooked by someone wearing wet clothing to ensure ritual purity (Khare, 1976). A young bride obliged repeatedly to cook meals in wet clothes in the cold winters of northern India soon became ill and sometimes died. Despite vigorous campaigns against the custom of dowry, brides continue to suffer if their families have been unable to raise the requisite amount. The affines of a young woman who died from multiple burns in Amritsar in 1979 were arrested for murder, and social workers concluded that dissatisfaction with her dowry was the cause (Observer, Foreign News Service, May 6, 1979).

Numerous suicides occurred among young brides all over China (Smith, 1899/1970). A girl might flee to her own family and be persuaded to return, but her family was powerless to protect her at a distance, though they often demanded ruinously grand funerals of her affines under threat of demanding an inquest. Undoubtedly there was an element of revenge, as well as escape, in the knowledge that her affines would be humiliated and her own family seek redress, with the added threat of her angry ghost to cause anxiety (Wolf, M., 1975). In 1935, when statistics in China were grossly incomplete, there were 1,353 suicides recorded in 244 counties, of which 20 per cent were women. In 1950, of 936 cases of loss of life handled by the People's Courts in Shansi, 66 per cent were women--either killed or suicide (Yang, 1959).

An examination of records for Taiwan showed that Chinese women were at least as likely as men to kill themselves, with a very high rate among girls between 1905-1915, dropping to a still high 28.7 per 100,000 for the 20- to 24-year age group by 1940. Most of these were recently married. The rate declined after the age of 35, when women were fully occupied in raising their own children, but since 1940 there has been a steady increase in suicides by women over 45, reflecting economic changes conferring independence (including the choice of their own brides) on young men. Mothers began to feel that their hold over their sons was threatened if conflict arose with their daughters-in-law. A far lower suicide rate occurred among Hakka than among Hokkien women. This is attributed to the greater independence and security enjoyed by Hakka women; the substantial sum they brought as dowry remained their exclusive property (Wolf, M., 1975).

The miseries of married life caused a revolt among sericultural workers in Kwangtung during the nineteenth century. Single women and young married women who refused to consummate their marriages formed into bands of sisterhoods which were mutually supportive and protective, able, on the basis of their economic independence, to refuse the future which society had traditionally ordained for them (Topley, 1975). A whole band committed suicide when one member was forced by her parents to honour a childhood betrothal (Smith, 1899/1970). Even today, a silk-producing commune of 72,000 people has 2,000 women in their fifties who never married (Melinda Liu, Far Eastern Economic Review, July 6, 1979).

Modernity and independence are improving prospects for young women, but the change is not swift. A survey in 1953 showed that

64 per cent of Japanese women wished they had been born men. By 1973 this had decreased to 50 per cent; of those glad to be women, over 60 per cent were below the age of 20 (Bando, 1977). Today the young Chinese bride can quickly prove herself by work in the fields (Whyte, 1977), and ill-treatment of a Korean bride is modified by the recognition that comfort in old age depends on a harmonious relation with her (Brandt, 1971).

7
Widowhood and Divorce

WIDOWHOOD

Early marriage, particularly in south Asia, has often meant that there was great disparity between the age of bride and groom. The Indian ideal has been that the bride should be one-third the age of her husband (Basham, 1954). While this may not have been generally observed, the difference in age has resulted in early widowhood which, for higher castes in the Hindu world, has, at least from mediaeval times, meant social death. Remarriage was prohibited from about 600 A.D. and by 1000 A.D. the prohibition was extended to child widows. This was the norm among high castes. By the nineteenth century lower castes wishing to raise their status also prohibited remarriage, but later relaxed the ban (Altekar, 1959). Remarriage seems always to have been common among lower castes (Dube, 1963) and still is (Bose and Sen, 1966; Jacobson, 1977; Srinivas, 1976). Self-immolation was expected only of high-caste women, but widowhood has been a particularly unhappy state for most. The Laws of Manu are explicit on the behaviour expected of a widow:

> A faithful wife who wishes to attain in heaven the mansion of her husband must do nothing unkind to him, be he living or dead. Let her emaciate her body . . . but let her not, when her husband is deceased, even pronounce the name of another man. Let her continue till death, forgiving all injuries, performing harsh duties, avoiding every sensual pleasure and cheerfully practising the incomparable rules of virtue. A virtuous wife ascends to heaven even though she have no child if, after the decease of her lord, she devote herself to pious austerity (quoted in Dunbar, 1949).

The reality for the well-born closely corresponds to this ancient prescription. A widow, economically dependent on members of her husband's family, could be ill-treated and abused, sometimes blamed for any unhappy occurrence in the family. She had to work hard and put up with all kinds of indignities and humiliations from senior, sometimes even junior, household members. And if this were not sufficiently degrading, she was considered inauspicious. To see

her in the morning or face her while going on a journey or some
mission was a bad omen. Her presence on any auspicious occasion was
a harbinger of calamity. She had to keep herself away, even from the
marriage of her own children (Altekar, 1959).

Chastity was imperative and if seduced she, not her seducer, was
blamed; her husband's family may even have induced her to commit
suicide. Legislation permitting remarriage has remained ineffective
in the face of such traditions. The educated young are beginning to
accept the remarriage of a young woman "if economically helpless,
passionate or childless" (Kapadia, 1966). Significantly, this con-
cession is made to prevent sexual irregularities, not as a woman's
fundamental right. Small wonder that women are unable to contemplate
remarriage when, instead of blaming their parents or society for the
disparity in age which led to their widowhood, they passively
attribute their state to punishment for misdeeds in a past life and
resign themselves ungrudgingly (Kapadia, loc. cit.).

Islam requires widows to remarry, but older societal norms
prevail in south Asia. The age gap at marriage in Bangladesh almost
ensures widowhood (Ellickson, 1976). In one village studied, 19 per
cent of the female population over 16 years of age were widows
(Ellickson, 1975) and, throughout Bangladesh, there is a sharp
increase in the number of widowed females above 34 years of age. In
the 1961 Census, 41 per cent of women in the 40 to 59 age group were
widows (Khatun and Begum, 1975). Among women past childbearing
engaged in Food for Work Activities, 20-25 per cent are widows who
cannot rely on their children for support (Chen and Ghuznavi, 1977).
Young widows and divorcees often remarry, but older widows generally
remain in their husband's home to ensure receiving a share of his
property (Abdulla, 1976; Jahan, 1975).

The chaste widow has long been a heroine of Chinese fiction and
remarriage was almost unthinkable. Her suicide brought honour to her
memory and was common in the past. The conventional law is expressed
in the saying: "She who is lucky dies before her husband." In The
Dream of the Red Chamber (translated as The Story of the Stone, David
Hawkes, Penguin, 1973), the widow of Jia Zhu, who had died young,
behaved strictly according to the ideal. Despite the luxury of her
surroundings, she was "able to keep herself like 'the withered tree
and dead ashes' of the philosopher, shutting out everything that did
not concern her and attending only to the duties of serving her
husband's parents and bringing up her child. Whatever leisure this
left her was devoted to her little sister-in-law and cousins, accompanying them at their embroidery or hearing them recite their
lessons."* Undoubtedly, it was easier for the wealthy to observe
Confucian norms. Popular sayings attest to the fact that among

---

*The strict traditions governing a widow's life remained until
the turbulent period when China entered the modern world during the
1930's. Cousin Mei, in Pa Chin's novel The Family (published in
1931, and translated by S. Shapiro for the Foreign Languages Press,
Peking, 1958), is wholly reconciled to a hopeless future, though she
wistfully observes the struggle for freedom from restrictive norms by
her peers.

non-élite groups, remarriage did occur: "A maiden marries to please her parents, a widow to please herself"; "If heaven wants to rain or your mother to marry again, you cannot prevent it."

If a non-gentry widow remarried, rights over her lay with her husband's family, rarely her own; ritually she remained part of her own family only in mourning her parents (Freedman, 1958). The poor remarried out of economic necessity. Despite this, in 1947 widows ranged from 1 in 3.15 to 1 in 4.15 of all married women, showing that a woman saw great disadvantages in remarriage. She feared especially that her children would be ill-treated by her deceased husband's family to which, of course, they always belonged (Yang, 1959). In the People's Republic of China, widows have the right to remarry, even though some still feel this to be wrong, and young men are reluctant to marry a widow (Parish and Whyte, 1978). Early this century young widows in Taiwan tended not to remarry, but many bore one or more children out of wedlock, thus retaining rights to their husband's property (Wolf, A., 1975).

Remarriage appears to have been common for Korean widows until the late fourteenth century, and the adoption of Confucian mores in this respect was slow. Remarriage has always been easier for lower-class women (Deuchler, 1977). It is claimed that there is no objection to the remarriage of widows in Korea today, but in practice this is rare; the Confucian ideal of the chaste widow remains in force, and women do not wish to lose the access to their children which remarriage automatically involves.

In Japan, widowhood averages 8.4 years, and unhappiness is reflected in the suicide rate among elderly women of 54.7 per 100,000, the second highest in the world. This must be understood against the background of the position in society of the aged in general, rather than specifically of widows. In 1970, 63.5 per cent of all Japanese families were of the nuclear pattern; in 1920 the figure was already 54 per cent. Despite this, 80 per cent of old people still live with their relatives (Tanaka, 1979). It is claimed that financial insecurity over the age of 60 is not a major preoccupation (Nakagawa, 1979), since the National Welfare Annuity Scheme (Kosei Nenkin) provides a couple with a pension more than twice that, in real terms, received in Britain, more than Swedish or German pensions and more in real terms than American pensions. Widows whose husbands were company employees will receive 60 per cent of the salary he received for the 3 years before his death as pension. However, not all are so comfortably situated; self-employed couples each contribute to a compulsory National Pension System, started in 1961. In 1979, the monthly contribution was 3,300 yen. Women (and men) over 65 years old who have contributed for 40 years received just under 800,000 annually, in 1979, adjusted annually according to the cost of living. A widow between the age of 60 and 65 years receives 50 per cent of this sum. Those who, for reasons of dire proverty, were unable to make monthly contributions still receive a (lesser) pension. Farming widows are disqualified from receiving pensions if, in the absence of dependents, their total income remaining after meeting farming costs exceeds 700,000 annually; with one child under 18 years this sum is raised to 920,000 yen, and with 2, 1,118,000 yen. A widow before the age of 60 receives 1,660,000 yen annually;

with one dependent child she receives 1,922,000 yen, and with 2, 2,182,000 yen.

Despite these provisions, it was calculated that in 1973 there were 626,000 households headed by women with children under the age of 18, and 63.5 per cent of these had an annual income of less than 600,000 yen (UNESCO, 1976). There were 2,400,000 widows aged from 40 to 64, and 70 per cent had an annual income of less than 600,000 yen. In 1978, the average monthly income of a salaried household was 304,562 yen, representing a disposable income of 270,307 yen (Japan: Statistics Bureau, 1979). Clearly, an annual income of 600,000 yen for widows with children (even in 1973) is inadequate, particularly when it is remembered that sundry expenses, covering education and social costs, amount to 53 per cent of total expenditure, in 1978, of families whose household head is over 50 years of age. Widowhood is likely to coincide with the period of costly higher education of children.

Since, however, 70 per cent of all agricultural work in Japan is performed by women, it may be assumed that a high proportion have husbands receiving a salary; they consequently will receive a comfortable income as widows. For these, distress relates more to fundamental social changes which have accompanied rapid modernization in Japan, particularly in the decades since World War II. As in other modern societies, there is increasing focus on the young, and the aged have lost the respect formerly accorded their seniority and authority. The change from habits of frugality to what has long been termed the consumer revolution, allied to a general rise in the cost of living and particularly to the high costs of education of children, tend to make the elderly feel that they are a burden on their children, whose outlook on life is necessarily very different from their own (Tanaka, 1979). It may be surmised that able-bodied elderly women in rural areas are better placed than are their counterparts in cities; they play a major role in agricultural production and consequently may feel that they do make notable contributions to family welfare.

It has been seen that suffering caused by the loss of her husband has in the past been greatest among élite classes of women in south and east Asia; in this respect at least, lower socio-economic groups permitted their women to remedy their position, even though they suffered economically from the loss of property rights, and psychologically in the loss of access to their children. Legislation and education are combining to remove the stigma of remarriage in modern times.

DIVORCE

The availability of divorce divides Asia into 3 distinct regions. The west covers the south Asian subcontinent up to the borders of Burma but excluding the central and eastern Himalaya, Sri Lanka and tribal groups. The east, formerly including China, now covers Taiwan, Korea and Japan. In both these regions women have been unable to escape from an intolerable marriage. The third region, southeast Asia, has always made divorce relatively simple, even if easier for men than for women.

Divorce in southeast Asia usually allows the mother custody of her children, particularly if they are small; if older, they are permitted to choose with which parent they wish to live. Divorce was common in the pre-Christian Philippines and remains so among tribal people there (Infante, 1969). A husband had to return bride price if he were at fault and the woman, if culpable, had to pay him twice that amount, though there were and still are regional variations within the Philippines. If a Thai husband leaves his wife, he may take the movable portion of the joint property, plus whatever cash may be needed to make up the value of his share, leaving his wife the home and land which are her inheritance from her parents. Wife and sisters can live comfortably without the husband (Hanks and Hanks, 1963).

It has been suggested that a high divorce rate in Malaysia fosters lesser commitment to the family, which is seen as impermanent, and greater attention to the purchasing of jewellry or land registered in the names of women and their children (Swift, 1963). A study among Malays in Singapore led to the conclusion that the frequency of divorce was supported by general toleration and legal facilities; lack of strong economic deterrents; easy, low-cost remarriage; a woman's ability to rely on close kin for practical and moral support; freedom of access to children by both parents; and the ease of having children adopted, should neither parent wish to keep them (Djamour, 1965). However, since the time of Djamour's study, there has been a growing disapproval of divorce, coupled with legislation in Singapore and some Malay states making divorce more difficult and making attempts at conciliation mandatory. While Islamic law makes divorce easy, modernizing trends within Islam stress the Hadith tradition that God finds divorce the most offensive of all acts tolerated by Him (Tsubouchi, 1978).

In the predominantly rural and traditional state of Kelantan, only in villages remote from towns is divorce still treated as a routine matter. In the recent past the rate was as high as 80 per 100 marriages and today it is 56 per 100, with a clear decrease in frequency in coastal districts more open to modernization (Tsubouchi, 1972, 1978). The elasticity of household structure and lack of a sense of belonging inherent in bilateral kinship systems are considered major contributions to frequency of divorce. In one village studied, the imam handles the notice of divorce and the husband is required to pay a M.$12 registration fee to the religious court, of which the imam receives 40 per cent (Tsubouchi, 1978). This considerable sum must represent a disincentive to attempts at conciliation. Divorce was common in the first 10 years of marriage and among those who had married outside their villages (Tsubouchi, 1972). Even though most divorces were actually obtained by men, more women than men initiated divorce by asking their husbands to undertake proceedings. This confirms the findings of Rosemary Firth (1966) who stated that when asked the reason for divorce, many men said "because the woman wanted." It was suggested to an anthropologist in this same area that the recent involvement of women in remunerative economic activities was doing much to counteract the former high divorce rate; women had far less time to allow their thoughts to wander, while greater family income reduced discord over money matters (Narendran, 1975).

In the more modernized west coast state of Melaka, the activities of the State Religious Department (set up in 1960), aimed at discouraging divorce, have led to a marked decline in the rate since 1962. In one village studied, efforts by village religious leaders have reinforced the state legislation and the divorce rate is now down to 10.2 per cent (Maeda, 1978). Kin marriage rarely ends in divorce, but 54.5 per cent of marriages to non-kin are dissolved.

It is clear that the Islamic sanction of divorce was grafted in southeast Asia onto an older tradition which tolerated the rupture of marital union. Among the aboriginal dwellers of the Malay peninsula, the Negrito and Senoi permit divorce by mutual consent, and women may themselves initiate divorce (Carey, 1976). Among the Ibans of Sarawak, divorce may be by mutual consent, by payment of fine, or following desertion or infidelity (Komanyi, 1973). Divorce is accepted among most tribal groups (Lebar, Hickey and Musgrave, 1964; Lebar, 1972; Lebar, 1975).

There has been a decline in the divorce rate in Indonesia since 1965, especially in the Javanese cultural centres of Jakarta and Yogyakarta (Tsubouchi, 1978). In Java, the divorce rate above the age of 35 does not rise as steeply for those in upper income groups as for others, and some stigma against divorce amongst these women is expressed as indicating a lack of control (Geertz, 1961). The poorer are more independent of their husbands economically than are those of the middle classes who do not work for pay and for whom divorce is consequently more serious, economically and socially. The majority of poor divorced women who do not remarry are entirely self-supporting (Hull, 1976b). Women who marry frequently are generally those with little or no education (Singarimbun and Manning, 1974), or those who marry early. By far the highest proportion of unconsummated marriages occur among those who marry early—some 37 per cent of those marrying before 15; among those with less education; and in arranged marriages. Many girls still marry before their first menstruation. Achehnese women of Sumatra have introduced into the marriage contract conditions which automatically give them divorce (Jayawardena, 1977).

Thus, divorce and several marriages have traditionally been acceptable to Malay and many Indonesian people. Hindu norms make it rare on Bali; so also among the Christian Batak (Ihromi, 1973). There is a high rate of divorce among the matrilineal, matrilocal Minangkabau of Sumatra. In central plains Thailand, there is low tolerance of discord and divorce takes place easily for what might be thought flimsy reasons (Phillips, 1966). Marital instability has been related to a lack of long-term relationships inherent in central plains Thai society (Piker, 1969). This is an extension of Embree's well-known characterization of Thai society as "loosely structured" (Embree, 1950), in which people are more concerned with behaviour than the obligations inherent in social structure, as in Japan.

The informal arrangements governing marriages in the Dry Zone of Sri Lanka are easily dissolved (Leach, 1960). Dissolution of marriage is common in Burma, frequently caused by the conflicting demands of family allegiance. This involves only the loss of the conjugal bond, not of a kinship network (Nash, 1965).

It can be seen that where marriage is of primary importance only to the nuclear family, divorce has generally been tolerated in Asia.

Elsewhere, where the alliance of the groups from which the young couple comes is important, divorce has always been strictly limited. If a Japanese women left her husband's home before the new legislation of 1945, she automatically lost access to her children. A Chinese girl, whose formal leaving of her natal family was symbolized in ritual, might well have nowhere to go and could expect no economic support if she were cast out.

Childlessness was not considered adequate grounds for divorce in fishing villages in southern Taiwan, because of the availability of adoption or, among the wealthy, the possibility of taking a concubine. In the few cases where concubines had been brought into the home, however, it was seen that the first wife had left of her own accord (Diamond, 1969). Even if a wife committed adultery, divorce was rare, because of the costs involved, as well as the subsequent cost of remarriage.

Confucian society provided women with neither ideological nor legal grounds for divorce in Korea (Deuchler, 1977). The Korean woman who divorces today has no right to access to her children (Koh, 1978).

Under the 1950 Marriage Act of the People's Republic of China, divorce was to be by free choice if both partners desired it, or after mediation and a local court decision if only one did so. These liberal provisions have been modified in recent years and lengthy mediation is recommended, even if both partners seek divorce (Whyte, 1977). New legislation presented to the Fifth National People's Congress in 1980 will make divorce procedures easier where mediation has failed. The division of child custody and property is negotiated by both parties, and the local court has the obligation to safeguard the woman's interests. A year after the 1950 Marriage Act was passed, 76.6 per cent of divorces were brought by women (Yang, 1959). This shift from tradition has been observed recently in south China, where 80 per cent of cases were initiated by women, who remarry quickly. It is more difficult for a divorced man to find a wife. The rights of women to the contribution of her work points during the marriage are, however, ignored; she takes only clothing and personal property with her. The children usually remain with the father, or at most she is permitted to take only younger female children. When the marriage has been of short duration, some commune cadres even insist on repayment of bride price before a divorce is granted (Whyte, 1977).

Concern is being expressed in Singapore at the rapid rate of increase in divorces among Chinese; there has been a five-fold increase since 1968. A study is to be made to discover the reasons for this increase, which is believed to be due principally to early marriages of young couples too immature to be able to plan adequately for their future (Straits Times, April 15, 1978). It may be noted that employment rates for both men and women are high (see Table 7.1). In 1977, 39 per cent of the workforce was female (Aline Wong, Straits Times, Sept. 16, 1977), indicating the widespread availability of economic independence for women unable to tolerate an unsatisfactory

TABLE 7.1
Singapore: Economically Active Population by Principal Occupation and Sex, 1966 and 1973

	1966				1973			
	Total	Male	Female	% Female	Total	Male	Female	% Female
Professional and technical	37,580	21,468	16,112	42.87	53,294	31,387	21,907	41.11
Administrative, executive and managerial	10,337	9,815	522	5.04	17,052	15,509	1,543	9.05
Clerical	66,948	52,981	13,967	20.86	103,396	62,735	40,661	39.33
Sales	86,954	75,310	11,644	13.39	61,239	47,087	14,152	23.11
Agriculture, fishing and forestry	19,391	14,832	4,559	23.51	3,237	2,585	652	20.14
Transport and communications	47,508	45,869	1,639	3.44	32,150	31,818	332	1.03
Services	118,916	75,805	43,111	36.25	64,934	44,061	20,873	32.14
Craftsmen, production and other workers	156,170	129,567	26,603	17.03	246,237	149,523	96,714	39.28
Miners, quarrymen	993	968	25	2.51	--	--	--	--
Total, All Occupational Groups	544,797	426,615	118,182	19.38	581,539	384,705	196,834	33.85

Source: 1966 Sample Household Survey, Singapore; Singapore, Ministry of Labour Annual Report, 1973. From Wong, 1975.

marriage.

Judicial divorce is available to either partner in Japan by court proceedings, but divorce by agreement with formal registration makes up 90 per cent of the cases. If the couple has not reached agreement, mediation may be sought at the family court. Mothers usually take custody of children, but 60 per cent of mothers take over the entire financial burden involved; 14 per cent of fathers bear the entire costs and only 4.7 per cent of couples share costs. Only 4 per cent of divorced women wished to remarry, while 67 per cent of men in the same survey would remarry (Bando, 1977).

In south Asia, divorce carries considerable stigma. It is rare among the middle classes in Bangladesh, but may be more common in villages than had been realized (Abdulla and Zeidenstein, 1977). In one village studied, 16.5 per cent of all marriages ended in divorce (Jahan, 1975). Infertility and infidelity are the only grounds for retaining the bride price on separation. Divorce brings stigma to the whole kin group, and other daughters will not be sought in marriage (Bertocci, 1974). National law permits divorce, but village tradition gives this right only to men (Ellickson, 1976).

In India, childlessness is considered sufficient grounds for divorce. Among lower socio-economic groups the most common cause of divorce is illicit relations, but among higher socio-economic groups, disharmony is the most often cited cause (Damle in Kapadia, 1966). Different surveys have shown that women favour divorce and would seek it if they could visualize supporting themselves. This is true of both educated women and women of traditional backgrounds with higher education (Kapadia, loc. cit.). Opposition to divorce is found not among particular classes, but among older people, irrespective of social status. The older generation still expects a wife to put up with an impotent, insane or diseased husband, while younger people are aware of obligations by both husband and wife. The young believe that if disharmony is fundamental, it is in the interests of both partners and their children that they should have the freedom to part. Yet, as with widow remarriage, many Indian women are conditioned to accept inequity as the norm. "Woman is an advocate of traditional behaviour, even at her own cost." The majority considers divorce right if a woman misbehaves, but very few if a man misbehaves (Kapadia, loc. cit.). Divorcees are impure, and structurally peripheral to society (Mathur, 1974). If socio-economic independence has been attained, a woman may remarry outside her caste, with class criteria becoming important in mate selection. It must be emphasized that such cases are few.

A review of ethnographic material from other regions led to the conclusion that where patrilineal kinship was the norm, rates of divorce were low, while the divided loyalties implicit in bilateral societies were conducive of a high rate of divorce. In India, however, it is believed that the key factor to low rates of divorce is the lack of strong economic and social ties between a man and his affines (Kolenda, 1967). Peoples in the Himalayan foothill region have relatively high rates of divorce; men continue relations with their affines after marriage, often in the form of gift exchange, as, for example, among the Limbu, where it is concluded that harmony between daughter- and mother-in-law is the crucial factor in marital stability (Jones and Jones, 1976).

It may be concluded that in the past and still in varying degrees today, women of south Asia, traditional China, Japan and Korea were expected to endure early unhappiness in marriage which would be alleviated by the birth of sons; these would provide emotional satisfaction, even some authority, and would protect their mother's interests when they grew up. In the modern context, irrespective of legislation at the national level, a woman will resort to divorce only if traditional culture or a changed environment provides her with the security of property, at least that which she brought to the marriage, access to or care of her children and, above all, the economic means of supporting herself and her children. This she may derive from the possession of land or, increasingly, from the performance of some gainful activity.

Photographs
Working Women in Rural Asia

Philippines: Threshing and winnowing rice. (Courtesy International
Rice Research Institute)

Above -- PRC, Kwangsi Chuang Autonomous Region: Commune members in Tienyang County cutting sugarcane. (Courtesy New China News Agency)
Below -- PRC, Shantung Province: Drying peanuts on a threshing floor. (Courtesy New China News Agency)

Above -- Hong Kong: Hakka women harvesting laichees for market.
(Courtesy Government Information Services) Below -- PRC, Yunnan
Province near Burma and Laos: Tai women weeding spring onions.
(Courtesy Francesca Bray)

Above -- Malaysia, Kelantan, Kampung Bunut Susu: Rolling latex.
(Courtesy Francesca Bray) Below -- Malaysia, Kelantan, Kampung Bunut
Susu: Sorting sireh leaves prior to insertion of betel paste for
chewing. (Courtesy Francesca Bray)

Malaysia, Kelantan, Kampung Bunut Susu: Making a basket container.
(Courtesy Francesca Bray)

India, Haryana: Woman with her crossbred cow and calf.
(Courtesy N. N. Bagga, National Dairy Research Institute)

Left -- India, Haryana:
Cutting fodder for cattle.
(Courtesy N. N. Bagga,
National Dairy Research
Institute) Below -- India,
Haryana: Churning milk
into butter. (Courtesy
N. N. Bagga, National Dairy
Research Institute)

Above -- Japan: Preparing land for sowing vegetables. (Courtesy
Y. Fujita, Japan Rural Youth Education Development Association)
Below -- Japan, Tokorazawa area: Farm wife, husband, and neighbor
picking tea by machine. (Courtesy Y. Fujita, Japan Rural Youth
Education Development Association)

Above -- Japan, Iwate Prefecture: Transporting padi seedlings to the fields. (Courtesy M. Nakajima) Below -- Japan, Iwate Prefecture: Filling gaps left by a rice-planting machine. (Courtesy M. Nakajima)

Philippines, Mountain Province: Inserting pattern sticks into a warped backstrap loom. (Courtesy Charlotte Coffman, Handweavers Guild of America)

8
Residence After Marriage

A major factor in the lives of Asian brides is the degree to
which they are cut off from the security and affection of their
natal homes. Anthropologists have always given special attention to
the relation between the givers and receivers of brides and the way
this reflects the status of the groups involved. There has been a
good deal of analysis of the reasons for different patterns, closely
linked to kinship, inheritance, position in the social hierarchy and
wealth. Very little attention has been given, however, to the
significance of different practices on the wellbeing and confidence
of the bride herself.

Social distance--the absence of sanction for a bride to visit
her natal family--can be as great a cause of distress for a young
woman as can physical distance. The south Asian bride has always
been able to look forward to visits to her parental home where she
could escape the restrictions of decorum and respectful behaviour
necessary with her affines. Jacobson (1977) has remarked on the
gentle "breaking-in" of brides in central India, where a girl may
spend perhaps a week in her affinal home when her marriage is con-
summated, returning to her own home for several months, spending
perhaps another 3 weeks with her affines before going back again to
her natal home. Even later she may spend several months at home each
year. Chinese brides also visited their parental homes (Fried,
1953).

In the strongly patriarchal societies of the south Asian subcontinent, in China, in Korea, from the Yi dynasty of the late fourteenth century, and in Japan, young brides were almost invariably
brought to the homes of their grooms. Part of the marriage ceremony
symbolized the breaking of the tie with the bride's parental home;
the girl belonged to a new household and family line. This still
holds true for the rural areas of all these countries today, although
fewer young people remain on the land in Japan, and some marriages
are taking place within the girl's village in the People's Republic
of China.

Only in exceptional cases is the rule of patrilocal residence
broken in east and south Asia, usually when a family is without sons.
In Japan, a child might be adopted, possibly a member of the same kin
group, who would be expected to take on the name of his adoptive

family and renounce his own (Nakane, 1967). In China, Korea and Japan, and also in south Asia, a son-in-law might be brought in to marry the oldest girl. Such arrangements implied a lower status for the man, since he had deserted his parental home. In Japan, such grooms were generally a younger son who would not inherit control of the ie under the system of primogeniture which prevailed; in both China and Japan, a marriage of this kind was a last resort for a young man of impoverished background (Nakane, 1967; Wolf, 1972). Two cases of a poor but promising groom moving into the wife's household occurred during a field study in a Korean village (Brandt, 1971), but parents prefer to adopt a kinsman's son to prevent the alienation of land. In the special conditions of Singapore in the past, an immigrant from China might stay with his locally-settled bride's family without incurring lower status (Wee, 1963). A son-in-law may live with his wife's family in Bangladesh, though this is rare (Abdulla, 1976). He has lower status, is dependent on his wife's family and his children, not he, inherit property (Bertocci, 1974).

These exceptions represent measures for continuing the family line, the principal aim of marriage. Even in modern China, marriages are mainly still patrilocal (Parish, 1975; Davin, 1975; Whyte, 1977; Parish and Whyte, 1978). There have been campaigns promoting uxorilocal residence (Croll, 1979). Some fishing villages in southern Taiwan appear to be unusual, since one-quarter of the wives had been born in the village and most had come from within 10 miles. The promixity of kin and long-standing friends was clearly of advantage to these women. Village public opinion is a potent weapon for help when women believe themselves unjustly treated by their affines (Diamond, 1969).

It was the custom among families of lower socio-economic status in China and Taiwan to adopt brides for their sons while they were still little, raising the girls as their own children. This avoided the expenses associated with traditional marriage and made relations between mother-in-law and daughter-in-law easier. Unstable marriages often resulted, however (Wolf, A., 1975). It may be noted that children raised together in the same unit in Israeli kibbutzim do not marry. A study of 3,000 marriages over 3 generations revealed that there had not been a single marriage between people raised together during the years from ages 3 to 6 (Shepher, 1971).

There is no clear pattern of settlement by young couples of tribal communities in southeast Asia in general. If bride price has been paid, residence may often be patrilocal, but many groups are matrilocal (Lebar, Hickey and Musgrave, 1964; Lebar, 1972; Lebar, 1975). The custom of bride service is common among swidden groups, and this automatically means that the groom will stay for a few months or even years at his bride's village. Among the Temiar of peninsular Malaysia, the couple moves between the longhouses of both parents until they decide where they are happiest (Noone, 1972).

Arrangements in southeast Asia among settled communities are flexible, except in the case of matrilineal societies such as the Minangkabau of Sumatra and in Jelubu, Malaysia, where men traditionally are brought into the household. The spread of education is weakening matrilineal adat in Rembau; the extended family is giving way to the nuclear, and residence after marriage is no longer

uxorilocal. Neolocal residence, often in association with urban
employment, is becoming increasingly prominent. Young couples in a
bilateral community of the state of Melaka spend the early months of
marriage staying alternately with both parents before deciding where
to set up home in relation to economic convenience. Land is inadequate, many young men are absent at work and marriage is mostly
uxorilocal, being 85 per cent in the case of marriage with first
cousins, 80 per cent with second cousins, 53.3 per cent with distant
kin and 62 per cent with non-kin marriages (Maeda, 1978). Residence
in Kedah and Kelantan showed a greater tendency towards virilocality,
related to the availability of land.

Marriage among the Achehnese of Sumatra is uxorilocal, and men
marry out of the area (Jayawardena, 1977). The father of the bride
supports the couple until the birth of a child, when a separate
household is established. Another observer finds that it is not
considered suitable for married daughters to remain with their
parents, but residence may be matrilocal (Ihromi, 1973). In east
Java, villagers insist that there is no bias, but again residence is
predominantly matrilocal (Jay, 1969).

In Bali, residence is virilocal; an adopted son-in-law is
legally treated as a woman and his wife is her parents' legal heir
(Geertz and Geertz, 1975). The harmony which reigns in the average
houseyard is attributed to the fact that the young bride is almost
certainly related to her sisters-in-law, or at least comes from the
same village.

In the Philippines, both parents may exert pressure on a young
couple, and availability of land may be the factor deciding residence. A virilocal pattern appears to be the norm, with an initial
period in the girl's home for the performance of bride service
(Murray, 1971; Mendez and Jocano, 1974). The young couple moves out
usually after the birth of their first child. In Malaysia, the
couple sets up a home when the marriage appears to be stable
(Strange, 1971), but there are no rules regarding residence, expedi-
ency being the main criterion (Strange, 1976a). Mothers and
daughters prefer to live near one another. The parents who are the
most well-to-do are likely to have the greatest pull (Husin Ali,
1975). Residence may be neolocal after the first few months,
although contribution to part of house building costs will be an
inducement to remain close to parents.

In central Thailand, daughters of marriageable age generally
attract in-marrying husbands bringing bride price, while sons leave
the parental home (Piker, 1975), giving them rights in the estate of
their bride's family. In the central flood plain, residence may be
with the parents of the bride, groom or neolocally, according to the
best opportunity, but with strong traditional preference for the
girl's family (Hanks and Hanks, 1963). A study of a village near
Chiengmai has led Potter (1976) to conclude that the matrilocal
extended family is the basic lowland pattern. Textor (1977) is
unconvinced that matrilocality is culturally defined and normatively
prescribed everywhere in lowland Thailand.

In Burma, ties of affection are important in determining residence, but young couples often reside with one set of parents for
economic reasons (Mi Mi Khaing, 1963). Matrilocal residence is

preferred, since the mother-daughter role is considered the keystone
of Burmese family life (Nash, 1965). Patrilocal residence invariably
brings difficulties; the word for sister-in-law in Burmese means
"stirrer-up." The existence of extended conjugal families with
married children residing with parents, or with siblings or cousins
living in the same compound, should not obscure the fact that the
underlying dynamic of family and household formation in Burma is the
drive for each married couple to set up its own compound (Nash, loc.
cit.).

Marriages in Laos were invariably uxorilocal (Levy, 1963).

In Bangladesh, brothers of the same household may farm together,
and share the produce, but they maintain separate kitchens, often
parting after the birth of the first or second child (Abdulla, 1976).
In north and south India, different marriage patterns mean that a
girl in the north must always leave her natal village, while in the
south she may remain, or live close by with kin (Mandelbaum, 1972).
Higher caste groups and wealthy rural classes have a wider network of
kin than do the poor, and a girl of high caste is likely to be at a
greater distance from her parents in north India than is one from a
lower caste. Rajputs may seek brides 30 miles away from their
village, while Chamars go no further than 20 miles (Das, 1975). A
similar pattern was found in Korea, where powerful upper-class rural
lineages sought their brides at greater distances than lower socio-
economic groups (Deuchler, 1977).

Among the Limbus of Nepal, a new bride spends several weeks in
her father-in-law's home, returning to her natal home for a year, or
more, moving in with her new family after the birth of her first
child (Jones and Jones, 1976).

In north central Sri Lanka, uxorilocal marriages are almost as
frequent as are virilocal, despite strong preference for the latter.
It is significant that 82 per cent of brides had come from within 3
miles of their husband's village, but 42 per cent of uxorilocal husbands had come from over 6 miles, avoiding the humiliation of being
frequently seen, in their lowered status, by members of their own
village (Leach, 1961).

It is clear that the southeast Asian bride experiences none of
the sense of isolation, loss of affectionate parents and siblings
and, above all, none of the awareness that she is on trial and her
abilities and behaviour likely to be found wanting, which have so
commonly been the lot of the east Asian and south Asian brides.

BREAK-UP OF JOINT HOUSEHOLDS

A sharp distinction between extended and nuclear families in
Asia has been shown to be artificial, since there is a cyclic pattern, the extended household prevailing while children are young
until the early years of their marriage, when the nuclear form may
occur until the marriage of their own children. The splitting of an
extended household is a traumatic event in patrilineal societies and
strong personalities, either the male head or his wife/widow, direct
much of their energies to the maintenance of the ideal. It must be
stressed, however, that this ideal can be followed only by family

groups with adequate economic resources, usually based on land, to support all members.

It has been suggested that conflict between brothers with equal rights to shares in the father's land has been the traditional cause of break-up in China (Freedman, 1970a). The split generally occurred after the birth of children, particularly those of the second son; tension between the daughters-in-law and anxiety regarding the rights of their children are considered a more likely cause of fission among traditional Chinese families (Wolf, 1972).

Rivalry between sisters-in-law is usually blamed for the break-up of extended families in south Asia, but this may equally be due to resentment of younger brothers at their subordinate status (Davis, 1976). A wife's rank in the household is largely determined by that of her husband, and this can also be a source of trouble between sisters-in-law. Rivalry may occur between sisters on account of differences of wealth and the status of each within their affinal families, particularly when one has married an older son who takes over control of the household and another has married a younger brother. "Not to be head of one's household is to be a 'nose-pierced cow,'" runs a Bengali proverb, indicating such a woman always moves at the will of another.

In India and China, the break-up may first take the form of separate cooking arrangements, proceed through the building of partition walls and finally result in the building of a separate home. In the People's Republic of China, the impossibility of migration to the cities and the high cost of building homes have combined to keep married sons as dependent on their fathers as in the past; it may take up to 10 years to save enough to build a separate home, and extensions are often made to the existing dwelling (Parish, 1975). Even when not sharing budget and food, brothers often live in the same compound or adjacent buildings, as in the past (Parish and Whyte, 1978). Where feasible, households do not long remain extended, for quarters become cramped as children are born and older brothers marry. The bride's additional earnings contribute towards the building of new quarters. And within 3 to 4 years after marriage, unless the groom is the only son, the young couple is accounted for separately in the matter of work points, private plots and rations. Both branches continue to co-operate in household work and child care. Families divide relatively early, and do not await the death of a parent. Where there are several sons, the older ones move out, and the youngest continues to live with his parents, though all brothers share in their support (Whyte, 1977). The joint family emphasis of the past has given way to the stem family with associated nuclear families (Parish and Whyte, 1978).

The distance a young girl may travel from her parental to her new home and the degree of familiarity of her surroundings play a large part in the degree of dislocation and disorientation these may produce in the early years of marriage. Young wives with some education are given a greater chance of influencing the upbringing of their children, family diet and health where they have some independence from affines, particularly their mother-in-law. Their sense of security and self-confidence enhances their ability to make decisions in an environment where they do not feel embattled and under constant--possibly adverse--judgement.

Do patterns of residence, in fact, help in the understanding of differences in female status within Asia? It seems that there is a relation in southeast Asia between absence of clear preference for virilocality and the oft-attested dominance of women. It is equally apparent that son preference is far less marked among uxorilocal communities where parents know that security in old age will come from their married daughters living near or in the home, than where virilocal marriage is the norm (see also Chapter 9).

9
Number of Children in the Family

The distribution of rural health care over large parts of Asia does little to protect women and children from organic, parasitic and infectious disease. The worldwide reduction of epidemic diseases has, however, made it more likely that some children will survive into adulthood. Children are essential for sacramental and economic reasons for the family and, in patrilineal societies, for the well-being of women who gain real acceptance in their husband's family only with the birth of a child. Emotional satisfaction and hope of security in old age are chiefly derived from children.

Higher fertility is associated with higher socio-economic status, the better nutritional status this brings the mother and better access to health care. In both the Philippines and India, families with larger landholdings and houses better than the average, in both rural and urban areas, have more children than those less well off. There is a positive relation between fertility and literacy in developing countries (Friedlander and Silver, 1967), despite the common assertion to the contrary by demographers (Hull and Hull, 1976). In Indonesia, there is a positive correlation for the majority of women. There is also a considerably lower level of infant mortality with each rising level of education. Upper income women can expect around 5, and lower-income women around 3 living children at the end of their childbearing periods. Part of the disparity is explained by marital disruption, which is more prevalent among lower socio-economic groups, sometimes accounting for one-fifth of the reproductive period. Among higher socio-economic groups, marital disruption accounts for only 9 per cent of reproductive life. Poorer women also practise post-partum abstinence for longer periods, although this is beginning to decline among younger women (Hull and Hull, loc. cit.). Poorer women have a shorter period of fecundity. The ratio of surviving children born to upper-class women is 25 per cent higher than among the poor.

It is difficult to make a comparative assessment of the success of family planning measures in different Asian countries because of the differences in density of information/planning clinics from, say, a city-state such as Singapore to a country such as Indonesia, with great differences within the country in concentration of population and availability of contraceptive advice and facilities.

In the People's Republic of China, provinces with a number of model communes which have attained a rapid degree of decline in fertility show a considerable drop in fertility over the province as a whole (e.g. in Kiangsu and Hopei). Provinces with fewer such model communes have been less successful, while certain provinces, such as Szechuan and areas with a high proportion of non-Han inhabitants, are lagging. It is doubtful whether the aim of reducing fertility to 10 per 1,000 by 1981 will be achieved (Banister, 1978). Socio-economic changes in the leading southern and eastern cities (full-time employment of women outside the home; universal education; good medical care; expensive and demanding child-raising; extremely overcrowded housing) are sufficient to reduce fertility without an intensive birth control campaign, but elsewhere there would have been little decline without a strong campaign to counter traditional values held by the older generation (Banister, loc. cit.). The campaign is reinforced by the fact that all methods of contraception are free, while those undergoing surgery are given a number of days off, lost work points being reimbursed. Some sanctions against larger families are applied, since benefits for a third and subsequent children are eliminated (Banister, loc. cit.). In Kwangtung, it has been concluded that much of the success of family planning campaigns is due to peasant perceptions that fewer sons are needed to provide the family with surviving sons, to shortage of land and to the presence of more midwives and doctors who provide contraceptives, rather than to administrative pressure from above (Parish and Whyte, 1978), though it is expected that this aspect will have increasing impact on birth rates in the future.

Vice Premier Chen Mu-hua, reporting on population growth to the Fifth National People's Congress, stated that in 1978, 17,000,000 infants were born, of which 50 per cent were the third child or above in the family. China aimed at reducing population growth to 5 per 1,000 in 1985 (NCNA June 29, 1979/SWB July 3, 1979). In an article in The People's Daily, she said that China aimed at zero-population growth between 1985-2000, by means of taxation and other disincentives to be applied to couples with more than 2 children. Couples with one child will be awarded a coupon providing priority for entrance to nurseries and kindergartens and free medical care. Between the age of 4 and 14 years a son receives a subsidy of Rmb. 5 per month, and a daughter Rmb. 6. One child will receive an adult's grain ration, and households with one son or 2 daughters will receive priority in labour recruitment (Far Eastern Economic Review, Oct. 5, 1979).

It is clear from these rewards that China recognizes the effect of son preference on population growth rates. If a second child is born, the above benefits are withdrawn, and medical expenses recovered; 5 per cent of total family income will be deducted from welfare expenses, 6 per cent for a fourth and 7 per cent for a fifth child. Parents must pay for confinement and medical expenses for the third and additional children. No coupons for commodities or subsidiary foodstuffs will be available for a third or additional children before the age of 14, nor will additional land for private plots be provided (F.E.E.R., loc. cit.). It has been recognized that social insurance must be provided to the aged who have had no children (NCNA June 25, 1979/SWB June 28, 1979).

Family planning efforts are reported to be reaching more young couples in Malaysia where in 1970, 59.2 per cent of acceptors were below the age of 30, with a median age of 28. Half of the acceptors have 3 or fewer children, with a median of 4.4 in 1969 and 3.6 in 1970. In 1970, 71.6 per cent of acceptors had only primary or no education, and 49.5 per cent had an income of M.$300 per month or less, showing that the lower socio-economic groups are coming to accept contraception (Malaysia, National Family Planning Board, 1970). In 1974, 33.3 per cent of acceptors were below the age of 25 (Malaysia, National Family Planning Board, 1974). This source gave 85 per cent of acceptors each year coming below the monthly income of M.$300, and in 1970, 87.2 per cent of acceptors had primary or no education, thus demonstrating the level of efforts in the rural areas. However, there are fears that the total number of women practising some form of birth control is well below national targets. A study in 1976 by the National Family Planning Board and Statistics Department showed that while 78 per cent of currently married women of childbearing age approved of family planning, only 16 per cent of these were using contraceptives. It is hoped to reach 550,000 new acceptors during the period 1976-1980, but a World Bank review team in June, 1977 considered that far fewer would actually begin contraception and, in particular, the poor would be least likely to be reached. The heightened sensitivities of a plural society further complicate the work of the National Family Planning Board. There is a strong positive correlation between a clinic's ability to gain and maintain acceptors of family planning when personnel are able to maintain good rapport with local political and religious leaders (Fong, 1976).

In Korea, rural women are better informed about contraceptive methods than women in urban areas, reflecting the national focus of family planning efforts (Lee, 1974). The adoption rate by women in rural areas has risen more swiftly than that of urban women, especially among those in the 30-39 age group.

RESPONSIBILITY FOR CONTRACEPTION

It is usually left to the Asian woman to take steps to limit the size of her family, provided she can overcome the resistance of her husband and affines. The preponderance of tubal ligation as the means of birth control in Shanghai is seen as continued inequality between women and men in bearing responsibility for contraception; cadres report that men insist on women undergoing surgery because of their uneasiness about vasectomy. Less than 10 per cent of acceptors underwent vasectomy, while 44 per cent underwent tubal ligation in 1971. The disparity is lower, however, in suburban communes where contraception as a whole is more recent (Banister, 1977). The preponderance of women family planning workers may be one reason for the fact that contraception is overwhelmingly a female responsibility in China (Banister, 1978). In Vietnam also, men refuse vasectomies because they fear the operation will weaken them (Gough, 1977). Pressure is thus placed on women, since accommodation is denied to parents with more than 3 children and those holding government jobs risk losing them at the birth of their third child.

The majority of Thai men consider contraception a woman's responsibility (Luechai, 1975), fearing loss of strength and inability to work following vasectomy.

Similar findings come from India, where the compulsion used in rural areas to meet target quotas for vasectomies was perhaps the single most important factor in the defeat of Mrs. Indira Gandhi's Congress Party in 1977.

WILLINGNESS TO LIMIT FAMILY

There is abundant evidence that poor women regard large numbers of children as a burden to themselves and to the children for whom they cannot provide adequate attention, food, clothing or education. "So many women come to me and touch my feet, begging for a medicine which will stop them from having more children," said a midwife in rural Bihar (Stokes, 1975). However, nowhere in Asia can it be claimed that all poor rural women desire smaller families and fewer births. A survey in Pakistan in 1968-1969 revealed that 90 per cent of women knew about birth control, but fewer than 3 per cent were practising some form (Sebo, 1975).

Resistance to family planning in north Bihar was shown to be due, as elsewhere in India, to the sacramental and economic value of sons, to the prestige and political power they bring and to the fact that in order to achieve a 90 per cent chance of having 2 sons living past the age of 6, each couple had to contemplate at least 5 births. Thus, there was no incentive to restrict families to 2. Moreover, there was a strong disincentive, in the form of time lost and cost of going to a clinic, the time needed for recovery and the possibility of infection. The poorest were least likely to accept contraception, to visit western medical practitioners, to be literate and to know of contraceptive opportunities. Muslims in Bihar, irrespective of caste and class, objected on religious principles (Blaikie, 1976). Women in Punjab village in Pakistan said birth control was interfering with God's work (Khan and Bilquees, 1976).

In Bangladesh, only middle-class urban women are likely to practise contraception, but family planning is considered acceptable by the poor in rural areas, provided methods are quick, simple and easily available. Women are motivated not by hopes of a higher standard of living but by hopes of a better chance of survival for themselves and their children (Sattar, 1978). The obstacles in rural areas are, however, great. Following a devastating cyclone which carried off the majority of children in one village, the religious leaders blamed the adoption of female education and of family planning measures. That family planning clinic has remained closed ever since (Adnan, Islam and the Village Study Group, 1977).

The consensus of Islamic scholars is, however, that there is no Koranic injunction against birth control, though sterilization is forbidden unless another pregnancy is dangerous (Schieffelin, 1967). The spacing of births and their limitation are allowed and, under certain circumstances, abortion up to 120 days is permitted. The

economic wellbeing of children should be considered, though some
denounce birth control on the grounds of poverty, since children are
the responsibility of society and government.

A study on attitudes towards family size revealed that anxiety
over child mortality was a common reason for not wishing to limit the
number of children in Taiwan, the Philippines, Thailand, Korea and,
somewhat surprisingly, Japan (Arnold et al, 1975). In Thailand, the
highest number of children is found in families which have experienced the greatest infant loss (Nibhon, 1977; Thienchay, 1977).

Conflicting views on the desirability of limiting families are
often heard from the same people. In a Gujerati village, almost as
many fathers as mothers mentioned the advantages of having fewer
children from the standpoint of their physical care (Poffenberger et
al, 1975), and many women understood the drain on their health represented by many pregnancies. Thirty-nine per cent of women thought
family conflicts increased with an increase in family numbers. On
the other hand, men mentioned the economic advantage of having more
children because this meant there were more hands to earn for the
family, and women mentioned the constant fear that if they had only 2
children, both might die (Poffenberger et al, loc. cit.).

SON PREFERENCE AND FAMILY PLANNING

The preference for sons, which is so marked in south and east
Asia and among communities originating from these regions, is widely
believed to be a major influence on acceptance of planning measures.
However, a recent study of data from India, Pakistan and Morocco
seems to show that son preference may not affect actual fertility
levels (Repetto, 1973). Even those bearing sons early did not stop
having children, while those with few sons did not necessarily continue childbearing (Repetto, loc. cit.). A scale for measuring son
preference in different countries has been established (Coombs, Coombs
and McClelland, 1975), but the difficulties of precise estimation of
the wishes of men and women have been pointed out (Williamson, 1978).
None the less, preference for sons is clearly marked, particularly
among men, in certain Asian countries. A report by the Population
Reference Bureau showed that, in answer to the question of sex
preference of a new child in families already having an equal balance
of girls and boys, 91 per cent of men in Bangladesh and 78 per cent
of Indian men wanted another son. Wide regional differences are,
however, found in urban India, with a lower degree of son preference
in Maharashtra, Tamilnadu and Delhi than in Gujerat, Kerala, Jammu
and Kashmir (Williamson, loc. cit.). Education, religion, income,
family size and number of living are significant factors governing
son preference, while age, sex and marital status are not (Bhatia,
1978). Rural people have a higher degree of preference for sons than
those in urban areas, and there is a higher preference for sons in
north than in south India. The numbers of sons considered ideal is
lowest among Christians, highest among Muslims; while Sikhs favoured
the lowest number of daughters, Muslims again wanted the highest.

Preference for sons is far less marked in southeast Asia than in
south or east Asia. While among urban ethnic Chinese in Thailand,

son preference is pronounced, Thais, though wanting some sons, wish to have both girls and boys. The number of children in a family is more important than their sex in determining the acceptance of family planning, and the majority of Thai women with 3 children, both in rural and urban areas, did not wish to have more (Visid, Knodel and Alers, 1974). The ideal family size in rural Thailand is shown to be 3.94, with some relation between boy-preference and non-contraception (Buripakdi, 1974).

In a cross-cultural study of the value of children conducted in Taiwan, Korea, Japan, Thailand, the Philippines and among different ethnic groups in Hawaii (Arnold et al, 1975), it was found that continuity of family name is the reason most frequently given for wanting sons, except in Japan and the Philippines. Support in old age and various types of economic and practical help are frequently mentioned. In Thailand the ability of sons to "make merit" is important. Emphasis on the psychological satisfaction of sons while still children is more common among Japanese. If told they could have only one child, 39 per cent of Japanese women said they wanted a son, 31 per cent a girl and 24.4 per cent had no marked preference, but 65 per cent of men wanted a son, only 7 per cent a daughter (UNESCO, 1976).

The onus for producing sons traditionally falls on women. The acute distress caused to an Indian mother who has produced a series of daughters is vividly described in Prem Chand's short story, "A Desperate Case" (translated by David Rubin, The World of Premchand, Allen and Unwin, 1969). In Korea, "reminded that it is the man who provides the chromosome for a girl as well as for a boy, a young husband responded, 'Yes, but it's the woman's job to catch the right one'" (Cha, Chung and Lee, 1977). Women have always sought supernatural assistance in their efforts to produce a son, and failure to do so can lead to mental illness (Rhi, 1977; Koh, 1978). The number of children women regard as ideal is strongly connected with development-oriented values, attitudes to modernity and preference for sons (David and Lee, 1974). Son preference in rural Korea automatically inflates the ideal number and actual number of children women bear (Table 9.1). Seventy-three per cent of rural women said they would go on trying until they had a son, while in Seoul only 29 per cent would do so. Seventy-six per cent of women with 2 sons, 32 per cent of those with one and only 15 per cent of those without sons wished to stop bearing children. Son preference is stronger if women experience pressure from family members with a fatalistic outlook (Kong and Cha, 1974). Preference for sons in Korea has been reinforced by laws of succession and adoption even more rigidly patriarchal than those of China and Japan; in the former sons inherited equally, while in Japan if a first son was considered unsuitable, he might be passed over in favour of a younger brother. In the absence of sons, an outsider could be adopted. In Korea, only a single male bearing the same surname and from the same clan seat could be adopted as family head. The Civil Code of 1960 permits the adoption of a son-in-law or of someone with a different surname, but practice is changing very slowly (Koh, 1978). Thus, the burden on a Korean woman to produce a son has been stronger than elsewhere in east Asia. It is hoped that improving the legal rights of women may diminish son

TABLE 9.1
Korea: Ideal Number of Children

	Rural Village	Small Town	Other Cities	Industrial Cities	Seoul	Average
Number of boys	2.46	2.10	2.24	1.97	1.98	2.23
Number of girls	1.56	1.35	1.48	1.25	1.22	1.42
Ideal total	4.02	3.43	3.69	3.26	3.19	3.64
Willing to let husband take concubine if wife has no sons (percentage)	68	37	48	35	25	50

Source: Chung, Palmore, Lee and Lee, 1972.

preference (Lee, M., 1977).

Singaporean Chinese, especially the older generations, maintain a strong preference for sons (Chen, 1974). Economic utility, family lineage requirements and power are the main reasons for having sons in Taiwan (Wu, 1972), although this is not to the exclusion of daughters. A family with boy, boy, girl may be content, but one with 8 daughters will still go on trying for a son.

In India, even at fourth parity, only 25 per cent of women with no daughters want more children, but 79 per cent of those without sons do so. The percentage of Asian women wishing to stop childbearing rises sharply at the age of 30, irrespective of the number of their children, except in India among women with no sons. Son preference is strong in India, Korea and Taiwan, less marked in West Malaysia and urban Thailand and less pronounced still in the Philippines and east Java (Freedman and Coombs, 1974; Table 9.2). No strong gender preference for children is expressed by educated Thai youth (Robinson, Somboonsub and Suwannapirom, 1975).

Chinese women living in urban flats in what was until recently a rural area of Hong Kong consider the ideal family to be 2 girls and 2 boys; the birth interval after a first girl is shorter than after a boy, showing that boys are still considered important, if less so than formerly. Some men believe that daughters are more obedient and more likely to care for their parents than sons (Johnson, 1975).

Even in modern China the continuity of traditional preference for sons is evident. An article in The Chinese Medical Journal, quoted by Orleans (1978), reports that doctors at the steel city of Anshan have perfected a method for determining the sex of the fetus. Of 30 women who underwent abortions following this test, 29 had been told they would have daughters. Chou En-lai once told a visitor: "There are still a lot of old customs hindering progress. We must admit the hindrances and support the women--not throw cold water on them. Old customs take effort to overcome. Chairman Mao says 'Don't believe everything they say if you didn't look into it yourself.'

120

TABLE 9.2
Mean and Modal Number of Children and Sons Preferred by Women Aged
20 to 39 Years

| | Mean No. of | | Modal No. of | |
	Children	Sons	Children	Sons
India	3.7	2.2	3	2
Korea	3.7	2.2	3	2
Taiwan (1967)	3.9	2.1	4	2
West Malaysia (1966-1967)	4.8	2.5	5+	2
Philippines	?	2.7	?	2

Source: Freedman and Coombs, 1974.

In some places it is still like the old days. First there is a girl
born, then a second, third, fourth, until there are nine girls. By
that time the wife is forty-five, and only then can she stop trying
for a son. Is this equality?" (quoted by Sidel, 1972).

The Population Reference Bureau, giving Japan, Singapore and
Hong Kong as examples of countries which have successfully reduced
family size, expects son preference to change more slowly than other
attitudes towards fertility (Williamson, 1978).

IDEAL FAMILY SIZE

The total number of children that rural women consider adequate
or ideal to ensure family continuity, help in the home and protect
them in old age varies from country to country and from one socio-
economic group to another.

In 1978 in the People's Republic of China officials campaigned
for 2 children per couple, claiming that the Gang of Four's agents
opposed instructions to this effect from Premier Chou and Chairman
Hua (Anhwei Provincial Service, Feb. 4, 1978). Following the Fifth
National People's Congress in 1979, it was stated that the national
aim was one child per family. The Fifth Five Year Plan aims at
reducing population by late marriage, longer intervals between births
and fewer children. The Kwangtung Conference on Birth Control and
Maternal and Infant Health Work claims that 71 per cent of women in
Kwangtung Province are practising birth control and natural increase
has fallen from 29.46 per 1,000 in 1965 to 12.6 in 1975 (Canton,
Kwangtung Provincial Service, Jan. 21, 1978). Against these claims,
however, it must be remembered that the economic status of a rural
family is raised in direct proportion to the number of its sons
(Parish, 1975). Such figures are considered representative of model
areas that have achieved unusual success, rather than average. The
birth rate for the country as a whole is estimated at between 22 and
25 per 1,000 in mid-1977, with population growth at about 1.4 per

cent (Orleans, 1978).

In Japan, the demographic picture has changed dramatically; before World War II the average births per couple was 5, while by 1972 this had fallen to 1.9. The birth rate has fallen from 28.1 per 1,000 to 19.4 in the same period (Japan, Prime Minister's Secretariat, 1976a). Childbearing ends early: 80 per cent of all births are to women between the ages of 25 to 29.

In most of Asia, however, the total number of children per family is invariably more than the two which are the aim of most family planning campaigns. Bangladesh women consider large numbers to be an essential insurance against the time when they are widows and require their children's support (Ellickson, 1976). In a Pakistani village, women who said they were content with a small family were under strong pressure from affines to raise more children (Khan and Bilquees, 1976). Burmese women say 3 is an ideal number, but do not complain until they have at least 6 (Nash, 1965).

Middle-class educated youth in Thailand consider the ideal family to be 2.5 children, while their parents considered 6.1 ideal (Robinson, Somboonsub and Suwannapirom, 1975). Most Indonesian women consider 4 to be ideal, 2 boys and 2 girls. Some 87.7 per cent of those interviewed in different parts of the country were ready to practise contraception, while 92.5 per cent wished their daughters to do so (Ihromi, 1973). The majority of poor Javanese women do not achieve their ideal family size, while half the women of upper socio-economic groups exceed their ideal. It has been suggested that this position reverses at higher levels of socio-economic development, but this has not yet been attained by most Asian countries (Hull, 1976a). The average ideal of 4 to 5 children is slightly lower among the upper classes, though many still want 5. In 3 areas of Sulawesi it was found that younger women gave 3.3 as the ideal family size, older women almost 4, with rural women favouring a slightly lower number than the urban élite (Komalig, 1975). Most were willing to try contraception on economic or health grounds.

In Taiwan, those with the traditional hope of living with and being supported by their children in old age tend to have fewer children (Yang, 1974). Rural Taiwanese mothers are interested in limiting the family only after the third or fourth child (Wolf, 1972). Experience with child mortality might delay initial acceptance of contraception; those with fewer than 6 children postpone contraception (Yang, 1974). There is evidence that the actual and ideal family size has reached an unacceptably high plateau (4.5 actual, 3.8 ideal), with son preference still running at 2:1. This is probably the major determinant of actual family size. The Population Council has provided a grant for a study under the title: Sociological, Anthropological and Psychological Study of Determinants of Family Size in Taiwan. The following variables are being considered: (1) internal-external control; (2) feeling of self-efficacy; (3) individual modernity; (4) authoritarianism; (5) need for affiliation; (6) need to raise social status through having children or sons; (7) differential fear of child mortality and attitudes towards children. These factors are being tested at actual, ideal and projected levels. The Behavioural Sciences Group at National Taiwan University includes, for the first time, psychologists working with those traditionally associated with family planning--sociologists, demographers, economists and anthropologists.

EDUCATION AND SOCIO-ECONOMIC STATUS OF MOTHER
IN RELATION TO FAMILY SIZE

It has been observed that primary and middle levels of education in rural Asia are correlated with more, not fewer children, even though these women are more disposed to practise contraception than those with no education or those who have dropped out early from primary school.

In Korea, fertility rates are lowered 7.9 per cent after primary education, 14.22 per cent after secondary and 16.29 per cent after higher education (Lee and Cho, 1976). In India, an inverse relation between education and fertility occurs only after matriculation (Rao, 1978).

In the Philippines, the anticipated decrease in number of children with improved socio-economic status and education is not found until mothers have graduated from Grade 6 or 7 of high school (Castillo, 1976a; Encarnacion, 1973). Rising income gives women better health and access to medical facilities and postnatal care, ensuring greater chances of survival. This has offset the reduction in births gained by postponed marriage associated with more education (Bulatao, 1974). Family size has decreased from an average of 6.46 in 1958-1962 to 5.89 in 1968-1972; in Greater Manila the average is 4.08, but in Mindanao more than 7, and on Bicol and Eastern Visayas more than 6 children per woman.

Eighty-one per cent of lower-income mothers and 85 per cent of their husbands favour limiting family size, but only 25 per cent practise some form of family planning (Gonzalez, 1976). Only 13 per cent of rural women use family planning methods, yet 84 per cent know of them (Monteil and Hollnsteiner, 1976). Among the poor, large families are favoured, without recognition of the declining health status which results (Gonzalez, 1976).

Births may, however, be more rationally planned in some areas than demographers have acknowledged. In villages in Java and Nepal, births are spaced at an average interval of more than 3 years, regarded as a mechanism which enables parents to achieve a relatively large number of surviving children while avoiding the extreme pressures on the household economy resulting from several very small, dependent children (Nag, White and Creighton Peet, 1978). Poor Javanese women have a knowledge of traditional contraceptive measures, and space births for both economic reasons and to avoid straining their own health (Singarimbun, 1974; White, 1967). Mortality among these infants and children is low, reflecting better care of such rationally spaced children.

In Malaysia, only in metropolitan centres is there a negative relation between fertility and income (Malaysia, National Family Planning Board, 1966-1967).

Respondents in 5 Asian countries gave economic reasons as a major cause for limiting family size (Arnold et al, 1975). However, poverty is not always seen as a barrier to good child-raising

(Guthrie and Jacobs, 1966). "God will provide" says a Bangladeshi woman (Ellickson, 1976). "God provides for the birds and the fish and the beast; he will provide for my children" is said in the Philippines (Flores, 1969/1970). A study of 39 rural secondary school students in India showed that they wanted fewer children than their parents, but in view of the traditional environment, fertility decline would be slow (Poffenberger and Sebaly, n.d.). In Asia as a whole, standards of education of women in rural areas are low (see Chapter 4) and traditional attitudes difficult to counter.

EMPLOYMENT AND FERTILITY

In Korea, the hypothetical negative relation between labour force participation and fertility does not always hold. Goldstein (1972) believes it is not so much labour force participation but other social and cultural variables which are effective. It has been suggested that if the mother/wife/worker roles are compatible, work will have little effect on fertility (Stycos and Weller, 1967). In Korea, the type of work is found to be important, agricultural work based on the home or unskilled work nearby being compatible with higher fertility. Urban working women show lower fertility rates at all ages than urban housewives, but in rural areas productive workers have higher fertility than those not working. Jobs which are urban and modern, and demand high levels of education and technical skills, do influence fertility. There is a correlation between lower fertility and employment only in some non-agricultural jobs (Lee and Cho, 1976). Female employment is considered to be a result of high fertility, not of demand for labour. There is a consistent rise in labour participation in the rural areas of Korea relating both to economic need and the availability of child care by older children. In 1970, 61.9 per cent of rural households were two-generation families, indicating that the traditional care provided by grandmothers was less available.

Fertility is lower among working women in Manila, but employment has little effect on the fertility of rural women. In developed countries, the relation between income and fertility is an inverse U, but in the less developed regions, the relation is positive (Bulatao, 1974).

In Hong Kong, there is virtually no difference in the size of families of women employed outside the home and housewives, but families of women employed full-time at all ages are considerably smaller (Chung, 1974).

The majority of female workers in both urban and rural Thailand are engaged in sales or farming, work which is compatible with motherhood. These women have the highest fertility (Nibhon, 1977). The cumulative fertility of female unpaid workers is as high as, sometimes more than, women not in the labour force. Employed women, particularly in urban areas, have lower fertility; they are younger, have been married for a short period, tend to marry later and practise birth control. They also lose fewer infants. Women with non-farm occupations have the lowest mean number of children, women working on farms the greatest, and the unemployed are intermediate.

The highest level of non-farm labour participation is likely to be found among those who have had more than 4 grades of education. Modernity, non-farm employment and lower levels of fertility are closely linked (Cook, 1977; Boonlert and Cook, 1976 and 1977). Women who engage in traditional marketing activities have also adopted family planning, since pregnancy interrupts economic undertakings. High fertility is not seen as leading to social prestige (Mougne, 1978).

PERCEIVED BENEFITS OF CHILDREN

We have shown that the benefits of sons are strongly perceived in communities in south and east Asia. Frequent mention has been made in this chapter of the economic advantages parents see in having larger families. In the People's Republic of China, the advantage of having male workers to gain work points for the family will make limitation of family size difficult in rural areas where unemployment or underemployment are not major factors.

A detailed study of the perceived value of children in different Asian countries, and in Hawaii, was undertaken by the East-West Population Institute, Honolulu. The responses given by rural Asians are given in Table 9.3. For most rural people the economic advantage is most frequently mentioned, with respect both to current economic contributions and security in the parents' old age. Emotional benefits were also salient, but less important than other benefits and less frequently mentioned. Two related psychological benefits are important in 3 east Asian countries: "pride in children's accomplishments," and "children to carry out the parents' hopes and aspirations." It was thought that these rural parents might have been frustrated by their own life circumstances and hoped their children would fare better (Arnold et al, 1975).

Daughters are desired mainly for the psychological satisfactions and practical help they provide while still children; companionship for the mother, behavioural and personality traits and help with the housework are the most common reasons for welcoming girls.

A frequent reason for not wanting fewer children is the need for companionship among children, the wish to avoid having an only child and the need to foster character development.

Reasons for not wanting more children are also mainly economic. Parents mention rearing problems, including discipline, tiredness of parents and emotional strain. Children do not restrict alternative activities of rural parents to the same extent that they do in urban areas, but this reason is given by some parents in Taiwan, Thailand, Japan and by Hawaiian Filipinos (Arnold et al, loc. cit.).

Educated middle-class young Thais consider that children bring love and warmth, make for a happier family and give one a sense of pride at being needed (Robinson, Somboonsub and Suwannapirom, 1975). It is expected that children will have to be supported financially until they have completed their education, between 20 to 23 years of age, and 84 per cent of men would postpone having a family until they had the economic means to support one.

In rural Hong Kong, children are seen as a way of "avoiding

TABLE 5.3
Why Rural People Want Children

Country	Reasons and Percentage of Replies				
Korea	Continuity of family name--59	Companionship, comfort, care in old age--17	Conformity to social norms--13	Proof of fertility, masculinity, femininity--12	Pride in children's accomplishments--10 Economic help in old age--10
Taiwan	Continuity of family name--56	Unspecified help in old age--32	Don't know--9	Companionship, avoidance of loneliness--6	Conformity to social norms--6 Instinctive, natural to have children--6
Japan	Children as heirs, someone to inherit family wealth--32	Prime value in life a--22	Happiness for family--22	Companionship, avoidance of loneliness--11	Happiness for individual parent--9
U.S. (Hawaii) Filipino	Companionship, avoidance of loneliness--67	Unspecified help in old age--44	Happiness for individual parent (general)--43	Love, affection--11	Continuity of family name--6
Philippines	Companionship, comfort, care in old age--32	Happiness for family--27	Help in housework, family chores; practical help--20	Economic help (old age not mentioned)--20	Play, fun with children; avoidance of boredom--17
Thailand	Continuity of family name--38	Companionship, comfort, care in old age--19	Help in housework, family chores; practical help--18	Don't know--18	No reason given--14

[a]Translated from the Japanese expression iki-gai--literally, "one's life worthwhile." The response is similar to the English expression "goals and incentives from children," but because it implies an emphasis on present satisfactions from raising children it has been coded as a country-specific response category.

Source: Arnold et al, 1976.

loneliness, bringing happiness to the home, giving a couple something to talk about, giving spice and colour to daily life, continuing the generations, reciprocating for having oneself been raised, because it is fate, or to avoid criticism" (Johnson, 1975). In another study in Hong Kong, joy, security and improvement of husband-wife relations were the chief emotional benefits of children (Chung, 1972). Women who perceive conflict with their careers limit the number of children. Many, however, believe that relations with their husband are unchanged after having children.

Irrational factors, such as a belief in a new child "bringing luck" may also affect views of family size, effectively removing responsibility from the parents. Moreover, fundamental psychological needs, which are not fully perceived, influence the desire for children. Children are expected to hold marriages together in the Philippines, their number enhancing the effect. No one will belong to the mother as much as her children; they confer emotional satisfaction and security which are all the more important if her relation with her husband is unsatisfactory (Lapuz, 1977).

ECONOMIC BENEFITS OF CHILDREN

It has been suggested that shortage of land in rural Java, increasing the intensification of subsistence agriculture and of non-crop cultivation and non-agricultural pursuits, has led to a greater requirement for family labour and the perceived need for more children (White, 1967; 1975). A study of demographic history in Java has shown that in the past, high labour requirements for individual families have been at variance with national requirements for the reduction of population growth rates (White, 1973; 1974; 1975). Recent investigations have shown that, however limited the available opportunities for productive labour, each individual household obtains a greater share of these opportunities by increasing its size. The positive relation between total work input of children in a household and the household's economic performance is relatively independent of access to land for wet-rice cultivation (Nag, White and Creighton Peet, 1978). A Household Studies Workshop conducted by the Agricultural Development Council (de Tray, 1977) discussed evidence that children, sometimes very young children, contribute significantly to the welfare of families, much of the contribution taking place within the home and thus unperceived by those studying income. The contribution of children to total family income might be as high as 25 per cent of the total.

Boys in a Javanese village work for 3.6 hours daily at the ages of 6 to 8 years, 4.7 hours from 12 to 14 years (when many attend school) and 7.9 hours above 15 years. Girls from 6 to 8 years work for 3.5 hours daily, 8.7 hours from 12 to 14 years and 10.2 hours from 15 to 19 years. In a Nepali village, boys from 6 to 8 years work for 3.7 hours, 7.5 hours from 12 to 14 years and 9.5 hours from 15 to 19 years, while girls 6 to 8 years work for 4.9 hours, 9.9 hours from 12 to 14 years and 11.3 hours from 15 to 19 years (Nag, White and Creighton Peet, 1978; see also Chapter 14, Tables 14.5 and 14.6).

In assessing the economic costs and benefits of having children, it is necessary to adopt a broader definition than normal of economic activity. This should include not merely production of crops, but the construction of a house, fetching of water and fuel, food processing and preparing, craft work, and medical, spiritual and administrative activities (Nag, 1972). A method for calculating economic benefit based on caloric output and caloric gain has been evolved.

Throughout rural Asia it may be assumed that parents are aware of the psychological and material implications of the size of their families. Demographers in Java conclude that the need for children is part of a perception of the family "as a co-operative institution of support, assurance, livelihood and personal fulfilment" throughout life (Hull, 1976a).

BIRTH CONTROL AND COMMUNICATION BETWEEN SPOUSES

It has been suggested that the pattern of acculturation in the Philippines, involving sex segregation and same-sex friendship, may impede psycho-sexual development in marital relations. This may lead to lack of interpersonal empathy and conjugal communication which are essential in the rhythm method, the only means of contraception widely sanctioned in the Catholic rural Philippines (Liu, 1971). More than 40 per cent of Filipinas never discuss the number of children they desire with their husbands, and this percentage is much higher in rural than urban areas (Castillo, 1976a). Since sex segregation and same-sex friendship after early childhood are found in most of Asia, this theory is obviously highly significant to family planning. It has not, however, been systematically studied on any scale in Asia as a whole.

An investigation has been conducted in Lebanon in which it is found that sexual inequality and incompatibility are likely to be more critically disruptive to the decision-making processes regarding birth control among women who are poorly educated or who have low rates of participation in activities outside the home (Chamie, 1977). Highly educated women and those in occupations outside the home environment are more likely to identify sources of information which do not depend upon the husband's explicit participation; they may practise contraception without his knowledge, or may seek to influence his opinion. A more egalitarian sexual relationship occurs between couples in which women have higher levels of education.

"Although sexuality does not act upon birth control behaviour in isolation from other aspects of marriage, we found sexual compatibility, responsiveness, and to a lesser extent, equality, to be associated with the use of more effective or permanent birth control methods" (Chamie, loc. cit.).

Comparable studies among different ethnic groups within Asia would be of great value. Cross-cultural extrapolation is inadvisable. Bengali women of high status, all of whom had higher education, never discussed the sexual act with their husbands, since tradition precludes this (Roy, 1975).

Women in Hong Kong who communicate frequently with their husbands, discussing their worries, events at home and work, have fewer

and desire fewer children. This is also true of families where decisions are made by the wife, or by husband and wife jointly. Women
who have had a courtship of 2 years or more start contraception at
lower levels of pregnancy than women whose marriages are arranged by
their parents (Chung, 1974). Women who worship deities and their
ancestors, and who have strong son preference, have larger actual and
ideal families than those without religions, or than Protestants or
Catholics (Chung, loc. cit.).

The percentage of those who had never used contraception in
Japan declined from 64 per cent in 1950 to 13 per cent in 1975. The
most favoured method is the condom (generally purchased by wives from
female sellers in the home), followed by the rhythm method. Both
methods require a high degree of co-operation by the husband.
Between 93 and 95 per cent of women said their husbands were in
agreement on the need for contraception (Uchida, 1978).

In India, on the other hand, as in many other parts of the
developing world, males exercise authority in sexual matters; their
lack of co-operation in contraception has been documented in several
states (Rao, 1978). The fear has been expressed that women will gain
freedom to have relations with other men if contraceptive devices are
made available to them. The inadequate involvement of men in family
planning campaigns has been shown to be a crucial obstacle to their
success.

The extent and nature of modesty or embarrassment have a negative correlation with communication between spouses in Singapore.
Seventy-one per cent of Malay women express embarrassment at being
examined by a male doctor and at any mention of sex with their husbands. Husbands are more important in family decisions among Malays
and Indians, while decisions among other groups are mostly made
jointly, especially among upper socio-economic groups. These all
have a higher proportion of acceptors of family planning. Chinese
couples have a higher degree of communication between spouses than
Malay or Indian couples on all but religious matters; they are most
likely to practise family planning (Chen, 1974).

In Thailand, males working in agriculture between the ages of
20 to 29 tend to make major decisions on birth control, while older
couples decide together. In families with a monthly income of less
than 400 baht, men decide on birth control measures, but above this
income the decision is made jointly. Men are more apt to make decisions during the first few years of marriage, later on the couple
makes them together. Seventy-eight per cent of respondents approve
of birth control, chiefly for economic reasons. See Table 9.4.

The Women's Development Institute of Ewha University, Korea, has
noted the crucial importance of pressure from other family members on
decisions to limit the number of children. If a woman perceives that
her husband, other family members, elders and her community support
birth control behaviour, innovative behaviour and non-authoritarian,
non-fatalistic behaviour, she tends to be active in fertility control
(Chung et al, 1972).

It is clear that the relation between levels of education, work
participation, family background, the prevalence of traditional
attitudes and the quality of her relation with her husband all influence a woman's attitude towards birth control in complex ways. These

TABLE 9.4
Thailand: Responsibility for Birth Control

	Decision on Family Size (percent)	Practising Birth Control (percent)
Husband alone	45.3	22.0
Together, husband dominating	8.4	11.0
Together	31.4	38.5
Wife alone	3.6	13.8
No freedom of choice	8.4	

Source: Luechai, 1975.

factors together may exceed in importance the effect of economic
factors on limitation of family size. So far, more is known of the
effect of economic factors on family size than of other variables.

10
Division of Labour
and Decision-Making

It is generally assumed that the participation of women in the labour force of a developing country will follow a U-shaped curve. Women are employed in agriculture in large numbers. This is followed by a decline and, as the modern economy expands, by a rise in the number of women employed. Most Asian countries are at the early stage where a high proportion of women are employed in agriculture. It has been suggested that where women play an important part in production, particularly if this brings in grain or cash income, their role in family decision-making is important. This seems to be confirmed in most of southeast Asia. Where convention prevents women from working outside the home, care of livestock, processing of the harvested crop and craft and other pursuits may still provide them with the status of contributing materially to family income. Even in wealthy Chinese and Indian families, where a woman has been expected to obey rather than discuss, an older woman who has raised children and run a household successfully is consulted (perhaps only privately) by her husband. Chinese women still have a strong influence over their sons in rural Taiwan (Wolf, 1972), as they had in traditional China. The effect of the power to influence decisions within the family on a woman's concept of her own individuality and self-confidence need not be elaborated.

Regardless of the extent to which society tolerates the making or influencing of decisions by women, their overt role in community--village or other unit--is usually minimal. The difficulties of persuading women to speak out at meetings on matters in which they were vitally concerned in the early days of the People's Republic of China are described by Hinton (1972). Even today, in a model brigade at Taching oilfield, where women form 85 per cent of the labour force, they have only 16 per cent of the places on the party committee (MacFarquhar, 1977). Indonesian men carry out most public performance of family responsibilities, and women those in the home (Papanek et al, 1974; Ihromi, 1973). Women rarely take part in panchayat meetings in India (Mandelbaum, 1972). There may be exceptions among more primitive groups; Iban women share rights and duties with men in daily life, and participate in decision-making in the longhouse (Komanyi, 1973). (See Chapter 4, section on political participation). As a general rule, however, no matter how important the Asian woman's role in production, she is able to influence only decisions affecting her family.

With these basic generalizations in mind, it is useful to look at the traditional division of labour and share in making decisions between men and women in different parts of Asia. It has been claimed that the liberation of women will come about only when society's conception of what is fitting for either sex to do has been fundamentally changed, starting with the sex-typing of roles which everywhere takes place early in childhood. Women in Communist countries are doing "men's jobs," from driving buffaloes in Vietnam to building bridges in China. The result of this is that women get less sleep than men, have less time for leisure and relaxation and less time for taking part in local organizations and community leadership (Whyte, 1977). In Phu Kanh Province, Vietnam, women carry out irrigation activities and produce fertilizer, take the lead in combating drought and eradicating pests; 75 per cent of the women in the province have become members of the Women's Union (Hanoi Home Service, March 10, 1977). However, "because of their experience in domestic work and child care, it is expected by both male and female Communist leaders that many women, as in other countries, will work in education, medicine or food industries, and because their physical strength is on average less than that of men, that more of them will enter light than heavy industry. The emphasis is less on job parity than wage parity and freeing women from housework" (Gough, 1977). Women represent 65 per cent of medical workers, 54 per cent of educators, 59 per cent of those in food industries, 65 per cent of workers in light industry, 65 per cent of agricultural workers and those in petty trade, but only 25 per cent in heavy industry and 25 per cent of those in forestry, for which they receive equal pay. Economic independence gives them authority in the family (Gough, loc. cit.).

Nowhere, however, are men doing women's jobs; the Vietnamese Women's Council advocates the sharing of tasks (Bergman, 1975). Chinese school texts describe a small boy enabling his mother to pick more cotton by collecting his younger brother and doing the cleaning (Martin, 1975). Others tell of a boy sweeping the home before doing his homework; another shows a girl driving a tractor. Recommendations have been made in Japan to reform education so as to avoid sex-typing of roles, to persuade men to help in the home and women to participate more in community life (Japan, Prime Minister's Secretariat, 1976b). A fundamental change in the attitude to sex-typing of jobs has not yet occurred, however, in 2 of the world's most revolutionary re-organizations of society, the Chinese commune (Davin, 1975; Sidel, 1972), or the Israeli kibbutz (Padan-Eisenstark, 1975).

After strong initial resistance, men in a Shensi village agreed to look after children while women attended political meetings (Myrdal and Kessle, 1973), but rural women in China generally do less productive work than men because of the demands of the home and child-raising (Davin, 1975; Sidel, 1972). Men consequently receive a daily average of 7-9 work points, while women average 6-7. Women do not generally take part in decisions affecting the allocation of labour, the distribution of produce and other resources of production of the team or brigade (Croll, 1976), though some participation does occur

(Davin, 1975). Women were chairpersons of 4,300 of 5,000 People's
Councils at the village level in Vietnam (Bergman, 1975), their
prominance in public life perhaps a reflection of the absence of men
at war. Before the American withdrawal from Vietnam, women in North
Vietnam performed 70 per cent of all agricultural work. In this
region they were heads of 3,580 of 17,900 agricultural co-operatives,
and heads of 13,783 rural production units (Gough, 1977).

A remarkable exception to the almost universal sex-typing of
roles and the minimal contribution of men in the home is found on the
island of Cheju, Korea, where women divers make the chief financial
contribution to the family budget, men meeting subsistence needs from
agriculture, assisted by women. Men are expected to help in child
care, prepare food and do housework and, indeed, take over the
running of the home entirely during the absence of groups of women
divers on the mainland or in Japan at certain seasons. Role reversal
is accepted because many men are raised in divers' families. Many
household heads are female. Men over 61 are expected to stay at home
and look after the children. Even in upper-class families of agri-
culturists in the centre of the island, women are involved in marketing. Women are active in community leadership on Cheju (Soon,
1977b).

An attempt will now be made to give a cross-section of the
division of labour in rural Asia. Material has been chosen from a
wide range of studies, in many of which division of labour was not a
primary concern. Some are quantitative, some merely descriptive, and
precise details are unavailable. Micro-studies, however incomplete,
have been preferred, since they give a more real picture than gross
national or regional statistics which are frequently of doubtful
accuracy, do not record local socio-economic variations and a "housewife's" productive work outside the house itself, however crucial for
family survival, is usually ignored. The selection presented here is
not, however, intended to be taken as typical of countries, or even
of regions; some cover only very small samples. We have sought only
to present some of the considerable body of material, which can be
abstracted, in order to see what rural Asian women do and how far
they are able to make decisions. Probably in no other sphere of
woman's life is precise knowledge of her activities so deficient, and
in no other sphere is it so important that more be known. Many
studies show an inadequate distinction between socio-economic and
occupational groups. Moreover, economic and social changes are constantly modifying the work carried out by women, and the findings of
older studies may no longer apply at the present time.

SOUTH ASIA

Pakistan

On a normal day outside the planting or harvesting seasons, a
typical Punjabi woman works for 14 hours. At least 5 hours a day are
spent in animal care, collecting, carrying and preparing fodder.
Other major daily activities are milking, churning and cooking food
and carrying it to the fields for men. During the wheat harvest,

women spend 10 hours a day in the fields. They also take part in
husking, winnowing and storing wheat. They help transplant rice and
in sowing. The picking of cotton and chillies are major annual
activities. Women living in <u>katchcha</u> houses (the majority) have to
renovate them twice a year after the end of the rainy seasons. A
variety of home crafts are practised, mostly for home use. Preserves
and pickles are also made for the family's use (Khan and Bilquees,
1976).

Rural women work unveiled in the fields. Purdah is not strictly
observed, although women are confined to their immediate neighbourhood; older women do the shopping, while younger ones attend to
domestic work (Gani, 1963). Men perform the heavier agricultural
tasks, those considered most essential; women do not help artisan
husbands--cobblers, blacksmiths, goldsmiths or carpenters (Saghir
Ahmad, 1974). Dairying is an important activity for women and children (Hirashima, 1977). One village girl complained that a woman
might earn half the family's share from work done during harvest, but
this was not considered a job, nor the wheat her earnings (Khan and
Bilquees, 1976).

In the North-West Frontier Province, the location of a farm job
is an important variable in influencing the participation of women.
(See Table 10.1.) Syeds, Rajputs and Pakhtuns observe purdah very
strictly. Jats and Arians are less strict, and women do field
chores. Peshawar and Mardun have a predominantly Pakhtun population,
but Hazara is more heterogeneous and more liberal in behaviour. A
typical farmer grows 4 grain crops; wheat, maize, beans and pulses.
These are stored for year-round family needs in clay bins holding
from 100 to 600 kilograms; these bins are constructed by women.
Wooden bins may also be used. The investigator noted that material
gathered by male agricultural extension workers, through interviews
with male farmers, probably led to an underestimate of women's work
in the following table, since these farmers do not readily volunteer
information about women members of their families (Malik, 1977).

Feeding the livestock usually includes pasturing animals, harvesting green herbage from the fields, chaffing, processing feed
concentrates and feeding in the manger. The first 3 jobs are usually
done by men; the remainder inside the family compound by women.
Women always pasteurize milk, ferment it for <u>dehi</u> (yoghurt) and process butter. The removal of ears and husking of maize is done in the
field, shelling both in field and home. Rural women are actively
involved in all tasks done in the compound, but men make all decisions pertaining to the disposal of surplus grain, its timing, location, price and person to whom it is sold; women may determine the
amount available, and place it in sacks for disposal. Two-thirds of
the farmers reported that women undertook the tedious job of drying
grain, done once or twice by laying it in the sun on rooftop or
houseyard, and replacing in containers. In Peshawar and Mardan,
where availability of irrigation absorbs all the labour of men in the
fields, women contribute more to livestock activities than in Hazara,
where there is less irrigation and consequently less continuous work
in the fields.

In the tribal areas of Waziristan, Kurram, Khyber, Swat, Dir,
Chitral and Malakand, it is reported that 87 per cent of all farm

TABLE 10.1
Pakistan, North-West Frontier Province: Participation of Women in Farm Activities in Selected Tehsils (percentage of families)

Farming Activity	Hazara Division			Mardan Dist.		Peshawar District		
	Haripur	Abbottabad	Manshera/Batagram	Swabi	Mardan	Charsadda	Nowshera/Peshawar	Average
No. of Sample Farms	32	44	44	26	34	26	34	240
1. Cleaning seed	81	59	70	62	62	58	71	66
2. Drying grains	47	73	80	46	79	69	71	68
3. Selling grains	9	0	5	0	0	0	0	2
4. Feeding livestock	28	52	39	46	76	58	56	50
5. Milking dairy animals	34	52	32	62	91	92	100	64
6. Harvesting and husking crop	28	55	39	0	0	0	15	23
7. Shelling cobs	22	25	32	65	38	38	59	38
8. Thinning/weeding	16	27	41	0	0	0	0	15

Source: Malik, 1977.

workers are adult males, women only 9 per cent. The proportion of
adult males ranges from 65 per cent in Swat to 81 per cent in Kalam.
In Malakand no woman has been reported as working on the farm. It is
acknowledged that answers from prestige-conscious men have biassed
these replies (Ashraf, 1963).

India

According to the 1971 census, 17.35 per cent of the total labour
force is female, representing 11.86 per cent of the total female
population. However, these figures, which have declined steadily
over recent years, do not include the high proportion of rural women
whose families are involved in cultivation, who contribute to production, but are recorded as housewives (INCCU, National Institute of
Public Co-operation and Child Development, 1977; India, National
Committee on the Status of Women, 1974). Employment in the organized
sector for both men and women is less than 10 per cent of total
employment. Only 6 per cent of all female workers are in the organized sector where, theoretically, they are protected by labour legislation. Over half the rural female workers are landless agricultural
labourers; 33 per cent are self-employed in agricultural enterprises
and 4 per cent in household enterprises (including spinning, weaving,
oil-pressing, rice-pounding, leather and tobacco pressing, etc.).
The female rate in all these undertakings has declined since independence, and has remained constant only in plantations, probably due
to the special aptitude of women in this sector (Rao, 1978).

The sex-typing of jobs in India gives women a lesser incentive
to move to the towns than in most Asian countries, since work in
textile factories,* and in clerical/secretarial posts, has been
almost exclusively reserved for males. In 1961, 93.7 per cent of the
workforce in Lucknow, and 96 per cent of that in Kanpur, were male
(Gould, 1974); men leave their wives in their homes to be cared for
by kin and raise children. Only 9.1 per cent of all employed women
in 1971 were working in factories, and 80.1 per cent in agriculture
(ICSSR, 1975). Labour force participation of women, both Muslim and
Hindu, is lower in predominantly Muslim areas, although 40 per cent
of all Scheduled Caste and tribal women in those same areas are
employed, all in low-status, low-income jobs (Joy and Everitt, 1976).
This indicates that the rural female labour force will probably
remain rural, unlike in other countries where there is migration of
young people to the towns for jobs. However, there has been a marked
change in some major cities, such as Bombay and Delhi, where many
women work as secretaries and receptionists.

Poor women all over India work in the fields; in the north those
not compelled by economic necessity to do so undertake much of the
processing of the crops in the family compound. Women predominate in
rice cultivation in the south.

---

*By contrast, in Japan women accounted for over half the total
factory labour force until the 1930's, over 80 per cent being in
textile-related industries; even in the 1970's, they still account
for over half the workers (Jones, 1976-1977).

Studies of the use of time by rural employed and unemployed
mothers, carried out by Lady Irwin College, New Delhi, from 1965–
1966, revealed poor management of time in relation to tasks (INCCU,
1977), as shown in Table 10.2. It will be seen that the unemployed
rural women in this sample were not required to assist their husbands
in the fields.

Women in tribal communities do much of the field work. In Naga
villages in the past, men organized for war and women worked in
swiddens, often far from home, in constant anxiety at the threat of
attack by headhunters. In these areas women might have to climb 500–
1,000 feet to the nearest water point, as most villages were on top
of hills. Women cooked, brewed rice beer, husked grain and wove
cloth, while supervising children. Women had considerable say in
village councils (Elwin, 1958/1975). Among the Gonds, husband and
wife are the predestined pair for sowing with plough and seed-drill,
no other team being permitted. Men broadcast pulses and small mil-
lets, and women drop the seed of large millet and maize into seed
drills on the plough. They grow vegetables, apply manure and weed
crops in groups while men drive a special weeding plough between the
rows. Young men guard the crops at night, women and children during
the day. Women reap by hand, but sorghum is winnowed by men (von
Fürer-Haimendorf, 1974).

Though women collect water from the well all over India, ecological stringency in a village in south India has produced a

TABLE 10.2
India: Daily Management of Time by Rural Women

Tasks	Employed Women	Unemployed Women
Cooking	3 hours/day (17.64%)	4.30 hours/day (30%)
Fuel-related tasks	15 minutes/day (1.47%)	1 hour/day (6.66%)
Washing utensils	1 hour/day (5.88%)	2.30 hours/day (16.67%)
Child care	1 hour/day (5.88%	2.30 hours/day (16.67%)
Sweeping house	15 minutes/day (1.47%)	1 hour/day (6.66%)
Personal and leisure	45 minutes/day (4.41%)	3.30 hours/day (23.33%)
Paid work	10.45 hours/day (63.2%)	--
Total	17 hours/day (100%)	15 hours/day (100%)

Source: INCCU, 1977.

deviation from the norm. The extreme inaccessibility of water during
the dry season at Elephant makes it very difficult for men to obtain
wives; only the most circumspect behaviour, including the collecting
of water 500 feet down in the valley, keeps the women content (Beals,
1962).

Tribal women and those among the lower strata of society play a
greater part in decision-making than do those of upper strata rural
and traditional urban dwellers (Dube, 1963); women in the latter
groups are not expected to work outside the home, while the former
engage in agricultural production. Among progressive urban couples
authority is shared more or less equally (Dube, loc. cit.; Srinivas,
1977). Educated men are willing to concede the right of their wives
to work outside the home only if there is adequate time left for this
after home activities (Kapadia, 1966). Mothers of mature years in
the middle classes enjoy considerable respect and authority in the
family, and have a say in decision-making. On the whole, however,
women play only a marginal role, except for decisions affecting their
daughters. The institution of purdah further withdraws a woman from
the family decision-making forum; 72.61 per cent of women in Haryana,
62.18 per cent in Rajasthan and 60.78 per cent of women in Delhi
observe purdah in the presence of their husband's kin (ICSSR, 1975).
Young mothers have more control over their children, especially their
education, pay less deferential respect to elders and their husbands
than previously, and have more power to control decisions regarding
their personal lives and on matters relating to food (Minturn, 1976).

Bangladesh

Only 2 per cent of the labour force is female, with a further
half million women, mostly destitutes, employed in agriculture outside the organized sector. Ninety-five per cent of the female population lives in the rural areas. Women are divided into 3 groups:
(1) destitutes, who beg or hire out as labour; (2) the wives of landless farm labourers or daily wage earners, sharecroppers and small
farmers with less than half a hectare of land, who make up about 70
per cent of all rural women; they do not usually work for wages nor
do they hire help in the household; (3) wives of owners of larger
plots of land, of traders and para-professionals, who are able to
hire labour and domestic servants. The last group, some 15 per cent
of the total, comprises women who are educated, who have some leisure
and are the first to take opportunities for employment and training,
but who at the same time place high value on female seclusion
(Sattar, 1978). A detailed analysis of women's activities throughout
the agricultural cycle, together with associated household tasks and
preparation for festivals, is given by Sattar (1975).

The work done by women is a major topic of misinformation. They
undertake all seed preservation and storage, post-harvest rice processing, grain storage, vegetable and fruit growing, poultry raising,
livestock care, food processing, food preservation, household manufacture, maintenance and repair and fuel gathering (Kabir, Abed and
Chen, 1976). Almost all this work is done behind the compound wall.
In weaving and fishing communities, they spin thread and make nets.
Yet a rural farmer, asked what work his wife does, may reply "none."

139

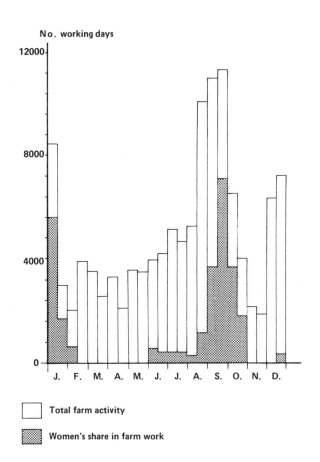

FIGURE 10.1   Bangladesh, Comilla District: Total agricultural
activities and contribution by women in four villages, 1974 (Martius
von Harder, 1977).

Women often do no agricultural work, and rarely work in the fields. However, economic necessity does drive women into seeking work outside the home. Of 303 women who joined Food for Work projects, one-third were married, one-third widowed, 19.1 per cent unmarried, 6.9 per cent divorced and 7.3 per cent deserted. There was an unexpectedly high proportion of those below the age of 20, mostly single, who had a high number of dependents such as incapacitated parents (Chen and Ghuznavi, 1977). Only 60.4 per cent of husbands of those married were the principal family earners, and none were cultivators or owned land. Most were day-labourers, doing earthwork, cleaning and cooking or house repair for payment in cash or kind. Bangladeshi men claim that if a woman earns money, it will cause conflict and break up the family--she will spend it on frivolous things. In fact, money earned is spent on survival (Kabir, Abed and Chen, 1976).

Seclusion prevents women from going to market, either to buy or sell. Nor do they work in the fields, but once the crop is brought home, they do all the work--threshing (men may help--Khatun and Rani, 1977), winnowing and husking (Ellickson, 1976; Bertocci, 1974; Martius von Harder, 1977; see Figure 10.1 and Tables 10.3a and 10.3b). Women cultivate vegetable gardens for subsistence and care for animals. They may keep cows or goats belonging to others in return for an offspring which can be sold for cash. Rice processing reveals the efficiency and managerial capacity of women and their ability to avoid waste by the extensive use of by-products. They use home-grown fruits and vegetables for subsistence and to barter (together with rice) for home needs in the market (Khatun and Rani, 1977).

Purdah is observed particularly in wealthy rural homes where women have separate quarters, starting from the age of 10 (Bertocci, 1974). As an adult, a woman emerges only to draw water or dry padi. Women move fairly freely at work within the village, but not beyond.

Decision-making rests firmly with men, and women have little power to influence men once these are out of the home. A father decides on whether a girl will be educated or not, and if so, what type of study she should pursue. A father or husband decides whether a woman may seek employment, and in what field (Jahan, 1975). However, working-class urban women are more assertive than rural women, and decision-making is more egalitarian among élite groups where women are highly educated, particularly if they also work (Jahan, loc. cit.).

A more egalitarian relation also exists between rural tradeswomen and their husbands. These families come from monocrop areas which are insufficient for subsistence. The men work as day labourers. Women obtain goods from town tradesmen and attempt to sell them in the villages. Small communities live on boats, returning to their villages only for harvest. These women do not wear a burqa; they may market on the way back to their community after spending the entire day attempting to sell their goods. Obviously, they are required to make decisions alone, but they remain outside traditional Bangladeshi norms (Martius von Harder, 1977).

TABLE 10.3a
Bangladesh: Expenditure of Time by Adult Female Household Members in
the Household Sphere, by Day and Year

Task	Total Expenditure of Time Per Day (minutes)	Expenditure of Time Per Person Per Year in Days	
		Total	Percentage[a]
Food preparation[b]	240	104.3	28.6
Fetching water (five pitchers at 20 litres)	25	10.9	3.0
Fuel collection (drying and storing)	15	6.5	1.8
Washing	8	3.5	1.0
Upkeep of house and courtyard	8	3.5	1.0
Clothing (repair)	1	1.5	0.1
Trading[d]	4	1.9	0.5
Production of:[e]			
Chirra (38 seers per year per household	8	3.4	0.9
Pitah (46 seers per year)	46	19.8	5.4
Muri and Khoi (19 seers per year)	2	0.9	0.2
Rice preparation:[c]			
Winnowing	2	0.9	0.2
Parboiling	5	2.1	0.6
Total	364	155.4	42.5

[a]As proportion of total time expenditure, 11.1 per cent of total
being devoted to family, 42.9 per cent to agriculture (see Table
10.3b).

[b]Including preparing fire, cutting vegetables and washing up
from average of 2.0 warm and 0.6 cold meals per day.

[c]Average yearly requirement per family is 41 maunds of rice
(1 maund = 82 pounds).

[d]Negotiations with female traders in own compound, or with male
traders via children and men.

[e]Rice preparations of different kinds. 1 seer = about 2 pounds.

Source: Martius von Harder, 1977.

TABLE 10.3b
Bangladesh: Expenditure of Time by Adult Female Household Members in
the Agricultural Sphere, by Day and by Year

		Expenditure of Time Per Person Per Year in Days	
Task	Total Expenditure of Time Per Day (minutes)	Total	Percentage[a]
Threshing[b]	3	1.5	0.4
Drying	12	5.1	1.4
Storage	1	0.5	0.1
Husking	263	114.2	31.3
Vegetables:			
Preparation for market	2	1.0	0.3
Drying for storage and			
preparation for home use	5	2.0	0.6
Livestock:			
Preparation of feed[c]	51	22.2	6.0
Cleaning stall	10	4.3	1.0
Care of poultry	10	4.3	1.0
Total	357	157.9	42.9

[a]As proportion of total time expenditure.
[b]Preparing rice--average 41 maunds per family per year.
[c]Yearly average of 1.7 feeds per day.

Source: Martius von Harder, 1977.

Nepal

    Women collect firewood and dry leaves in the forest for fuel,
and bring water to the home. They spade and hoe the fields, carry
manure to the land and dry, store and mill grain. In 1971, the
female labour force participation rate was 57.77 per cent, one of the
highest in Asia, particularly for the 15- to 24-year age group.
About 98 per cent of working women are employed in agriculture (Rana,
1978).
    Limbu women in east Nepal work with men in the fields during
planting, cultivating and harvesting. At other times men work at
building, repairing roofs, erecting racks to store grain, making
baskets, frames for looms and pens for animals, while women bring
them all the materials needed. Only men work with oxen, and women
follow with hoes to smooth out the earth, tidy the fields, repair
terraces, plant seeds and transplant rice. Men, women and children
weed. Until recently women worked with cloth--spinning and weaving--
and straw, while men worked with bamboo. Women cook in the home but
men do so on the trail and help in preparations for festivals.

During the slack agricultural season, men may leave home on trading ventures or go to India for seasonal work; many men serve abroad in Gurkha regiments. Women brew beer, distil liquor and sell the produce (Jones and Jones, 1976).

While outwardly deferrent, women have strong influence over decisions by means of their close relations with their children (Caplan, 1974). They instruct and discipline daughters and serve as a channel of communication between their sons and their husband. The absence of men has led to a greater sense of independence; many women now assume much of the work load and decision-making, even when their husbands are at home (Jones and Jones, 1976).

Sri Lanka

Women are more important in economic activities in the dry zone than in the wet zone. As family income rises, women and girls are withdrawn from labour, working only on the family farm during seasonal peak times. The head of the family decides who will do what work (Wickramasekara, 1977). Men may work their land with family labour, the wife being excluded from threshing (Leach, 1961). In the dry zone, a Sinhalese husband and wife may work together in the fields, but there are no other occasions upon which they may be seen together in public with propriety (Leach, 1960).

The introduction of coffee in the mid-nineteenth century, followed by tea and rubber, brought a large immigrant population from south India, and for the first time, women undertook labour for wages. Sinhalese women, however, did not participate, and continued their traditional unpaid family work (Kannangara, 1966). In 1966, two-thirds of all employed women were in agriculture and related occupations, 8 per cent in manufacture and industries, 2.5 per cent in trade and financial services and 17 per cent in government and business services; 63 per cent of urban employed women come in the last category. In the rural areas, 42 per cent of working women were employed in agriculture, 23 per cent in government and business, nearly 4 per cent in trade and finance, and 15 per cent in manufacturing and industries. These figures show the traditional female preferences for teaching, nursing and cottage industries (Kannangara, loc. cit.).

In 1971, 70.4 per cent of rural women were engaged in agriculture and related activities, while 55 per cent of the urban female workforce were engaged in community, social and personal services and 14 per cent in manufacturing, showing little change since 1966 (Table 10.4).

The overall female activity rate is influenced by the high rate of participation in the plantation sector, where women form 53.1 per cent of the total labour force; 59.6 per cent of the female labour force is engaged in agriculture and forestry. The paid female labour force has increased from 13.3 per cent in 1959 to 16.9 per cent in 1969-1970, but 42.6 per cent of women in the working age group are classified as engaged in home duties. This indicates the continued importance of traditional roles for women and the part they play as unpaid family workers (Devadas, 1978).

TABLE 10.4
Sri Lanka: Employed Females Aged 10 Years and Over, by Industry (1971)

Major Industrial Groups	Total No.	%	Urban No.	%	Rural No.	%
1. Agriculture, hunting, foresting and fishing	01,231	61.9	8,875	8.0	492,356	70.4
2. Mining and quarrying	1,044	0.1	77	0.1	967	0.1
3. Manufacturing	99,290	12.2	15,579	14.0	83,711	12.1
4. Electricity, gas and water	250	0.0	146	0.1	104	0.0
5. Construction	1,214	0.2	413	0.4	801	0.1
6. Wholesale and retail, trade, restaurants and hotels	23,329	2.9	8,487	7.0	14,842	2.1
7. Transport, storage and communication	3,366	0.4	1,761	1.6	1,605	0.2
8. Financing, insurance, real estate and business services	1,717	0.2	1,224	1.2	493	0.0
9. Community, social and personal services	131,743	16.27	61,038	55.0	70,705	10.2
10. Activities not adequately defined	47,287	5.8	13,371	12.0	33,916	4.8
Total	810,471	100.0	110,971	100.0	699,500	100.0

Source: Sri Lanka, 1971 Census.

SOUTHEAST ASIA

Burma

Tasks are shared and orders given with equal frequency by both
sexes in Burmese homes (Nash, 1965). There is great overlap in the
sexual division of labour. Men can sew, cook, baby-tend, wash
clothes and shop for food. Women can work in the field, drive bul-
lock carts, chop wood and be prominent in market transactions. There
is no clear pattern of authority. In public the husband is supposed
to be dominant, but women are not shy, backward or deferential. In
the home they speak out freely.

Women hire out for agricultural labour. In rice cultivation,
men plough and harrow and pull up the seedlings, while women transplant, often in gangs. When gangs are large, for transplanting,
pulling up, harvesting, milling and cleaning rice, a gang leader is
employed, who may be either male or female. At peak times wives and
children help in the fields. Men cut the rice with scythes, and
women and young people winnow.

Women may be tailors as well as men, and women may sell food at
festivals, while others keep small "stores" in their own compounds.
Stores are petty businesses run by older women or widows who are able
to stay at home all day. They replenish their stores from the
nearest town once or twice a month (Nash, loc. cit.).

A woman's role is flexible, and can be fitted in with household
duties (Mi Mi Khaing, 1963).

Laos

In traditional Laos, before involvement in the Indochina conflict and its aftermath, men ploughed or harrowed the rice-field, and
women and children followed with a receptacle for catching fish from
the furrows (Levy, 1963). Men usually sowed the seed, harvested and
threshed the crop, but thinning and pricking out seedlings was done
by women. Hunting, felling of wood, all bamboo work, building,
carpentry and house-building were men's jobs. Women husked rice, did
the housekeeping, looked after livestock, fetched water and did the
weaving. Healing was formerly a male preserve. Petty trading in
village shops was mostly in women's hands; they grew or purchased
from middlemen the fruit and vegetables they sold in markets.
Pottery making and blacksmithy were men's crafts (Halpern, 1964).

Vietnam

Traditionally women looked after livestock and worked in the
fields (Vietnam Resource Centre, 1974). Today they plough, use
mechanical pumps, select seed, breed animals and carry out technical
innovations, all activities usually associated with men in other
countries.

In the past, wives of the scholar gentry were important in
commerce and the management of property; wives of civil servants were
similarly active under the French. Confucian norms did not influence
the peasant classes; women had higher status than among the élite,

with stress on equality resulting from the important role they have played in production. Women looked after livestock, spun and wove in addition to field work (Vietnam Resource Centre, loc. cit.). The sense of equality was reinforced by custom, whereby young men had to work for 3 years for a girl's parents before being allowed to marry her. Political upheavals have placed women in charge of home, fields, market, business and commerce (Hoang van Co, 1955).

In rural north Vietnam, women make up 60-80 per cent of the labour force. Seventy per cent of public health workers, 60 per cent of teachers and about one-third of Vietnamese scientists are female (interview with Madame Nguyen Thi Binh, Far Eastern Economic Review, June 20, 1980).

Cambodia

In the past, women played an important role in production and their views were consulted in family decisions. They were often more active and ambitious than their husbands, attending to business and taking an important part in economic life.

Men generally prepared the nursery and padi land, while women broadcast the seed and transplanted rice. Families harvested jointly; animals were used for threshing and women winnowed and stored the grain. Fruit was often sold to buyers while still on the tree, and sugarcane sold in the field; purchasers were responsible for harvesting (Delvert, 1961).

Malaysia

Husbands do 51.7 per cent of the work involved in padi farming, their wives 25.6 per cent and hired labour at seasonal peaks another 22.7 per cent. The preparation of nursery and fields is a man's job, as are ploughing, harrowing and hoeing. Transplanting is mainly a woman's job, while weeding and manuring are done by both. Men and women cut the crop at harvest, men thresh and transport and women winnow and clean the grain. Men and women tap rubber, women work on smallholdings or mat-making. Young women work outside the family plot only with other family members. The landless work largely for wages (Purcal, 1971). Underemployment is more acute among women than men; 60.9 per cent of women work less than they would wish, whereas only 37.8 per cent of men are underemployed (Malaysia, FFPA, 1976). In matrilineal Jelubu, Negri Sembilan, rice growing is a woman's job and tapping a man's (Swift, 1963). Men plough alone; women harvest in a group working on their own and group members' land (Husin Ali, 1975), although paid labour is beginning to eliminate such mutual help. In Kelantan, where women are renowned for their independence, men as well as women transplant padi (Bray, 1977).

Women fetch water; boiling it is the first task of the day. Many work outside the home in a Trengganu village, some in fish-drying business, making belachan, growing vegetables for sale or making cakes for sale and hawking them (Strange, 1971). The weaving of pandanus mats and sewing are female jobs. Men fish, caulk and paint their boats. Some women bargain with middlemen for their husband's catch. Men are middlemen in fish, women for cloth and

pandanus. Both sell coconuts, both may be shopkeepers. In this
village planting and harvesting are women's jobs, while men tap
rubber. Both may work in vegetable gardens and sell the produce
(Strange, loc. cit.). In another Trengganu village men chop the
firewood gathered by women and girls for the cooking stove (Wilson,
1970). In Kelantan, fishermen's wives see their husbands off, having
made ready the meal they take with them; they carry their gear to the
beach and are there on their return to help bring in fish and boats,
while another meal awaits them in the home. This greatly limits
women's ability to work outside the home (Firth, 1966).

A farmer and his wife hire out as a family group for harvesting
and planting in a region which does not exceed 10 miles from their
home. This has not changed, despite improvements in transport.
Female specialization in planting is beginning to change with the
hiring of labour in contract groups, either male/female, all male or
all female. Group threshing is chiefly done by men. Sex is not a
cultural hindrance in seeking wage labour, though women tend to earn
less. Work is done on a contract basis for a specific operation and
area (Fredericks, 1977).

A good Malay wife performs domestic duties, cooks, runs the
household and looks after children without nagging, while her husband
is the provider (Swift, 1963), an ideal which does not correspond to
the reality of shrinking landholdings and the taking up by women of
any pursuit which brings in some income. Women influence decisions
about where to build a new house, the choice of spouse for their
children and even influence economic decisions (Swift, loc. cit.).

The oldest woman in a Selangor household allots such tasks as
fishing and care of children to other family members. The only
domestic job done outside the home is washing, in the absence of a
family well (Wilson, 1967). Women over 40 years are allowed greater
licence in behaviour and are important in decision-making. The functioning of clusters within the village depends on the interactions of
women. Whether and where to tap rubber is usually decided by women;
they discipline children. Nominally their status is inferior, but
they strongly influence decisions.

Women play an important role in the petty marketing economy,
particularly in the northeast. In 1875, Swettenham noted that the
market in Kota Baru was dominated by women (Burns and Cowan, 1975).

Among the aboriginal peoples of the Malay Peninsula, Negrito men
are responsible for training boys, especially those over 5 years,
while women train girls who accompany them on food-gathering expeditions (Carey, 1976). Hunting is a purely male pursuit among Negrito
and the cultivating groups, the Senoi and Jakun. Negrito women con-
struct wind shelters once men have cleared the site. Only men deal
with outsiders, for example in the sale of jungle produce. Senoi
women plant small gardens for the use of their own family. Among
most swidden cultivators of the peninsula, men fell trees, women and
children clear undergrowth. The man uses the dibble, women insert
the seed; weeding and the harvesting of maize, tapioca and rice are
done by women (Carey, loc. cit.).

Iban men of Sarawak, East Malaysia, will not sow, reap or weed,
while women do not fell trees, build farm huts or make tools,
although the absence of men on traditional long journeys leaves their

wives with responsibility for all agricultural activities (Komanyi,
1973). A Malay woman may speak freely to other men only after the
age of 40, whereas an Iban girl grows up as an equal member of her
society and participates in every aspect of life as an adult. Women
actually have more say than men in decisions during the absence of
their husbands. There is a lack of marked sex-typing in socialization patterns.

As might be expected in a plural society where different ethnic
groups have, for historical reasons, been associated with either
fully rural or urban residence, there have been differences in the
degree to which women are employed in different groups. In 1957,
one-quarter of Malay women and 17 per cent of Chinese women aged 15-
64 were employed in agriculture; the Malay figure was probably higher
(Hirschman and Aghajanian, 1980). Only 3 per cent of Malay women, 5
per cent of Indian and 12 per cent of Chinese women were employed in
the non-agricultural sector. By 1970, the proportion of Malay women
in agricultural employment remained the same, though there were more
older and fewer younger women so occupied. The number of Chinese
women in agriculture had declined, and the total of Indian women,
mostly working in estates, had fallen by 50 per cent. There were
marked increases in all groups of women employed in non-agricultural
pursuits, especially among the young. Increasing urbanization,
higher levels of education and later age of marriage are closely
associated with employment in the modern, non-agricultural sector.
It is expected that cultural variables regarding the propriety of
employment for young women will decline in importance as the different ethnic groups are similarly affected by socio-economic conditions
(Hirschman and Aghajanian, loc. cit.).

Indonesia

It has been traditional for Indonesian women, even those of high
status, to work, though not outside the home except in agriculture.
Three out of 7 agricultural labourers in Java are women (Sajogyo,
1974). Socialization still aims at making a girl a good wife and
mother before all else. Studies undertaken in Java over recent years
have given a picture of the activities of women of different socio-
economic status with a degree of precision not generally available in
Asia (Stoler, 1971; Hart, 1978; Sajogyo et al, 1980). The Rural
Dynamics Study of Bogor Agricultural University has shown that rural
families depend on 4 or 5 occupations to ensure their livelihood
(Sajogyo et al, loc. cit.).

Ploughing, harrowing and hoeing are men's tasks in Java, during
a limited number of work days spread over relatively long periods;
harvesting is a female job, the most labour intensive of all tasks
(Stoler, 1976). Planting, threshing and care of animals are generally female jobs (Ihromi, 1973), although children play an important
part (White, 1976). Couples work together on small-scale jobs such
as weeding, the harvesting of perennial crops, processing of crops
for home or market (Jay, 1969), but larger work parties are usually
all male or all female. Women plant secondary crops, transplant rice
(men pull and bundle the shoots) and harvest. They thresh and store
the crop (Koentjaraningrat, 1960). Men build and repair the house,

repair farm equipment and the earthworks in field irrigation and do most of the daily tending of the crop. The spade, sickle, plough and parang are men's tools, the ani-ani a woman's. Husbands decide the farming plans, what land rights to seed or set out, what crops to plant and the means of cultivating and marketing. However, more enterprising wives contract for land rights and market crops virtually alone (Jay, 1969).

Women from large landownings oversee the harvest operations, control the number of women invited to work, fix their shares and preside over the threshing, bundling and distribution of shares to each. Poor men work as self-employed porters or long-distance carriers for the wealthy. Men and women sell garden produce; young men with high school educations, but little land, are becoming middle-range traders (Stoler, 1976).

The difficulty of establishing clear-cut lines of responsibility for decision-making has been revealed in the Rural Dynamics Study of Bogor Agricultural University (Sajogyo et al, 1980). Decisions are usually shared, with men intervening in domestic matters and women in agricultural and economic fields. Wide variations are the result of differences in personality. The conclusions of an earlier survey gave women an important role in decisions on the rites de passage of family members, particularly the marriage of children. Decisions on purchase of land, moving to a new house, education of children and their marriage were discussed together, though the husband's decision was final. Increasingly, older children were also taking part (Ihromi, 1973). The Bogor Agricultural University study revealed no rigid demarcation between the sexes in decision-making in any socio-economic group, though in one village when many men were employed outside agriculture, there was greater equality of responsibility. Women's decisions usually predominated in expenditures on food, but men took part in those on housing, education, clothing, household utensils and medical care. It could not be concluded that women were firmly in control of expenditure (Sajogyo et al, 1980).

Among the Achehnese, women perform domestic and subsistence work and men provide cash by tending fruit and vegetable gardens, cattle and buffalo. Women look after goats and poultry (Jayawardena, 1977).

In Bali, the equality of the husband and wife is underscored by the fact that they represent a unit for political citizenship and in worship. Decisions are mainly made jointly. There is no sharp division of roles socially, though men do the heavy work. Men may, however, look after children, and men cook the large ritual feasts. Balinese women spend much time working together in the houseyard. They share the rice-pounding for the nuclear families sharing the houseyard (an average of 2 to 3 nuclear families, ranging up to 20 families among the gentry). They share the tasks of going to the river for water, going to market, child care and the incessant preparations of offerings for temples, where rituals occur about once a week. Girls start helping from the age of 8 or 10 (Geertz and Geertz, 1975).

The Philippines

Women make up about one-third of the labour force, though female labour force participation rates have declined since 1957, more significantly in rural than urban areas, reflecting the female drift to the towns. Unemployment for rural women is about twice that for men (Castillo, 1976a). In 1973, the Department of Labour reported that 30 out of every 100 women were working in agriculture, but the figure is probably higher, since many classified as housewives also help in the fields (Monteil and Hollnsteiner, 1976). Sixty per cent of rural women are engaged in agriculture, and this has increased rather than declined in importance as a source of rural employment (Castillo, 1976a). Women do much of the petty marketing.

The rural Filipina must shop daily, though she sometimes buys at higher cost from door-to-door sellers. She chops fuel, though men and boys chop larger material. Older women may fish with rod and line in fields or nearby rivers. Men also trap fish. Women often work together at cottage industries after the mid-day meal; during the evening leisure periods, groups divide into men and women, a division learned early in life. Men may occasionally cook, tend to children or even market. Women are constantly busy, but rural men are clearly unemployed except for limited periods during the agricultural cycle (Fox, 1963). See Table 10.5 for the allocation of time by a rural housewife.

Fields are cleared and fenced by tribal men, but all other work is left to the women. In the past men's roles were above all in hunting and defence. Women care for chickens and pigs, fetch water, perform household tasks and fish by traps. Trade is carried on by women. Men might make baskets, while weaving is a woman's task, as is the making and selling of pottery. Building and repair of the home is usually a man's job (Infante, 1969).

Under the relatively new sagod system near Iloilo City, those who weed are given exclusive rights to harvest the crop, receiving one-sixth if they also thresh and clean the grain; this system has parallels throughout the Philippines (Ledesma, 1977). This means that a family is not paid for weeding, as before, but it does away with the free-for-all previously common at harvest, giving security of work and income while spreading risk over different plots, since agreements are made with different landowners. Women and children do the first and second weeding, while men do the heavier tasks of harvesting, threshing, cleaning and hauling. Women fatten pigs, an important source of income (Ledesma, loc. cit.).

The decision-making pattern is more egalitarian than patriarchal. The Filipina participates in the management not only of matters concerning household and family, but also of farming and livelihood (Castillo, 1976a). Women decide themselves whether it is necessary for them to find work to supplement family income (Illo, 1979). Among lower-class rural, semi-urban and urban families, women exercise the greatest influence in matters relating to household chores, care of children, discipline of daughters and allocation of monetary resources; men in matters relating to occupation, livelihood and discipline of sons (Licuanan and Gonzalez, 1976). Social and leisure activities are decided together, and there is often mutual

TABLE 10.5
The Philippines: Average Time Allocation by Women During Survey Week

Activity	Time (in hours)	Percent of Total Time	No. of Wives Who Performed Activity
A. Consumption Time	94.99	56.5	
Sleeping	62.17	37.0	10
Eating	9.06	5.4	10
Attending seminars, lectures, adult education classes	0.60	0.4	1
Other personal activities	22.45	13.4	10
Assisting relatives, neighbors with the housework without pay	0.72	0.4	4
B. Home Production Time	52.10	31.0	
B.1 Care of Children	9.55	5.7	
B.1.1 Care of Children aged 0-2	7.69	4.6	
Bottlefeeding	0.17	0.1	1
Breastfeeding	1.78	1.1	2
Feeding children aged 0-2	0.18	0.1	3
Care of children aged 0-2 other than feeding	5.56	3.3	4
B.1.2 Care of Children aged 3 and Above	1.86	1.1	
Care of children aged 3 and above	1.83	1.1	8
Assisting children with schoolwork	0.03		1
B.2 Other Housework	41.46	24.7	
Marketing, including travel time	1.10	0.7	5
Shopping, including travel time	0.76	0.5	5
Buying from sari-sari neighborhood store or peddler	1.34	0.8	8
Preparing food/cooking for household only	15.05	9.0	10
Fetching water/firewood	0.12	0.1	7
Feeding livestock/poultry	0.94	0.6	7
Taking meals to family members away from home	0.03		1
Gardening	0.10	0.1	3
Cleaning house, laundering and ironing, sewing and mending for household	21.94	13.1	10
B.3 Supervising Housework	1.06	0.6	

Source: Jayme-Ho, 1976.

consultation before decisions are made in either's sphere. Important decisions are more likely to be shared by those with higher levels of education (Gonzalez and Hollnsteiner, 1976).

A study of family power in East Samar showed that decisions are women-dominated when there are young children, but become more egalitarian after they have left the home (Contado, 1978). Most decisions are made jointly, but whereas the husband alone decides only major matters, his wife alone makes decisions on major, intermediate and minor matters; men often give in to avoid conflict.

Public decision-making remains a male sphere (Monteil and Hollnsteiner, 1976). There is low participation of poor rural women in any but church groups and government-organized welfare groups. In 1969, half the nation's unions had no women members, due to lack of interest, the transient nature of their employment and the burden of domestic chores.

Thailand

Thailand has the highest proportion in Asia of women recorded as being in the labour force (from 65 to 72 per cent, according to different surveys), holding the least skilled jobs at the lowest wages (Richard Nations, Far Eastern Economic Review, June 9, 1978). However, a survey in 1978 by the National Economic and Social Development Board indicates that 38 per cent of the labour force are women, of which 60 per cent, or over 3.2 million, are in agriculture. Forty per cent earn between 501 and 1,000 baht (U.S.$25-50), and less than 1 per cent more than 5,000 baht (U.S.$250) (Business Times, Singapore, Aug. 29, 1978).

In the central plains of Thailand, most tasks are performed by both men and women; both may plough, sow and act as midwives (Phillips, 1966). Women raise chickens. Grandmothers look after home and infants while the husband, wife and older children work in the fields. The husband may tend the buffalo, but children gather its feed in the evening (Hanks and Hanks, 1963).

There is no discrimination within the family between girls and boys. A girl is considered easier to raise, more helpful around the house and more likely to care for her parents in old age, whereas a son will help in farm work and increase his parents' store of merit by becoming a monk. Both girls and boys look after small children, cut grass, tend animals and work in the fields. Privilege is by age rather than sex. If necessary, adult men care for children and cook, and women may plough (Hanks and Hanks, loc. cit.).

An analysis of the pattern of decision-making in Thai families has revealed the results shown in Table 10.6. A survey of villages in north and central Thailand showed that decisions were generally made jointly; 58 per cent of couples decided together on the children's future; 57 per cent on family planning (in 36 per cent of families the wife alone decided); 40 per cent of couples, and 40 per cent of husbands alone, decided whether to borrow money and 50 per cent of couples decided together how to dispose of the products of family labour. Ninety-four per cent of women in these villages thought all decisions should be made jointly (Nantanee et al, 1977).

TABLE 10.6
Decision-making in Thai Families

Subject	Husband	Decisions made by (percentage) Husband Dominating	Together	Wife	Children
Education	46.7	10.0	31.7	2.7	4.3
Child's marriage	18.3	5.0	19.0	--	53.7
Child's occupation	36.3	6.3	17.3	--	35.7
House expenditure	31.7	5.7	22.0	31.3	
Major household equipment	45.0	6.0	25.7	10.7	

Source: Luechai, 1975.

EAST ASIA

China

In the People's Republic of China, women participate in labour in different degrees all over the country. Women in the south are more active in the fields than in the north, reflecting the heavier demands for labour in multiple-crop areas. This distinction was more strongly marked in the past, when women rarely worked in the fields in the north. The practice of footbinding (see map in Buck, 1937), more prevalent in north and central China than in the south, but from which only Hakka women were wholly exempt, severely limited mobility. Women have always worked outside the home in south China. Throughout the country, however, an upper- or middle-class woman would have brought shame to her family had she worked (Yang, 1959).

The proportion of labour contributed by women in traditional China varied according to ecological zone. Davin (1975) quotes Buck's analysis (1937), showing that in the double-crop region of Kwangtung, south Kiangsi and south Fukien, women performed 29 per cent of the agricultural labour; in the rice-tea area of northern Fukien, Chekiang, Kiangsi and southern Hunan, only 5 per cent; in the southwest rice zone, 22 per cent; in the Yangtze region of wheat and rice, 19 per cent; in the Szechwan rice zone 11 per cent; in the spring-wheat area north of the Yangtze 14 per cent; in the winter-wheat kaoliang area, 8 per cent and in the winter-wheat millet area, 5 per cent. Davin notes that this analysis fits with Boserup's conclusion (1970) that, where several irrigated crops are grown, high labour demands necessitate work by men and women, as in the southern regions of China. In north China and part of the south where plough agriculture predominates, women help only at peak times. The fairly high proportion of work done by women in the spring-wheat area (14 per cent) is explained by the high labour demand at peak periods in a

short growing season. Buck related labour contribution to the degree
of prevalence of footbinding, but was disturbed by this high figure
for the north. It may perhaps be explained by the fact that women
did most of the processing of the crops, once harvested.

At a village in Shantung Province, women worked outside for the
first time each year in June, threshing, drying and storing the winter wheat. Women cut seed heads from stalks of millet and kindred
grains in August, when the crop had been gathered by men and brought
to the threshing ground. All women worked at this time, and girls
worked for others for cash. Women helped thresh and stored the millet. They helped remove peanuts from the vines; girls hired out for
this job, and for oil-pressing. Mothers and their children cut sweet
potato vines in the nursery into sections suitable for planting;
daughters poured water into the holes where the vine was planted, and
mother and daughter filled them with earth. Women processed and
stored sweet potatoes after harvest, October being a time of intense
activity. They preserved and stored cabbage, turnips and string
beans for winter, but did not help with the cultivation of soybeans.
Fishing provided a minor source of income for many women (Yang,
1945).

Buck's survey listed tea-processing, pig and poultry raising and
craft and textile work separately, but even here, revealed fairly low
participation by women. Davin (1975) suggests that the time-
consuming nature of household work helped explain this. During the
last century the amount of time spent on the preparation of thread
and spinning for household clothing and bedding was considerable
(Smith, 1899/1970), and this would have been higher in the colder
regions of the north. Women did all the picking, spinning and weaving of cotton, as well as sewing. Girls and boys gathered fuel until
the girls were deemed too old to be outside the home. Women assisted
in the gathering of crops, and cared for the orchard and melon
patches (Smith, loc. cit.).

Women in the newly liberated areas of China after 1949 were
initially reluctant to do agricultural work. They lacked confidence
in their physical strength, their ability to learn unfamiliar tasks
and to acquire new skills (Hinton, 1972; Croll, 1979). The Women's
Federation at village level took a major part in persuading women to
overcome their diffidence, and special measures were taken to encourage them. As the process of collectivization proceeded from smaller
to larger co-operatives and thence to communes, opportunities for
women to work increased. The innumerable rural industries set up at
the time of the Great Leap Forward took many men away from agriculture, and further stimulated the demand for women to replace them.
Female labour participation reached a peak at this time, supported by
the provision of canteen and child care facilities outside the home
(Croll, 1979). Villagers disliked these measures and, as the fervour
of the Great Leap subsided, they were discontinued, being replaced by
more flexible arrangements. By 1962 women were averaging 24-26 days
work per month on commune lands, the remainder being devoted to home
duties (Andors, 1976). Croll (1979) quotes evidence that, despite
the prominence given to female work teams (usually composed of unmarried women) performing work traditionally done by men, women still
tend to concentrate on field activities demanding less physical

strength and less skill than jobs assigned to men.

Innumerable press and radio reports of women's participation in labour from all over the People's Republic are sometimes difficult to interpret. A report on March 29, 1978, for example, states that 95 per cent of the women in Kiangsu participated in labour. Does this simply refer to female labour at a given peak time; do 95 per cent of women work at some time during any particular month or year, or does this mean that 95 per cent of women in Kiangsu work full-time in the fields--a most unlikely conclusion? Some reports are more precise. Heilungkiang Provincial Service on May 14, 1978, reported that 25 per cent of the labour at the sowing of spring wheat was performed by women.

In Kwangtung today, there is still a considerable division of labour. Child care, laundry, meal preparation and other domestic chores continue to fall on the family unit, being performed mainly by women who rise before other family members. She prepares animal feed, the family breakfast, fetches water from stream or well for laundry and waters the private plot. Most able-bodied women work in the fields, unless there is no one to care for small children, or joint income is sufficient to release her. Men generally plough and do heavy tasks, while women weed. Women generally tend the family livestock and cut fuel from hillsides, while men usually work on private plots, except among Hakka communities, where women may do more than men. Marketing appears to be shared, men making major purchases, women buying daily items, though in some cases men do all the purchasing and in others women do it all. On the whole, men help little with domestic chores, though grandfathers may tend children. Sons help their fathers, while daughters help in the home (Parish and Whyte, 1978).

Men are still acknowledged as heads of households and make major decisions, although they may consult the others, both male and female, and there are variations in the pattern (Whyte, 1977; Parish and Whyte, 1978). The household head and his wife decide on which children will receive education and which shall be withdrawn from school. They decide jointly on the occupations of their children (Salaff, 1973).

Japan

The inadequate development of facilities for child care, the increase in the proportion of nuclear households and the consumer-oriented pressure of the mass media upon women to remain at home (the better to embellish it and their persons), together with subtle pressure by employers, have caused a two-peak employment structure for women. There is a high level of participation in the labour force by young, single women, followed by a sharp drop until middle-age, when there is again a sharp rise (Willing, 1977). The female labour force (38 per cent of the total, and 35 per cent of the total female population) is one of the highest in Asia and among capitalist nations. Some 46.6 per cent of the female population of working age (i.e. over 15 years) were working in 1974, representing a decline from 1955, when 56.7 per cent of working-age women were employed. The decline is due not to increased school attendance (14.2 per cent in 1960 and

156

14.7 per cent in 1974), but to an increase in the number doing housework only (65.9 per cent in 1964 and 68.4 per cent in 1974). However, unlike western countries where salaried women far exceed other
categories, only 58.7 per cent are salaried in Japan (in 1955 only
31.2 per cent), the others being self-employed or unpaid family
workers (Willing, loc. cit.). The fact that over 70 per cent of
agricultural work in Japan is performed by women helps explain these
figures.

The number of women engaged in agriculture fell from 8,550,000
in 1960 to 4,590,000 in 1976. By 1972 they represented 70 per cent
of all agricultural workers corresponding to a general exodus from
rural areas. Table 10.7 shows that most farm wives are engaged in
agriculture, and that two-thirds of them are the principal worker;
the smaller the holding, the more likely this is the case. The rapid
and widespread introduction of improved agricultural machinery has
led to the gradual reduction in the proportion of time spent on
agricultural tasks. The time gained is chiefly devoted to rest or
household duties (Table 10.8), but women would like to obtain additional income from work which can be done in their homes or from
part-time work (Japan, Prime Minister's Secretariat, 1978).

Korea

A study of 11 remote villages showed that women thought economic
activities outside the home were better carried on by men. Infants
are cared for by women, but men discipline children. However, if

TABLE 10.7
Japan: Labour Status of Farmers' Wives (percent)

	Wife as Principal Worker	Wife Works with other Family Members	Wife Helps Others	Occa-sionally Helps Others	Does Not Take Part in Farm Work
Total	32.3	33.7	14.8	11.9	6.1
Size of farm:	(hectares)				
below 0.3	42.1	12.2	7.9	21.7	16.1
0.3-0.5	49.3	17.0	12.0	13.9	7.8
0.5-0.7	41.8	26.8	12.7	15.0	3.7
0.7-1.0	32.1	37.8	18.8	8.7	2.7
1.0-1.5	26.3	45.9	16.7	8.1	2.9
1.5-2.0	19.4	49.2	20.9	9.4	1.0
2.0-2.5	12.5	58.3	19.2	4.2	5.8
2.5-3.0	14.0	44.2	23.3	14.0	4.7
Over 3.0	10.0	59.2	16.3	10.2	4.1

Source: Japan, Prime Minister's Secretariat, 1978.

TABLE 10.8
Japan: Expenditure of Time Outside Agriculture by Farm Wives
(percent)

	Wife as Principal Worker	Wife Works with Other Family Members	Wife Helps Others	Occasionally Helps Others
Actual:				
Rest	32.8	42.9	39.7	19.1
Non-farm work	32.8	22.2	28.1	43.7
Housework	23.5	23.4	26.8	24.0
Desired:				
Rest	33.2	43.0	42.9	33.7
Non-farm work	33.5	20.2	21.4	38.9
Housework	14.3	19.1	8.6	13.7

Source: Japan, Prime Minister's Secretariat, 1978.

housework is chiefly done by women, economic activities outside the home and child care are shared. In joint families, tasks inside the home and those outside, which require strenuous effort, are performed by men, but many other tasks are shared between the generations and sexes. Child care falls mainly on women (Choi, 1969).

Children take jobs from about the age of 8, and work full-time from about 15 on. Men appreciate help from their sons, and women from their daughters. Groups of kin, all male or all female, work together on an exchange basis (Brandt, 1971).

Emancipation from the sex-typing of roles is occurring more swiftly for jobs traditionally performed by men than for those by women. Women are now able to do many tasks formerly considered the preserve of men, but are still obliged to shoulder a considerable proportion of essential activities within the home, including child care. In Vietnam and Japan, women have been admitted to men's jobs in the absence of men--at war in Vietnam, or in urban employment in Japan. In the rest of Asia work done on a contract basis by hired labour from outside the village is blurring formerly clear divisions between male and female jobs.

In south and east Asia, young women with some education are no longer accepting their traditional exclusion from decision-making, and deference to mothers-in-law in this respect is diminishing (Minturn, 1976; Bernstein, 1976). In southeast Asia, women have always had an important role in making family decisions, together with opportunities for paid work. Increasingly, children are being consulted on matters concerning their own future.

11
Women as a Source
of Family Income

Throughout Asia women make an important contribution to family income. The lower the socio-economic level of the family, the greater the proportion of total income contributed by women. Only in Japan does this finding not apply; there, the higher the income group, the lower the proportion of total household income contributed by the household head. In the lowest income group in 1978, 88.5 per cent of the budget was provided by the household head, while in the highest income group, 76.8 per cent came from the head. Wives contribute 3.2 per cent of income in the lowest income groups, and 10.5 per cent in the highest group (Japan: Statistics Bureau, 1979). This is clearly a reflection of the employment of women from higher socio-economic groups in professional and management occupations.

In most other Asian countries women are expected to work only if necessary for family wellbeing. This often makes it difficult for higher-status women to work. In the Philippines, however, traditional economic roles make allowance for both husband and wife to engage in economic activities. "The Filipino woman in the business and in the professional world is as familiar and as acceptable" as is the woman who spends her time exclusively in the home. "Comparisons have been drawn between her and her Asian sisters with the resounding conclusion that she is years ahead of them in this area. Her western counterpart may be startled to hear that such inclination for achievement is entirely compatible with her feminine image" (Lapuz, 1977). At lower socio-economic levels, where women must work for family survival, they are admired, though their husbands may suffer some stigma having been unable to support the family (Illo, 1979).

Rural women in Thailand are rarely exclusively housewives. Studies of 10 villages in central Thailand and 10 villages near Chiengmai in the north showed that 92 per cent of the women were earning an income, and 96 per cent thought that women should contribute to the family budget (Nantanee et al, 1977).

The contribution of Asian women is often in the form of unpaid labour—work on subsistence plots which would otherwise be beyond the capacity of the husband alone. Their work obviates the need for hiring and paying labour which the family budget could not tolerate. Rural unpaid female workers in the Philippines are 45.4 per cent of all employed females (Mangahas and Jayme-Ho, 1976). In Thailand in

1960, 82.1 per cent of the female workforce represented unpaid family labour, and this figure was still 76.7 per cent in 1971. In the same year 41 per cent of the Indonesian female workforce, and in 1967/1968 30.9 per cent of the Malaysian female workforce, fell into this category (Manderson, 1978b). In 1977, over 45 per cent of the 38 per cent of women employed in Malaysia received no payment (Manderson, 1977b). Women often exchange labour at planting and harvesting, although their share may not be accounted as a full share.

More and more women, however, are bringing cash to the family budget, either from the sale of grain received as payment for labour on large landholdings, as cash pay, or small sums derived from a multiplicity of secondary pursuits such as weaving, sewing, mat-making and the preparation and sale of snacks. Markets in southeast Asia, from Burma to the Chinese border, are dominated by women selling small quantities of fruits and vegetables, grown themselves or bought from others. Their profit margins are very small, the proceeds needed for subsistence, so there is no possibility of investing money for expansion and increased profitability. Small-scale selling in the open market of a district headquarters in Kelantan, Malaysia, appeals especially to the lowest economic sector of the community--single, divorced or abandoned women (Winzeler, 1976). Old widows and young divorcees engage in snack-making, because little expenditure is required, but their profits average only a quarter of their expenditure (Narendran, 1975). Women who run small sundry shops have a total monthly income of only $30 to $300, from which new supplies must be purchased. Women who sell fish caught by their husbands have an income which fluctuates greatly, averaging $32.20 daily. This must be shared with crew members and cover the costs of renting a boat, paying for diesel and mending the nets. In the Philippines, women are self-employed "in low income, low prestige, traditionally feminine types of work" which permit them to look after home and family (Gonzalez, 1977). In the People's Republic of China, the work done by farm women in handicrafts, embroidery and weaving may yield an annual income exceeding that of an able-bodied man (NCNA, July 10, 1979/SWB, Aug. 15, 1979). Village women in northwestern India look after the buffaloes which provide milk for the 844 co-operatives of the Kaira Milk Union; milk money constitutes half the income of their households, compared with about 20 per cent in families which do not belong to co-operatives (Dixon, 1978). Asian men, willingly or tacitly, accept that their wives must work; they know that family survival depends upon it.

THE NEW HOUSEHOLD ECONOMICS

It is obvious that women who work outside the home are obliged to maintain a fine balance between the amount of time they can spend on gainful activity and that which they must devote to their families in order to meet basic welfare needs. The greater the economic necessity for cash, the less are they able to provide adequate care to their families. Many Asian women manage their time adroitly, though in order to do so they have a long working day and inadequate rest. The Agricultural Development Council Household Studies

Workshop, 1976, agreed that women's time is efficiently allocated in most traditional households, and efforts to move women from accepted roles into "modern" roles must take account of the importance of women as "earners" in traditional forms of household activities (de Tray, 1977).

The term "new household economics" has been coined in an attempt to shift the emphasis from traditional market production to a combination of market production and home production. The average time spent by mothers on home production is at least 3 times that spent on market production in the Philippines (Jayme-Ho, 1976). Measures of family welfare based on market production alone may thus underestimate a household's true welfare considerably. This underlines the importance of using social indicators as measures of welfare to supplement traditional measures of income and wealth. Welfare indicators, such as family health, reflect the integrated effects of home and market production time, as well as consumption time.

The household is taken as the producing unit of the basic welfare needs of the family; one input is time, as a productive resource, while another is "market-purchasable goods." The basic assertion of the new household economics is that productive activities in the home are no less significant economically than those outside the home. It is thus important to study the allocation of time between home and market production, and between production and consumption (or leisure). The fact that in the Philippines almost one-third of a woman's time is spent on home production, 3 times more than the 12.4 per cent spent on market production, demonstrates the degree to which her activities are overlooked in surveys of the labour force. A study of the use of time by employed, home-employed and unemployed women shows that it is the women employed in the home who are least able to spare time for their children or housework (Table 11.1).

In America, the production of housewives in 1973 exceeded 60 per cent of family money income before taxes, and 70 per cent after deduction. The value generated by the home sector seems to account for over one-third of output produced at market, and is probably higher in less advanced countries (Gronau, 1977). Gronau (1976) has prepared a model for household allocation of time and consumption patterns. The family rather than the individual, is emphasized as the decision-making unit; total family income rather than individual income is considered (Mangahas and Jayme-Ho, 1976). The application of the new household economics in evaluating the contribution of women is just beginning, in Asia as elsewhere. It has been recommended that women's economic contribution in Japan be reassessed, to include housekeeping and child-raising (Japan: Prime Minister's Secretariat, 1976a). Women's contribution to such essential items of family comfort rise in proportion to the contribution to family income made by others.

MULTIPLICITY OF SOURCES OF INCOME

Concentration on labour expended in producing the staple crop has led to consistent under-evaluation of the time spent on other activities by both men and women (White, 1976; Table 11.2). The

TABLE 11.1
The Philippines: Average Time Allocation During Survey Week by Women Without a Young Child, by Major Activity and by Employment Status

Activity	Employed at Home		Employed Away from Home		Not Employed	
	Time (in hours)	% of Total Time	Time (in hours)	% of Total Time	Time (in hours)	% of Total Time
A. Consumption Time	84.79	50.47	94.08	56.00	109.17	64.98
B. Home Production Time	42.08	25.05	52.42	31.20	58.83	35.02
B.1 Care of children	0.33	0.20	4.00	2.38	2.58	1.54
B.1.1 Care of children aged 0-2	--	--	--	--	--	--
B.1.2 Care of children aged 3 and above	0.33	0.20	4.00	2.38	2.58	1.54
B.2 Other housework	41.42	24.65	47.17	28.08	56.25	33.48
B.3 Supervising housework	0.33	0.20	1.25	0.74	--	--
C. Market Production Time	41.13	24.48	21.50	12.80	--	--
C.1 Traveling time	--	--	3.25	1.93	--	--
C.2 Working time	41.13	24.48	18.25	10.86	--	--
TOTAL	168.00	100.00	168.00	100.00	168.00	100.00

Source: Jayme-Ho, 1976.

TABLE 11.2
Java: Percent of Working Time Devoted to Various Activities by Adult
Men and Women (aged 15 and over) in a Sample of 20 Households,
November 1972-October 1973

	Activity	Percent of Total Working Hours Men (N = 31)	Women (N = 33)
1.	Childcare	4.2	9.3
2.	Housework	0.9	9.4
3.	Food preparation	1.2	24.5
4.	Firewood collection	2.4	0.8
5.	Shopping	0.5	2.5
6.	Handicrafts	5.1	20.9
7.	Food preparation for sale	3.9	3.7
8.	Animal care and feeding	15.2	1.3
9.	Trading	8.3	12.9
10.	Garden cultivation (own)	8.4	0.9
11.	Sawah cultivation (own)	21.7	3.7
12.	Gotong royong	8.8	1.4
13.	Wage or exchange labour (agricultural)	3.4	6.9
14.	Wage or exchange labour (non-agricultural)	12.8	1.5
15.	Other	3.2	0.3
	Average hours of all work per day:	8.7	11.1
	Average hours of directly productive work per day (No's. 6-15 only):	7.9	5.9

Notes to Table 11.2
    Category No. 2, "Housework" includes fetching water, washing
clothes, sweeping, cleaning, washing utensils etc.; No. 3, "Food
preparation" includes the drying of rice and other crops for home
consumption, handpounding and cleaning rice, and cooking.
    No. 7, "Food preparation for sale" includes all activities in
the production for sale of tempe (fermented soy-bean cakes), dawet
(a boiled drink made from rice or arrowroot flour, coconut milk and
coconut sugar) and gula Jawa (coconut sugar), but not the time spent
in selling them or buying ingredients (No. 9) or the collection of
firewood for cooking them (No. 4).
    No. 10, "Garden-cultivation" includes only work on the house-
hold's own garden (see note to No. 13).
    No. 11, "Sawah cultivation (own land)" includes work on owned,
rented and sharecropped land.
    No. 13, "Agricultural wage--or exchange labour" includes all
agricultural work done on land farmed by another household, whether
for a cash wage or a share in kind (as in harvesting) or on an unpaid
labour-exchange basis. There were a few cases of wage labour on
pekarangan, but the great majority was in the sawah.

164

TABLE 11.2 (cont'd)

Notes to Table 11.2: (cont'd)
    No. 14, "Non-agricultural wage-labour" includes work on local
development projects, carrying goods for wealthy traders, brick-
making, carpentry and haircutting when these were done for wages.
"Gotong royong" includes unpaid work in village projects, and unpaid
reciprocal labour for another household (especially housebuilding and
repair), but not unpaid exchange labour in agriculture (No. 13).

Source: White, 1976.

picture throughout Asia is increasingly of a multiplicity of occupations being carried on by different family members, a lower-return
occupation being dropped in favour of a higher-return activity when-
ever opportunity presents itself. For the landless and near-
landless, this means "a lot of work to do, with very low returns"
(White, loc. cit.; Table 11.3). Similar results have been found from
a survey of poor households in Bangladesh (Farouk and Muhammad, 1977).
In Thailand in the past, women took employment to tide the family
over periods of hardship, but increasingly this is becoming a regular
feature (Hanks and Hanks, 1963). A Korean family owning less than
one hectare of land derives 48.2 per cent of its income from non-
agricultural sources, to which all members may contribute (Soon,
1977a). In a village where both fishing and rice-growing were major
occupations, women obtained extra income by oystering, collecting
shellfish and gardening (Brandt, 1971). Lower-class women in Korea
have greater occupational freedom (as well as sexual and social
freedom), but suffer greater economic and political hardships than
the well-to-do. Throughout Asia, the poorer the household, the
greater the proportion of income generated by the working mother
(Popkin and Solon, 1976).
    A universal measure of wealth in rural areas is the possession
of land. The possession of assets, particularly land, makes participation in labour unattractive unless returns are perceived as being
commensurate with the effort expended. The possession of adequate
stocks of grain makes it possible for households to avoid employment
during slack periods when pay is low. Those with few assets, particularly the landless, have no such option; they are obliged to work
long hours for low pay in order to meet minimal subsistence needs
(Hart, 1977, 1978).
    In a village in lowland central Java, a household of 5 people
needs to control at least 0.5 hectares of double-crop rice fields to
attain an adequate level of income from its own production assets
(Class I in Table 11.4). The middle-class (II in Table 11.4) own
or operate a minimum of 0.2 hectares, required to meet minimum household rice requirements. Class III controls less than 0.2 hectares or
no land at all. There is a strong direct relation between class
status and the absolute and proportionate amount of time spent by
women on housework (Table 11.5). More than 40 per cent of the time
spent by Class III households on income-earning activities is

TABLE 11.3
Java: Estimated Returns to Labour in Various Occupations, at Early
1973 Wage and Price Levels[a]

Occupations	Returns to Labour (Rp./Hour)
1. Rice cultivation	
(a) Owner-cultivator : 0.5 hectare	50
(b) Owner-cultivator : 0.2 hectare	25
(c) Sharecropper : 0.2 hectare	12 1/2
2. Garden cultivation	25
3. Agricultural wage labour	
(a) Plough (own animals)	70–90
(b) Hoe	9–11
(c) Transplant	6–7
(d) Weed	9–11
(e) Harvest	16–20
4. Non-agricultural wage labour	
(a) Carrying/construction	10
(b) Craftsman (carpenter)	15
(c) Weaving factory	7
5. Trade	
(a) Women on foot (capital = Rp. 1000)	5–10
(b) Men on foot (capital = Rp. 1000)	15
(c) On bicycle (Rp. 8000–12000) Capital = Rp. 3000	20
6. Preparation of food for sale	
(a) Gula Jawa (own trees)	5–6
(b) Gula Jawa (sharecropping)	2 1/2–3
(c) Lontong	3 1/2
(d) Tempe	5
7. Animal husbandry	
(a) Ducks	5–12
(b) Goats	1–2
(c) Cattle (own)	4–6
(d) Cattle on gaduhan (sharecropping) basis	2–3
8. Handicrafts	
(a) Tikar	1 1/2
(b) Kepang	3

[a]Rp. 415 = U.S.$1.00.

Source: White, 1976.

TABLE 11.4
Lowland Central Java: Allocation of Household Working Time Between Males and Females

CLASS		Averages (hours/household)				Income—Earning Activities		Housework	
		(Hours per Month)[a]							
		Own Production	Trading	Wage Labour	Searching Activities	Total Hours	Percent	Total Hours	Percent
Peak Month:									
Class I	Female	18.1	29.9	42.7	5.2	95.9	23.6	153.1	95.8
	Male	271.0	15.0	22.0	1.6	309.5	76.4	6.7	4.2
Class II	Female	10.5	36.3	92.9	32.3	171.1	32.8	116.3	93.3
	Male	103.8	9.0	186.3	51.1	350.1	67.2	8.4	6.7
Class III	Female	2.3	12.9	153.5	26.5	195.1	40.1	94.9	92.0
	Male	17.9	0	237.1	36.2	291.2	59.9	8.2	8.0
Slack Month:									
Class I	Female	25.6	25.8	8.6	16.1	76.1	19.0	136.7	82.0
	Male	290.0	13.6	15.0	4.8	323.4	81.0	30.0	18.0
Class II	Female	5.3	55.4	41.4	20.3	122.4	27.5	113.8	90.2
	Male	81.7	5.3	123.5	111.6	322.2	72.5	12.4	9.8
Class III	Female	5.9	8.6	138.4	42.6	195.5	41.9	97.7	90.5
	Male	21.6	0	104.6	144.5	270.7	58.1	10.2	9.5

[a]Including travelling time but excluding child care.

Source: Hart, 1977.

TABLE 11.5
Lowland Central Java: Average Hours Per Month Spent Working[a] by
Individuals According to Age, Sex and Class

Age Group	Class	Peak Month			Slack Month		
		Income Earning Activities	House-work	Total	Income Earning Activities	House-work	Total
Females:							
6-9	I	0	2.4	2.4	0	1.3	1.3
	II	2.5	1.1	3.6	0	6.8	6.8
	III	6.8	2.7	9.5	2.7	0.2	2.9
10-15	I	27.8	13.3	41.1	37.8	36.6	74.4
	II	62.5	49.1	111.6	36.5	35.7	72.2
	III	107.2	27.3	134.5	164.2	31.0	195.2
16+	I	63.0	107.2	170.2	46.6	93.8	140.4
	II	116.9	76.6	193.5	88.2	78.9	167.1
	III	118.9	64.4	183.3	111.2	67.7	178.9
Males:							
6-9	I	0	0.7	0.7	0	0.4	0.4
	II	0	0.5	0.5	0	1.3	1.3
	III	8.4	0.7	9.1	24.2	4.6	28.8
10-15	I	43.2	1.3	44.5	47.2	1.9	49.1
	II	103.2	2.3	105.5	100.4	3.0	103.4
	III	87.3	6.7	94.0	123.2	3.8	127.0
16+	I	198.0	3.9	201.9	205.9	20.0	225.9
	II	214.4	5.1	219.5	194.7	7.7	202.4
	III	242.2	4.4	246.6	217.8	6.7	224.5

[a]Including travelling time but excluding child care.

Source: Hart, 1977.

performed by women, while Class I men undertake 76 to 80 per cent of
all income-earning activities; these mostly relate to supervision of
hired labourers, whereas Class III labour is concentrated on heavy
manual labour. The long hours worked for low pay during the slack
season by women of the Class III group (Table 11.5), especially those
aged from 10-15 years, guarantee minimal household income, enabling
men from this group to undertake the riskier but more remunerative
occupation of fishing (Hart, 1977).
    Greater family welfare is revealed by the greater proportion of
time women in Class I spend on housework. Meals are cooked more
frequently and are more elaborate, taking longer to prepare. These

housewives are able to take advantage of lower prices and the greater variety of food available in a nearby town, whereas Class III mothers must make purchases quickly on the way home from work in the village. School attendance rates for children in landless households are considerably lower than those in wealthier households (Hart, loc. cit.).

In a south-central Javanese village, 75 per cent of households have to meet subsistence needs at least partly or wholly outside the cultivation of their rice land (Stoler, 1976). Subsistence is partly met by harvesting on the land of others; they receive from one-quarter to one-half or more of the grain they harvest from the land of relatives; from neighbours with whom reciprocal exchange is necessary, they receive from one-sixth to one-eighth. From labour hired to those on whom women had claims neither of kinship nor of neighbourly exchange of harvesting opportunities on their own land, they receive only one-tenth to one-twelfth of the grain they harvest. Those without wealthy kin or land have to work harder and longer than any to obtain the same quantity of grain (Stoler, loc. cit.).

The relative proportion of income derived from gardens by small, medium and larger landholders is nearly the same, 22.27 per cent, but for the poor it is the largest source of income. The poor are unable to give more time to gardening because of the demands of other remunerative occupations, such as harvesting of padi. The smaller the holding, the more important the production of coconut sugar as a source of income, but this activity is so time-consuming that it precludes other work (Stoler, 1977). The smaller the holding, the greater the intensity of labour input. People with less than 0.1 hectares sawah obtain 21 per cent of dietary intake from cassava, those with 0.2 hectares sawah only 4 per cent. Basic foods are in short supply among families owning less than 0.1 hectares sawah; their total intake is 25 per cent less than those with 0.2 hectares and rice consumption 65 per cent less. They therefore supplement meals with more green vegetables and pulses from the home garden, and their vitamin A status is better than that of those consuming rice. Those with 0.2 hectares sawah are able to purchase tempe (soybean curd), a good source of protein; their intake is 45 per cent higher than the poor group. There is, throughout Asia, a close correlation between level of income and quality of diet (Whyte, 1974).

In 1963, half the women in a fishing village in Kelantan, Malaysia, had a paid occupation, compared with 1940 when only about one-quarter worked for cash (Firth, 1966). In the same village in 1974, 61.8 per cent had gainful occupations, though these had changed from market gardening and care of poultry to occupations related to the newly introduced crop, tobacco (Narendran, 1975). Older women preferred to combine fish selling and tobacco growing, while younger women favoured dressmaking and tobacco grading at tobacco stations. Dressmaking, snack making and running small sundry stores are occupations which depend greatly on the availability of cash in the village, which in turn is related to the ability to catch fish and thus, ultimately, to the monsoons (Narendran, loc. cit.). In a village in the neighbouring state of Trengganu, in 1965 only 3 women had no source of income apart from their husband's contribution (Strange, 1971), and 92 per cent were working. In 1975, when the population had increased, 91 per cent were working (Strange, 1976b).

In Thailand, where decreasing availability of land is disrupting kindred association based on exchange of labour and services in rice agriculture, reducing traditional subsistence, women are taking greater advantage than men of alternative sources of raising cash (Piker, 1975). They engage in vegetable and market-gardening, poultry production and retail buying, frequently coming to city markets to purchase supplies or deliver produce (Hanks and Hanks, 1963). Studies in north and central Thailand showed that 43 per cent of women worked on their family rice fields; 3 per cent hired out; 12 per cent grew other crops and 3 per cent raised animals, especially chickens and pigs, and tended vegetable gardens (Nantanee et al, 1977).

In Bangladesh, women whose families own less than 2,000 square meters of land contribute 33 per cent of family income, while women from larger landholding households contribute only 15 per cent. Bangladeshi women rarely bring in cash income, their contribution being indirect. This could be improved by the expansion of vegetable growing, coupled with adequate marketing channels (Martius von Harder, 1977).

In Taiwan, members of families holding less than 0.5 hectares predominate among those who supplement their incomes in a variety of non-farm activities located near their own homes (Table 11.6). A study of farms in the Taichung rice-growing region, where holdings averaged 1.19 hectares in 1960-1962 and 1.18 in 1970-1972, showed that the percentage of non-farm receipts to total farm household income was only 11 per cent in 1960-1962, while in 1970-1972 this had

TABLE 11.6
Taiwan: Non-farm Jobs of Farm Household Population in 1975, by Employment and Sex

	Male	Female	Total
Total	897,659	558,009	1,455,668
Employed	762,007	461,160	1,223,167
Agriculture, forestry, fishery and animal husbandry	307,375	174,921	482,296
Mining and quarrying	15,476	7,534	23,010
Manufacturing, water, electricity and gas	179,317	152,483	331,800
Construction	58,927	8,784	67,675
Commerce	16,717	13,245	29,962
Transport, storage and communications	32,137	4,000	36,137
Other services	152,058	100,229	252,287
Work for own account	127,267	49,884	177,151
Family handicraft	8,385	46,965	55,350

Source: The 1975 Agricultural Sampling Survey of Taiwan.

risen to 31 per cent. Purchased inputs were substituted for family
labour in farming, which was allocated to non-farm activities as
opportunities expanded. There is a clear inverse relation between
size of farm and degree of dependence on non-farm income sources for
most holding classes. Without non-farm employment, the income of the
smallest landholding households would have been 33 per cent below the
actual level, while that of the largest holdings would have been only
6 per cent (Chinn, 1979).

REGIONAL VARIATIONS IN FEMALE PARTICIPATION
IN REMUNERATIVE OCCUPATIONS

The degree of participation of women in cash-producing activities varies across Asia. More women work in the fields in south than
in north India, and actually outnumber men in some of the fertile
rice-growing districts of the south (Beteille, 1975). Even in the
north, however, women must contribute as best they can when opportunities present themselves. The income earned by women employed on
earthwork in Maharashtra is essential to enable their families to
cross the poverty line (India, Planning Commission, 1978a). In
Bihar, men would need to be fully employed and women agricultural
labourers employed for 60-80 per cent of the year, and their total
combined income spent on food for them to achieve the minimum
calorie intakes required by the Indian Council of Medical Research
(Rodgers, 1976). In fact, employment is highly seasonal. Moreover,
unemployment affects female agricultural labourers (one-third of the
total agricultural labour force in India) more than men. During
1964-1965, men in agricultural labour households were gainfully
employed for an average of 242 days, and women for only 160 days
(Gulati, 1976).
The Indian Planning Commission has contested the findings of the
1971 Census that the proportion of women workers had declined from
28 per cent in 1961 (it was 33.7 per cent in 1911); there had been
gross under-estimation of female participation because of the emphasis on primary occupation. In fact, the rate has remained at 28 per
cent, while numbers have increased and are expected to continue to do
so. While chronically unemployed men outnumber women, unemployed
women on a weekly or person/day basis far outnumber men, revealing
the essentially part-time nature of woman's work. Forty per cent of
the unemployed are women, indicating that the labour market continues
to discriminate against them (India, Planning Commission, 1978a).
A major influence on the ability of women to improve family
income by their own activities is the prevalence of purdah in the
northern part of the Indian subcontinent, and among Muslim communities in peninsular India.
In a review article on purdah, Papanek (1973) quotes an unpublished Ph.D. thesis by Florence McCarthy indicating that the burqa
was common in Comilla District, Bangladesh, although it had been
introduced only somewhere between the first decade of this century
and the late 1950's. Women felt their freedom of movement had been
greatly increased. The "portable seclusion" of the burqa has freed
women for gainful work in Pakistan (Papanek, 1971), but is not a

practical solution for agricultural work; women work unveiled among
their kin. While strict purdah is observed by the rich, poor women
roam the streets freely, are seen in the market and participate in
many low-skilled activities (Saghir Ahmad, 1974). None the less, if
purdah cannot be attained by wearing the burqa, then women will try
to confine their activities to the home compound. This helps explain
why a far lower proportion of Pakistani women are working than in
India (Sebo, 1975). Only 14.5 per cent of women over 15 are economically active, one of the lowest figures in the world, and, of
these, there is a far higher proportion of unpaid family workers than
elsewhere: in Pakistan 68.3 per cent, the average for Asia 36.3 per
cent (Papanek, 1971). Pakistan has an extremely high dependency
ratio, due to the large number of young children, but also to male
unemployment and low female participation (Bean, 1968). Purdah has
given nursing low status; teachers congregate at high schools and
colleges, which are not co-educational, rather than at primary
schools as in much of Asia. In Bangladesh, impoverished widows must
seek to support themselves by petty trading, but lose prestige
because of this exposure (Ellickson, 1976). Those with children can
rely on their help, and a son may sell in the market rice husked by
his mother. Many income-generating activities are carried on inside
the compound (Abdulla and Zeidenstein, 1976).

"Traditional patterns of family life are becoming increasingly
difficult to maintain in the rural areas. Unmarried girls, young
wives, busy mothers, as well as older women, are being forced by
difficult economic conditions to seek some kind of employment"
(McCarthy, Sabbah and Akhter, 1978a). Seclusion is forced to give
way in extreme economic distress. Women on Food for Work projects
"are roughly one generation away from economic and social security.
When a family falls below subsistence, independence often breaks
down; these women enter a 'frightening independence'. Nothing in
their upbringing in the rural economy prepares them for this independence, or to be sole supporters. All that was the norm has been
taken away." Work opportunities are uppermost in their minds. They
will work anywhere. Social stigma does not matter (Chen and
Ghuznavi, 1977). After the good harvest of 1976, the proportion of
women on Food for Work projects fell from 30 per cent to less than 5
per cent (Sattar, 1978).

Chronic distress is a powerful inducement to women to defy
cultural norms in their effort to ensure family survival. However,
there have always been strong-minded individual women able to take
initiative, even at the expense of arousing social disapproval. The
life history of an elderly woman in a central Indian village, member
of a sub-caste second in prestige only to the Brahmins, whose husband, the village priest, was unable to meet family needs, provides
an excellent example of female enterprise (Jacobson, 1978). This
woman worked as a domestic servant for a wealthy Pathan family, being
careful to avoid contact with their water and other pollutants.
Later she was the first female village merchant:

> She was given a set of social roles, which she played very well,
> yet at the same time she asserted her own individuality and
> attempted to direct events in her own life in ways which many

around her did not. Clever and able, she guided her family
through many crises over the years. She worked hard as a field
hand, organized a small-scale salt-smuggling operation, and
brushed aside the marriage proposals of prosperous men seeking
to lure her away from her unambitious but good-natured mate.
Despite suffering near-starvation and disastrous losses, she
managed to keep her family functioning and even to remain a
strikingly cheerful person (Jacobson, loc. cit.).

Even in the most strongly patriarchal countries of Asia, women have
not presented a picture of meek conformity to socially accepted
behaviour and to the commands of their status-conscious husbands,
particularly when adversity has threatened the wellbeing of their
families.

Most Asian women, however, prefer work that can be done in or
near the home, to avoid conflict between their roles as homemaker and
wage-earner. A widespread source of income is the care of domestic
livestock and the sale of their produce. Women invariably look after
scavenging chickens, milk and feed cattle in the Indian subcontinent,
attend to poultry and often cattle in Indonesia and Thailand, to pigs
in Indochina and Taiwan. Women make major contributions to the care
of private plots and especially livestock raised by the family in the
People's Republic of China (Parish, 1975; Parish and Whyte, 1978).
Indeed, the household sector provides cash throughout the year,
instead of only twice yearly after summer and autumn harvests for
commune work. A woman fattens a pig for sale to the state purchasing
co-operative, the proceeds of which may equal those received from the
collective for the whole year (Parish, 1975).

In China, as in India, the participation of women in income-
generating activities varies according to region. While many of the
historical cultural obstacles to the ability of women to work have
been removed, more women work in the fields in the south than in the
north (Parish, loc. cit.), as in the past. Young wives are not permitted to take up factory work, on the grounds both of propriety and
of family status (Salaff, 1973). Some 40 to 50 years ago, women were
not allowed to attend markets in the New Territories of Hong Kong,
since it was considered improper for them to mix with men (Potter,
1969), a convention abandoned there, as it has been in Kwangtung,
where either men, or women, or both may market (Parish and Whyte,
1978). In Kwangtung it is calculated that women perform 40 per cent
of all agricultural work.

INEQUALITY OF PAY

There is ample evidence from all over Asia to show that women
engage, directly or indirectly, in a wide range of income-generating
activities. How well and how equitably are they paid? There has
been legislation on equality of pay in many countries, but this
affects largely the organized sectors of national labour markets, in
which low proportions of women, particularly rural women, are
involved. It is accepted as "natural" that women should receive
lower pay than men, even when they are performing the same task.

This is partly because it is believed that women's productivity is lower, despite much contrary evidence, and partly because it is assumed that women's income supplements that of men. This has a particularly adverse effect on women heads of household, who are a significant minority in many Asian countries. It has been estimated that 10 per cent of households in the Philippines are headed by women (Mangahas and Jayme-Ho, 1976). In 20 villages in north and central Thailand, 9 per cent of women were household heads (Nantanee et al, 1977).

Sixteen per cent of households in a Bangladeshi village were headed by women (Ellickson, 1975). There is widespread absence of men in Nepal, since many are serving overseas in Gurkha regiments. Twenty per cent of women surveyed in 3 villages in Limbuan were heads of households (Jones and Jones, 1976). It is significant that female labour participation rates in Malaysia are highest for divorced and, secondly, for widowed women (Malaysia, FFPA, 1976). About 19 per cent of rural household heads in Java are women (Sajogyo et al, 1980), predominantly among the landless (Hart, 1978). They spend nearly 80 per cent of their productive time in heavy physical labour, often far from home during the slack rice-production season, whereas women from families with land are able to withdraw from the labour market at this time. In the People's Republic of China, it appears that there are more female heads of household than previously; one sample in Kwangtung Province showed that 15 per cent of households were headed by women (Parish and Whyte, 1978). The economic standing of such households would depend greatly on the number of sons able to earn work points.

In some countries, unpaid family workers are beginning to perceive injustice in their situation. Korean women are campaigning for joint ownership of property, on the grounds that "The money may have been saved by the husband--but it could not have been saved without the help of the wife." Most, however, accept the necessity for their share in production as a matter of course.

The disparity in wages paid to men and women is often considerable. In Saemaul Undong (New Village) projects in Korea, such as road building, women receive far less than men. Average pay for women is 48 per cent of that for men throughout Korea. In India, lower pay for women construction workers is justified on the grounds that they work less since, in the absence of child care facilities, they bring their children with them (Sebo, 1975). Female agricultural labour may be preferred to that of men because they are paid less. Certain tasks, such as transplanting rice, have been almost exclusively theirs. Women receive less for this task in Java than men, but more than men for harvesting, a tribute to their greater productivity (Stoler, 1975). Female income per hour in 1977-1978 was 30-50 rupiah, and 50-80 rupiah for men (Sajogyo et al, 1980). Women invariably work longer hours each day than men. When Filipono men become unemployed, their wives seek any job for whatever wage can be obtained, and this may lead to men being replaced by women, or themselves receiving lower pay (Monteil and Hollnsteiner, 1976; Philippines, Department of Labour, 1974). In Japan, the overall disparity in rates of pay for men and women has diminished slightly, due to the increased level of education of female workers and increased job opportunities, from 42.8 per cent that of men in 1960, to 55.8 per cent in 1975 (UNESCO, 1976). This relates mostly to urban employment, and is complicated by the double peak in employment of women and the consequent break in service in a country where increments in pay relate to seniority.

On plantations throughout much of Asia, there is a different minimum wage for men and women, the actual wage depending on output. As the incentive pay is the same for men and women, the gap between the starting rate is often closed by deft female workers, particularly in rubber tapping and on tea plantations (ILO, 1970). In Malaysia, rubber tappers have received the same pay, irrespective of sex, since 1953, but male weeders earn M.$3.10 daily, compared with women's M.$2.60.

In Sri Lanka, women are considered as efficient as men in transplanting rice, weeding and harvesting, but receive 0.66 to 0.75 of the male wage, based on the supposed differential in productivity (Wickramasekara, 1977). In 1966, women's pay averaged half that of men in all sectors, with the least disparity in plantations (Kannangara, 1966).

While disparity in male and female pay is justified on the grounds of differential productivity, a further factor is the concentration of women in occupations which bring lower pay. This is largely due to their lower levels of education (Chapter 4). In Malaysia, for example, 64 per cent of women in industry earn less than M.$100 a month, while only 24 per cent of men come within this category (Figure 11.1).

These disparities have not yet been eliminated in Communist countries. In the People's Republic of China, fewer work points are granted to women on the grounds that they work fewer hours, devoting time to housework which still goes unrecompensed (Diamond, 1975). When task rates prevail, theoretically women should receive the same work points as men if they finish a task in the same length of time. However, if they are assigned tasks which receive a lower award than those assigned to men, they will receive fewer work points. When time rates operate, women generally receive 2 points less than men per day, from 6 to 8 instead of 8 to 10 (Parish and Whyte, 1978).

In Vietnam, women formerly received half the pay of men. The new regime has enunciated the principle of equal pay (Bergman, 1975). Higher pay for more skilled and heavy work has been adopted, the task rate also used in China. Theoretically this enables women to earn as much as or more than men, since, for example, transplanting padi is considered a skilled job (Gough, 1977). Fruits, vegetables, pigs and chickens are reared on private plots, occupations in which women were traditionally involved, and presumably still are. These are sold to the co-operative or peddled on the roadside in towns to buy extras for the family. The turmoil that began in 1978 makes it impossible, however, to obtain accurate knowledge of rural conditions, of the economic standing of families in general or of disparity in pay between men and women.

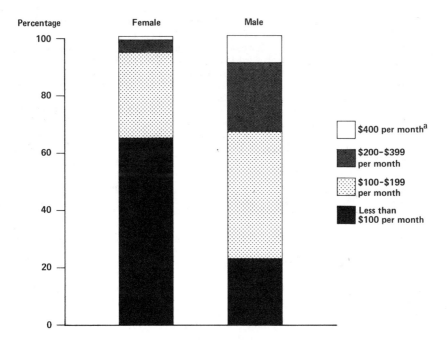

Source: Department of Statistics, Malaysia.
[a]U.S. $1.00 = approximately M. $2.00.

FIGURE 11.1 Malaysia: Employment by salary/wage group in all industries covered, peninsular Malaysia, 1972 (Malaysia, FFPA, 1976).

ROLE CONFLICT

For the poor, economic necessity dictates that women must seek
work for pay. The need for cash has been enhanced even for higher
socio-economic groups by increased requirements for consumer goods,
and for expenses related to the education of children, sometimes
school fees, but invariably books, and often uniforms. Both men and
women work longer hours than formerly, if they are able to obtain
work, and many seek employment during slack seasons formerly devoted
to rest, socializing or repair of home and equipment. For women,

this means less rest than for men, since even with other relations to help in the home, some tasks remain. Most of all, women have less time to devote to their children. For the favoured few, the ability to stay at home and care for children is a prestigious right (Hull, 1976b; Strange, 1971, 1976b). For most Asian women work, paid in grain or cash, or unrecompensed on family land, is essential.

Indian women participate in agricultural labour only if it can be combined with child care and housework, in such jobs as picking cotton, vegetable gardening, care of poultry and dairy farming (Dasgupta, 1977). Among 117 educated and uneducated married women working in Punjab, only 25 per cent felt they were devoting adequate time to their children. Role conflict was most sharply felt by women who were unable to make satisfactory arrangements for the care of small children. Educated women who work because they are interested in their jobs, or to gain economic independence, experience less conflict than women who work from necessity, probably because of more comfortable home circumstances; their children are, however, mostly left in the care of servants (INCCU, 1977).

In Java role conflict is expressed by many employed women (Hull, 1976a). Women do not work because they enjoy their jobs, but from economic necessity, and the highest proportion of female workers are married women. In the Philippines, 43 per cent of employed women are aged from 25 to 44 years, 40 per cent are aged 45 to 64 years and 26 per cent from 10 to 25 years (Philippines, Department of Labour, 1974). Among lower-class women in 3 localities, rural, semi-urban and urban, 60 per cent of rural, 74.3 per cent of semi-urban and 34.3 per cent of urban women were employed (Licuanan and Gonzalez, 1976). These figures represent availability of work; among those who were not working, unavailability of mother surrogates was given as the chief reason. More grandmothers (without responsibility for young children) than mothers had primary occupations. However, employed mothers were experiencing role conflict because of their inability to perform traditional roles correctly; they budgeted their time as rationally as possible in order to reduce conflict to a minimum. Most would prefer not to work and to devote more time to their homes (Licuanan and Gonzalez, loc. cit.; Gonzalez, 1977).

Educated city Malay women and wage-earning kampong women, who commute to work away from the village, both experience role conflict, being particularly concerned at spending little time with their children. This does not occur among village women who work on their fields or at crafts in the home, where they are able to look after their children at the same time (Strange, 1976b).

There has so far been little study of the actual effect upon the family of a woman's absence at work, though many assumptions are made, both regarding benefits and ill-effects. A study in the Philippines showed that the indirect effect of a mother's working is to increase expenditure on food from 1 to 5 per cent, especially on cereals and meats. Total diet is not significantly impaired, even when there is a concomitant reduction in time spent on the home garden. Total household welfare improves, but child welfare deteriorates, although there are complex interrelations which vary with age of child and ecological zone (Popkin and Solon, 1976; Popkin, 1978). Children of poor working mothers in Cebu had lower intakes of vitamin

A but higher intakes of protein and calories than those of non-working mothers; those in the 2 middle income quartiles also have lower protein and calorie intakes; those in the highest income group have higher protein and calorie intakes. The greatest difference between children of working and non-working mothers is in vitamin A intake, which is derived mostly from vegetables which are disliked, except in the form of time-consuming soups. There is increased incidence of xerophthalmia among children of lower-income working mothers (Popkin and Solon, loc. cit.).

Infants of mothers working too far from the home to be able to return for breastfeeding have lower weights than those being breast-fed. There is more anaemia, parasitic infestation and higher incidence of severe disease. The adequate replacement of mother's milk would cost U.S.$20 annually, while unskilled and semi-skilled women have annual incomes of only U.S.$76 and U.S.$130 respectively (Popkin and Solon, loc. cit.). The availability of girls aged 13 to 15 in the home is likely to reduce the incidence of breastfeeding, and that of girls aged 7 to 12 its duration (Popkin, 1978).

Further studies of the nutritional status of children of mothers working away from the home and those remaining at home, and of the development of personality among children of both groups, would undoubtedly show that some of the concern expressed by Asian working women is well founded in fact. Care of children during infancy up to the age of 3 is considered particularly important in the development of personality. Specialists in child development consider that the absence of the mother at this stage will result in the building of a close emotional bond with the mother-substitute, creating a subsequent barrier between mother and child. Neglect of small children at the place of work, characteristic among poor employed women, also leads to emotional suffering and damage to the development of personality.

Asian women are seeking work in ever-increasing numbers. At higher socio-economic levels their earnings are needed to maintain a standard of living formerly attainable from the efforts of heads of household alone, supplemented only at seasonal peaks by women. Poor women work for family survival. Among both groups economic benefits must be set against the emotional costs, to both mother and her children.

12
Who Holds the Family Purse?

It would appear that control over the family purse must automatically give some degree of authority, and this is often assumed to be so. However, some sociologists have pointed out that control over cash does not confer power, since poverty dictates expenditure until incomes are high enough to give some options (Hollnsteiner and Burcroff, 1975; Licuanan and Gonzalez, 1976). In east Java, a male anthropologist thought that women derived considerable authority from their control of family cash (Jay, 1969). This seems to be a subject worthy of further study.

In southeast Asia, women invariably hold the family purse and regulate spending. This may occur also in India, China and Japan. In the south Asian subcontinent, sanction for female control of the family budget goes back some 2,000 years to the Laws of Manu, not otherwise notable for high esteem of female qualities:

> She should always be cheerful,
> and skilful in her domestic duties,
> with her household vessels well cleansed,
> and her hand tight upon the purse-strings (Basham, 1954).

In modern Japan, it is usual for the wife to be in charge of family income and expenditure. Female control of the family budget appears to be more common in urban than rural areas. One survey showed that 97 per cent of women in urban housing developments, as against 66 per cent of rural housewives, received their husband's paycheck and gave him an allowance; he often did not know the amount of family savings (Lebra, 1976). A woman receives her husband's pay from him, pays all bills, buys food and makes most decisions on major expenditures, with perhaps some mutual consultation. She gives her husband a spending allowance and takes care of savings, investments, banking and budgeting herself (Vogel, 1978).

Traditionally, the head of the family in China made major decisions, but his wife informally managed family income, and still does (Salaff, 1973). However, 500 interviews conducted just after the Second World War indicated that the budget was controlled by heads of households, reinforced by the prevalent convention that it was indecent for women to appear in markets. In city areas women showed a greater tendency to manage their households, but even there men held the purse strings. Poorer women, particularly those in the south, appeared to have greater freedom; it was from this area during the nineteenth century that men had emigrated to seek work, leaving their wives to care for the family (Lang, 1968). In Kwangtung, team payments are handed to the family heads as total payment of a corporate unit, the family, rather than as individual payments, and those requiring funds must obtain them from the family head, usually, though not necessarily always, a male (Parish and Whyte, 1978).

Korean women play an important role in maintaining family finances; men are expected to be spendthrift, and women to compensate for this (Brandt, 1971).

In Burma, a woman's control of family finances is gradually being modified in urban areas, as men need ready cash for daily expenses (Mi Mi Khaing, 1963); in the rural areas she retains control. Men are content to be dependent in this way, provided the facade of male dominance is maintained. Women consider men economically irresponsible, likely to squander money on gambling, women, drink and other pleasures if they have the means (Spiro, 1977).

Javanese women believe that men are incompetent with money. Women consider that daily financial matters do not concern their husbands in Indonesia (Ihromi, 1973), a pattern which applies equally to middle-class rural women with some education and to the poor with little or none (Hull, 1976b). Out of 60 couples in rural Modjokuto, only one man dared to check on domestic expenditure, and men chafed at having to ask for pocket money (Jay, 1969). While men might decide on farming activities, women appear to have the power of veto if such decisions involve expenditure.

Thai women of the central plains have a controlling voice in expenditure--the stereotype is of a steady, sensible, tight-fisted woman and a wasteful self-indulgent man (Phillips, 1966). The authority of women over the budget of the family compound may be dwindling, however, since children earning an income are less inclined to turn it over to her (Hanks and Hanks, 1963). In the Chao Phraya delta, where a large part of the income comes from rice, the farmer himself controls the budget (de Young, 1966).

The wives of scholar officials in traditional Vietnam not only managed family finances but their estates also, while commerce was largely in their hands (Hoang van Co, 1955; Vietnam Resource Center, 1974). There are reports from modern Vietnam of women managing Commune finances (Bergman, 1975).

In Malaysia, men may keep enough cash for coffee and cigarettes, turning over the remainder to their wives (Strange, 1971). It seems natural to Malay peasants that women should control money, "for who should guard the money while we are away all day, if not the women?" (Firth, 1966). In Selangor, household income is managed by an older woman who does most of the spending (Wilson, 1967). In matrilineal Negri Sembilan in the past, men provided cash from rubber tapping and women subsistence from rice; men preferred to control expenditure and did the shopping (Swift, 1963). A recent study in this area shows that modern kinships are best described as bilateral, even though rice land is inherited through the matriline. Subsistence rice cultivation and rubber tapping are increasingly becoming of secondary importance to wages earned outside the peasant economy altogether, and rice cultivation, in particular, is now being carried on mainly by older people. The domestic economy, however, is becoming increasingly associated with women, into whose hands both rice and rubber land--and presumably their income--are falling (Kahn, 1977).

Control of finances in the rural Philippines is mainly in the hands of women, who decide how much should be saved (Castillo, 1976a). A public opinion survey conducted in different Asian capitals, asking whether it was considered that men or women should control the budget, found the greatest support for female control came from the Philippines. Family conflict arising from a man's propensity to attend cockfights or other activities from which women are excluded can be resolved by female control of the purse (Murray, 1971).

In the south Asian subcontinent, women have far less say in ordering family expenses. In India, they have no voice in budgetary matters, particularly in the rural areas, where the dependency ratio is higher than in urban areas. There are, however, exceptions. The senior wife in a joint Rajput household has generally controlled finances and their allocation, though there are signs that young wives, who are more educated than their mothers-in-law, do not accept her authority (Minturn, 1976). A Bihari midwife was proud of managing family finances (Stokes, 1975). In Andhra Pradesh a higher proportion of women participate in decisions regarding family expenditure than among Tamil women (Leonard and Leonard, 1981). In Bangladesh, men control the family purse, and women have little say in expenditure (Sattar, 1978). It may be asked whether women among lower socio-economic groups, who have greater mobility and who contribute in cash to the family economy, do not have a greater say in managing the household budget than do higher-status women, who make no direct financial contribution and are confined to the home and its surroundings.

Control of finances implies some degree of autonomy in the regulation of daily expenditure, even if poverty dictates that decisions take place only within a very narrow range. Decisions on the purchase of costly items or expenditure on the celebration of family ceremonies are likely to be made jointly, irrespective of who is in control of daily spending.

In areas covered by the green revolution, control of finances may be passing definitively to men. Credit, which is an essential component of the successful application of the new agricultural technology, is granted on the basis of landholding, and this, especially in south Asia, is usually in the name of a man (Palmer, 1978).

13
Agricultural Modernization, Technological Innovation and Female Employment

Modernization throughout Asia has brought advantage to different groups unevenly, élite urban groups, including some women, and large landowners, predominantly male, being the first to benefit. In Korea "development has bypassed a large section of the rural and industrial population—the working female" (Soon, 1977a), a conclusion which may be applied to most countries of the region. It may be asked, however, whether the increase of population, the growing inadequacy of landholdings to provide subsistence and the obligation to supplement income by all possible means have not affected Asian women more than "development" itself.

Little detailed information is yet available on the effect of technological innovation on women's opportunities for employment. There is some evidence that the generally lower levels of education equip women ill for learning new skills (ICSSR, 1975). Sex-typing of jobs, giving those of higher status to men, may transfer work which is traditionally the preserve of women to that of men as higher levels of technology dignify the task. At a seminar on the changing role of women in rural societies at the Fourth World Congress for Rural Sociology , 1976 (Castillo, 1976b), it was noted that mechanization in agriculture affected mainly the jobs performed by men; in many cases it led to men taking over jobs performed by women, or in the jobs being eliminated altogether. Mechanization in the developing world has often meant reducing the availability of jobs for women, rather than lightening their burden (Castillo, loc. cit.; Ward, 1970; India, Planning Commission, 1978a).

There have been numerous studies of the achievements of the green revolution in raising output, but few on the changes brought about in rural standards of living. In particular, the effects of the new technology on the lives of women must usually be understood by implication, since they are rarely mentioned. While conclusions regarding the benefits of the green revolution vary, most writers agree that the greatest advantages have accrued to those with the largest landholdings who are best able to assemble the increased capital necessary for the increased inputs involved. There are, however, great variations throughout Asia, quite apart from purely agronomic considerations such as the adequacy and reliability of irrigation water, the availability of essential inputs and knowledge

of their timely application. The range of size of landholdings in a
given area, the relative proportion of landless to landowners, the
distance from a larger centre of population, the feasibility of growing crops other than the principal grain crop, all these influence
the distribution of prosperity among rural communities. The availability of non-farm employment, particularly in small factories, has
an important bearing on agricultural wages; this, in turn, influences
the degree to which farmers adopt mechanization and chemical weedi-
cides and reduce the employment of human labour.

In a situation where access to the operation of padi land and
its benefits is already very unequal, the distribution of technology,
even if fairly equitable, cannot but contribute to the increase in
income inequality; this has occurred in Aceh, Sumatra and in Kedah,
Malaysia (de Koninck, 1979). Far from having an equalizing effect
among small farmers, the green revolution has aggravated inequalities. Smaller farmers have reached a stage where the productivity of
their labour decreases rapidly. In 48 per cent of Acehnese households, the net commercial balance of farm operation is negative;
costs of production are greater than the revenue obtained from sale
of padi, much of which must be kept for subsistence. Unremunerative
small holdings necessitate participation in labour for wages on other
holdings. The lot of marginal producers in northwest Malaysia seems
to be better; increasing integration of rural agricultural development with rural industrial development provides an outlet for excess
regional labour (de Koninck, loc. cit.).

A two-year study carried out by the Centre for Policy Research
at the Universiti Sains Malaysia, Penang, in the Muda region of Kedah
and Perlis revealed that in 1974, 9 combine harvesters replaced over
2,000 workers, while by 1980, 160 harvesters replaced 36,000 workers.
Eighty per cent of harvesting is now mechanized. It is expected that
even transplanting will be mechanized in the future. By 1990, some
20 per cent of the labour force in this region will be unemployed
(Report by Ho Kwong Ping, Far Eastern Economic Review, June 13, 1980).

An area in Laguna Province, the Philippines, which has been
subject to both advanced technological practices under the green
revolution as well as to crop diversification, and to industrialization which has offered alternative sources of income, has been
studied as an indicator of possible future developments elsewhere in
the country (Smith and Gascon, 1979). High-yielding crop varieties
were adopted in 1966, the increased care (fertilizer, weed, insect
and water control) being met by increasing the use of labour until
the mid-1970's. Labour per hectare was 84 work days per hectare in
1965, and 107 work days in 1975. From the mid-1970's, labour was
gradually replaced by the use of chemicals and machinery; by 1978,
labour use had fallen back to levels prevailing before the introduction of high-yielding crop varieties. This has been due to the
stabilization of prices of herbicides and a rise in the real agricultural wage. Family labour has declined dramatically, partly due
to mechanization and partly due to substitution by hired labour.
Farmers explain that weeding (like harvesting, threshing and transplanting) now has to be done in a short period of time, and family
labour is unable to cope.

Wives have not participated in field work to any significant

extent in this area. Most family labour is provided by sons over 18
years, and these put in only 7 days per hectare per crop. This has
remained unchanged since 1965, since adult sons are able to obtain a
higher income from factory work. While the annual income of farm
families rose by 47 per cent between 1965 and 1978, most of the
increase came from salaried non-farm jobs and non-labour sources of
income such as rent, interest, etc. This confirms the findings in
Taiwan (Chinn, 1979) discussed on p. 210. Farmers have become farm
managers rather than tillers of the soil over this period, and are
now able to hire labour. Smith and Gascon (1979) note that comparable changes in Taiwan took 40 years, but less than 15 in Laguna,
probably due to the difference in time span between the introduction
of agricultural innovations and the development of local industry.
It is concluded that the new rice technology cannot be relied upon to
provide continuing labour absorption in agriculture, since this is
significantly affected by ratios between the factors of production
(cost of labour, mechanization) and the selling price of rice.

In India, high-yielding crop varieties and mechanization have
reduced labour demand in ploughing and threshing, but have increased
all other tasks, especially transplanting and harvesting. In addition, many new jobs associated with machinery and the stocking and
distribution of fertilizers, seeds and insecticides have been created
(Dasgupta, 1977; Parthasarathy, 1977; Bautista, 1977). Most of these
jobs are, however, for men. For example, the widespread adoption of
combine harvesters will have a serious effect on rural employment,
since many in the workforce have been accustomed to earn a major
share of their annual earnings from harvesting alone. So far there
has been a decline in the number participating in the workforce and
an increase in the number of hours worked (Dasgupta, loc. cit.).

In Ludhiana District, Punjab, India, where most farmers possess
an average of 6 to 8 hectares of land, only 20 per cent of cultivators have 4 hectares or less, and the latter have experienced a serious deterioration in their relative economic position (Frankel, 1971).
However, in other wheat-growing states in north India, over 80 per
cent of all cultivating households hold less than 3.2 hectares. In
the rice-growing area of Thanjavur, Tamilnadu, where the majority of
holdings are said to be from 0.8 to 1.2 hectares, the aggregate gains
from the green revolution have been insufficient to provide funds for
investment in land development. Those with 2 to 4 hectares have done
better, and those with 4 hectares or more have made the greatest
absolute gains. There has been an absolute deterioration in the
economic condition of the small owner-cum-tenant cultivators, because
rising land values have increased rents and owners have resumed
possession of the land. The majority of farmers, some 78 to 80 per
cent of the population, have experienced a relative decline in economic position, while unprotected tenants have suffered an absolute
decline (Frankel, loc. cit.). The payment of wages in cash rather
than grain represents a fall in real income throughout India, further
aggravated by rising prices. Dasgupta (1977) feels that inadequate
attention is given to a labourer's total income when wages for work
with high-yielding crop varieties are considered. It must be asked
whether a truer comparison would not be between a household's real
income before the introduction of high-yielding crop varieties, when

women were able to find work, and after, when there are few opportunities. An analysis of employment during different stages of
mechanization on sample farms in Punjab showed that on those farms
using only bullocks for cultivation, 56 per cent of family labour was
employed; with the introduction of tubewells and farm machinery,
family labour was reduced to 46 per cent, and when tractors were also
used, family labour was further reduced to 24 per cent. Mechanization implies an increased demand for trained personnel and a reduction in that for unskilled manual labour, effectively excluding women
(INCCU, 1977).

In Java, an average farmer's net returns from high-yielding crop
varieties are not significantly higher than for traditional crop
varieties, because of increased costs. The landless have been only
marginally affected by the green revolution; they form 30-50 per cent
of the population, while another 20 per cent are almost landless,
according to the Agro-Economic Survey. Two-thirds of all rural
households in Java are below the poverty line (Sajogyo et al, 1980).
Opportunities for employment have been reduced, leading the Agricultural Development Council to conclude that the green revolution has
been cost-reducing (usually labour-reducing) rather than output-
increasing. At the same time, there has been a reduction in off-farm
employment (Collier, 1978).

What does all this imply for women? Before the adoption of the
high-yielding crop varieties, women were specialists in transplanting
and harvesting. This work is increasingly being done on contract by
men. The Rural Dynamics Survey conducted by Bogor Agricultural University reported that more than half the employed women work for
fewer than 35 hours per week on income-yielding jobs. In Java as a
whole, 50.9 per cent of women and 34.1 per cent of men who are
employed work fewer than 35 hours a week; The difference between men
and women is far greater in rural than urban areas (Sajogyo et al,
1980). In West Godavari, India, over three-quarters of the female
workers belong to labouring households. Even where productivity and
employment per hectare are higher, there has been little impact on
wage rates and seasonal unemployment (Dasgupta, 1977). Further south
in Thanjavur, only 11 per cent of women are in the workforce; they
are 12 per cent of agricultural labourers, and only 2 per cent of
independent cultivators (Gough, 1978). The padi yield per hectare in
Thanjavur increased from 2.1 tons in 1960-1961 to 3.1 tons in 1975-
1976, and double-cropping has risen from 21 per cent to 30 per cent
of all padi land. Why has the increased labour requirement that this
would imply been associated with a drop in the proportion of working
women in Thanjavur, when only 20 per cent of the rural population
owned any land in 1971?

Women in Java have been placed at a serious disadvantage by the
introduction of rice-hullers, since rice-pounding formerly provided
subsistence grain to women (White, 1976; Collier et al, 1977). The
introduction of the sickle has allowed a few men from other localities to take the place of many local female kin or neighbours working
with the traditional ani-ani; one man works with a tiller instead of
many women working by hand. A landlord need forego a smaller proportion of his harvest to pay these workers, and many women have seen
their opportunities for adding to the supplies of grain for their

187

families sharply reduced.

Double-cropping, with its acceleration of the pace of activities, has forced gleaners in Java, formerly the most underprivileged
old women and children but now increasingly women of all ages, to
follow the harvesters, rather than coming to the fields at their
leisure without asking permission. Tensions result, since gleaners
are not required to yield any part of their share to the landowner
(Stoler, 1975). Farmers with large holdings sell their rice before
harvest to middlemen, who assume responsibility for harvest management (the tebasan system). Harvesters are brought in from outside
the area, or local harvesters are greatly reduced in number. Costs
are reduced by as much as 42 per cent, and the number of harvesters
by 60 per cent; there has been loss of jobs on a huge scale (Stoler,
1977).

A survey of 48 villages in 28 districts in west and central Java
led Hayami and Hafid (1979) to conclude that, while farmers were
indeed aiming at greater control of the numbers harvesting their
crops, the severity of the effect of tebasan on rural employment
might not be as great as had been supposed. They found the tebasan
system existing together with the traditional bawon system, whereby
local harvesters have the right to harvest, in 18 out of the 48
villages studied. Where the ceblokan system (workers transplant and
weed without pay in return for the right to harvest) prevails, giving
the farmer control over the numbers he employs, the tebasan system
is not found. The employment of labour has been reduced by an
average of 12 per cent, and the harvesters' share has declined from
10 to 8 per cent, while the increased volume being harvested gives
them a greater income than previously (Hayami and Hafid, loc. cit.).

The average level of labour productivity in 3 villages in central Java ranges from 0.5 kilograms milled rice per work-hour with
local crop varieties to 1.2 kilograms with high-yielding crop varieties (Sajogyo, 1974). For labourers, however, returns have actually
declined, in one study by one-third, over the period 1968-1969 to
1972-1973 (Makali, 1974). In Kali Loro, central Java, a half day's
work by men in the sawah brought two-thirds of a kilogram of rice;
women earned slightly less than half a kilogram in 1972. In 1973,
they earned half a kilogram and one-third of a kilogram respectively.
Landless families have a lower income than those with land on which
there are opportunities for exchanging labour for a share of the crop
(Stoler, 1975). Thus, the most disadvantaged, both men and women,
have to work longer hours for lower returns.

These changes are partly due to population pressure, but more to
changes in political functions and in the sources of power of wealthy
villagers. The need has changed from that of a loyal following
within the village to a source of cash to be spent outside the
village on luxury goods and higher education for children leading to
better jobs. It is no longer necessary to redistribute wealth among
the more disadvantaged in the village, and lower-paid outsiders and
machinery often replace them (White, 1976).

Women have also lost their traditional job of husking grain to
the rice mills in Bangladesh (Kabir, Abed and Chen, 1976; McCarthy,
Sabbah and Akhter, 1978a). The labour exigencies of high-yielding
crop varieties, particularly the concentration of activities at peak

TABLE 13.1
Bangladesh: Time Required for Processing High-yielding and Local Varieties of Rice in Different Types of Households (days per year)

| | Time Required in Different Types of Households | | | | | | | |
| | Surplus Household[a] | | Subsistence Household[b] | | Deficit Household[c] | | Average Household[d] | |
Task	HYV	Local var.	HYV	Local var.	HYV	Local var.	HYV	Local var.
Threshing:								
With oxen	11.3	14.3	8.5	10.8	3.8	4.8	8.7	11.0
Foot thresher	16.1	12.7	12.1	9.5	5.4	4.2	12.4	9.8
Hand thresher	13.9	13.9	10.5	10.5	4.7	4.7	10.7	10.7
Winnowing with:								
Sieves	0.9	0.9	0.7	0.7	0.3	0.3	0.7	0.7
Fans	1.2	1.2	0.9	0.9	0.4	0.4	0.9	0.9
Wind	1.4	1.4	1.1	1.1	0.5	0.5	1.1	1.1
Parboiling with:								
Normal chula	9.0	9.0	6.7	6.7	3.0	3.0	6.9	6.9
Large chula	1.8	1.8	1.4	1.4	0.6	0.6	1.4	1.4
Drying:								
In courtyard	7.8	9.1	1.3	6.9	2.6	3.0	6.0	7.0
On concrete or asphalt surface	3.4	5.3	2.5	4.0	1.2	1.8	2.6	4.1
Storing	0.7	0.5	0.5	0.4	0.2	0.2	0.5	0.4
Husking	28.7	28.7	21.5	21.5	9.6	9.6	22.0	22.0

[a] Surplus household: family with average of 7.1 members and average rice requirement of 54.8 maunds per year. This quantity of rice must be processed after harvest for individual requirements.
[b] Subsistence household: family with average of 6.9 people per family and average requirement of 41.1 maunds.
[c] Deficit household: family with average of 6.4 people and average yearly requirement of 26.5 maunds.
[d] Average household: 6.9 family members, and average requirement of 41.4 maunds.

Source: Martius von Harder, 1977.

time, are believed to have caused more women to abandon seclusion to
work on the family plot (Germain, 1976). However, in the family
compound women work with traditional technology (Khatun and Rani,
1977; Martius von Harder, 1977). The extra work for women involved
in processing high-yielding crop varieties is shown in Tables 13.1
and 13.2.

In Korea, it is lack of modernization of the rural sector which
has penalized women. From 1960 to 1970, the number of women working
in agriculture almost doubled, and they averaged 13 hours work a day.
The out-migration of youths throws a further burden on older rural
women (Soon, 1977a). There has been a rapid exodus of males to urban
areas, leaving an onerous burden on rural women who need help with
mechanization, rational technology and co-operative farming (Lee and
Cho, 1976). Before mechanization in the People's Republic of China,
their lower physical strength was a barrier to women's work in agriculture; this is said to be diminishing.

The declining role of crafts and cottage industries in the face
of competition from cheap, mass-produced factory goods has increased
over several decades. This applies also to the former practice of
making snacks in the home and hawking them in villages or at market
centres, since competition from factory-made biscuits, cakes and ice-
cream has displaced them. The tendency has been countered in China

TABLE 13.2
Bangladesh: Comparison of Time Required for Processing One Maund of
Unhusked Rice of High-yielding and Local Varieties (in minutes)

Task	HYV				Local Varieties			
	I	II	III	IV	I	II	III	IV
Threshing:[a]								
With oxen	--	--	173	173	--	--	220	220
Foot thresher	247	247	--	--	195	195	--	--
Drying:								
In courtyard	119	--	119	--	140	--	140	--
On concrete or								
asphalt surface	--	52	--	52	--	81	--	81
Total	366	299	292	225	335	276	360	301

[a]Hand threshing is omitted, since there is no difference in the
time required for winnowing, parboiling and husking high-yielding and
local varieties.

I   threshing with foot thresher, drying in courtyard
II threshing with foot thresher, drying on asphalt or concrete
III threshing with oxen, drying in courtyard
IV threshing with oxen, drying on asphalt or concrete

Source: Martius von Harder, 1977.

by the location of small factories in rural areas, providing local
employment and meeting needs for consumer articles locally (Whyte,
1981). Rural industry provides goods to alleviate women's chores,
for example in milling flour or processing oil. Similar plans are
being prepared in India where, during the period 1961-1971, the number of women workers in modern urban industries grew from 6 to 10
times, while at the same time numbers employed in horticulture, livestock husbandry, food processing, the preparation of dairy products
and jute textiles declined sharply (India, Planning Commission,
1978a).

On plantations the widespread use of herbicidal sprays has
limited the work of women who formerly did weeding by hand; union
efforts in Sri Lanka have succeeded in banning their use. Tractors
are also being used for weeding between rows in coffee and sugar
plantations. The ILO Report to the Sixth Session of the Committee on
Work on Plantations (1970) reports that in Kenya labour requirements
for weeding on coffee plantations have declined from 2,380 work days
to 80 per year, while the use of chemicals for decouching has reduced
female labour demand by 75 per cent. It is not known to what extent
female labour on Asian plantations has been affected by these
changes. Higher yields from plantation crops have, however, greatly
increased the demand for labour at harvesting; on tea plantations the
season for plucking tea has been extended, spreading earnings over a
longer period. There has been a tendency to reduce the permanent
labour force on plantations and to increase the use of temporary or
casual labour at peak periods. The sex distribution on plantations
in India, Sri Lanka and Malaysia is fairly even, unlike that in
Africa and Latin America, and much of the labour force is permanent,
living on the plantations themselves. Problems here relate to the
full use of available labour throughout the year, and finding suitable employment for the children of the labour force, for whom there
are no longer openings on the plantations themselves.

There has, however, been a marked decline in employment of
estate labour during the 1960's, and this is reflected in a drop in
the number of Indian women employed in agriculture. Between 1957 and
1970, the figure fell by 50 per cent and there was considerable emi-
gration of Indians from Malaysia (Hirschman and Aghajanian, 1980).
It may be surmised that the replacement of rubber by oil palm on many
plantations was responsible for this decline.

The Indian state of Kerala has long imported cashew nuts from
east Africa, to supplement its own production. Large numbers of
women have been employed in the delicate task of breaking the shells
without damaging the nuts. Recent technological improvements have
led to the manufacture of efficient machinery. East African growers
have, therefore, sharply reduced their export of nuts to Kerala, and
the 486 cashew processing factories in India are now unable to
operate for more than 90 to 100 days annually. Large numbers of
women have seen their incomes reduced or eliminated (The Economist,
June 21, 1980).

The introduction of high-yielding varieties of crops and mechanization of traditional methods of agriculture have brought about

many changes in social relations and the allocation of labour in rural Asia. Many of these complex changes are not yet fully understood, but it is clear that women, particularly those of lower socio-economic groups, have suffered rather than benefitted from them.

14
Help for Working Women

A crucial factor in the ability of women to work, to improve their family's situation and to gain some measure of independence, is the availability of household help. Most important is someone to whom she can entrust young children, though in dire necessity, she will work even though child care is inadequate or lacking entirely, since the alternative is destitution. The problem of child care tends to be most acute in urban, nuclear families, especially in Japan (Lebra, 1976; Willing, 1977). In many farm areas in Japan cooking centres and day care nurseries are operated on a co-operative basis (Japan, Prime Minister's Secretariat, 1976a). In rural areas elsewhere in Asia, the problem is often mitigated by the existence of extended families or of parents living close at hand. Children are also often left in the care of older siblings while their mothers work in the fields.

Where help is lacking or is inadequate in quality, there can be serious repercussions on family health and nutrition, while social deprivation has a major influence on child development (Popkin and Solon, 1976). The presence of children aged 7 to 12 in a household greatly enhances labour force participation of rural Cebuano women (Popkin and Hart, 1975); girls aged 13 to 15 are more important for the care of young infants, and girls 7 to 12 for older infants and preschool children (Popkin, 1978). The presence of a small child does not reduce market production hours, but does reduce home production, thus probably affecting the quality of other home production goods—of welfare—in the home (Jayme-Ho, 1976).

Most women working in rice farming in Malaysia could put in the eight-hour day completed by their husbands if they had not been required to cook lunch; this demands 2 hours. But women with 5 children or more have little time available for work outside the home (Purcal, 1971).

In Vietnam, child care facilities have been more readily available in rural than urban areas, since children were evacuated for safety from the towns (Bergman, 1975). The Hanoi Home Service, on March 24, 1977 (BBC Summary of World Broadcasts, April 6, 1977), announced that in the Red River Delta, each co-operative would have a dispensary and the number of children kept in nurseries, now 20 per cent, would rise to 70 per cent, and those in kindergarten from 20 to

50 per cent. This was designed to increase the number of women in productive work from 45 to 70 per cent. Much domestic work is done by grandparents (Gough, 1977). Rural young women organize crèches, and only the elderly do not work (SWB, May, 1977).

In urban China, day care facilities are common at places of work, where mothers may come to breastfeed infants. In rural China, nursery schools and kindergartens tend to be combined (Sidel, 1972), and are organized at both the production team (hamlet) and brigade (village) level. Nurseries take children from about one month to 2 years of age, kindergartens from 2 to 6 years (in Vietnam this is from 2 months to 3 years and 3 to 6 years respectively). However, most rural children are taken care of by grandparents until primary school (Sidel, loc. cit.).

Early attempts at collectivization and the institutionalization of rural child care in the People's Republic of China have given way to more flexible arrangements as it came to be realized that housework and subsidiary production were as essential as collective effort. If women work in animal husbandry, collection of manure, handicrafts, afforestation and irrigation, they are allowed to remain near the home, in an effort to achieve successful integration of familial and productive roles (Andors, 1976). Rural industry aims at alleviating women's chores by the creation of flour mills and oil presses. The prospect of wives abandoning housework and children as well as their submissive role is not acceptable; there are many examples in fiction of women fulfilling their various roles with equal competency, showing that traditional virtues and roles are compatible with occupational skills (Eber, 1976).

Rural nurseries are often in the charge of older women no longer able to perform field work (Davin, 1975). Baby care costs half a work point daily, a toddler a whole work point and those requiring constant care one and a half work points. Communal eating facilities, which were stressed until about 1959 (Wong, 1974), were disliked, and are now used only at the busiest times of the agricultural cycle. Similarly, a number of places have temporary babysitting facilities during busy harvest and planting seasons (Parish, 1975). More nurseries and nursery schools are considered necessary under the Fifth Five-Year Plan (Fukien Provincial Service, Jan. 24, 1978).

The Socialist Labour Law of North Korea adopted by the People's Assembly on April 18, 1978, includes an article providing conditions enabling women to work. These are the operation of nurseries, kindergartens, child clinics and service clinics, as well as the organization of home-working teams and home co-operative associations by local and state organs (Pyongyang Home Service, April 18, 1978, SWB April 24, 1978).

Communist nations are finding the reconciliation of their aim of liberating women for productive work with the need to relieve women of household chores as difficult as are countries in the third and developed worlds. While 92 per cent of all women of working age in the Soviet Union are employed or studying, a report by the Soviet Academy of Sciences found that in 61 per cent of Soviet families, women did all the shopping (a time-consuming occupation where much queueing is involved); 64 per cent of employed women prepared meals, while only 4 per cent of men did so. Only 2 per cent of men helped with washing and ironing. Shopping and housekeeping take up to 6 hours daily, leaving women no leisure. The result has been a dramatic fall in birth rates, now causing concern to Soviet planners (The Economist, June 23, 1979).

Childrearing is not a male responsibility in Asia, though there are minor exceptions. In the Philippines, some tribal groups leave field work to the women, while men watch, tending children, even returning home to cook. This is seen as being an inheritance from the days when conflict was common and men had to be ready at the edge of their fields to defend the group (Infante, 1969). Role reversal on the Korean island of Cheju among communities of women divers has also been noted. Men in southeast Asia are ready to help bathe and dress children; more than half the fathers in a Philippine village did so (Mendez and Jocano, 1974). This is especially true when children are young.

A survey of lower-class women in rural, semi-urban and urban locations in the Philippines showed that fewer than half the males (husbands or sons) helped with household chores, but among those who did, help was given not only with the heavier tasks of chopping firewood, fetching water and house repairs, but with jobs such as cooking, child care and laundry. The latter tasks are those most reluctantly taken up, for reasons based on what Filipinos call machismo, but which have their counterpart in most of Asia, and indeed the rest of the world--fear of ridicule by their friends and the shame of being thought under the thumb of a woman.

In another study, only 27 per cent of Filipina working women were found to have relatives and/or servants helping them. Working wives have more children than non-working wives, and their age is not significant. Sixty-five per cent have an oldest child 11 years old or older, only 12 per cent have children below 5 years. For a woman to work, an older child is essential to assume responsibility. Moreover, the mother's occupation must not require daily absence, so cooking, sewing or laundering, hog-raising or managing a store are all favoured pursuits. Alternatively, women work part-time, or seasonally, making ad hoc arrangements (Castillo and Pua, 1963). The degree of help given housewives in a Laguna village by other family members is shown in Table 14.1.

While Thai women usually prepare meals, boys watch, and consequently men can cook if they have to. Men rarely fetch water, but may launder and iron their own clothes (de Young, 1966).

Only among the educated, urban, middle classes in India do men share some household chores if their wives are working (INCCU, 1977). Household help and child care are given by Gujerati men when the wife is sick and when there are no other women to help (Poffenberger et al, 1975). Women from rural villages around Delhi who were working in factories, chalk and stone quarries all had preschool children; many had no help in looking after them (INCCU, 1977).

The restrictions imposed by purdah make help essential, particularly for tasks outside the home, such as fetching potable water from a well outside the compound. A detailed examination of the effect of seclusion on women's activities and opportunities has been conducted in Bangladesh (Martius von Harder, 1977). When women at the lower end of the socio-economic scale have overcome their fear of the

TABLE 14.1
The Philippines: Number of Households in Which Housework Was Done by Persons Other Than the Wife, by Activity

| | Household Member | | | Non-household Member | | |
| | | | | | Others | |
Activity	Hus-band	Son	Daugh-ter	Rela-tives	Hired	Not Hired
Feeding children aged 0-2	1		1		1c/	
Care of children aged 0-2 other than feeding	4	2	2	1a/	1c/	
Care of children aged 3 and above	4		2			
Assisting children with schoolwork	1					
Marketing	2		1		1c/	
Shopping		1	1			
Buying from sari-sari store	1	8	6			
Cooking/preparing food for household	6	3	6	2b/		
Fetching water/firewood	5	4	3			
Feeding livestock/poultry	8	3	2			
Taking meals to member away from home		1	1			
Gardening	2					
Cleaning house, laundering and ironing, sewing and mending	3	4	6			

a/ Mother-in-law.
b/ Same mother-in-law as in footnote (a) and in a second house-hold, a niece.
c/ Neighbor.

Source: Jayme-Ho, 1976.

stigma of breaking purdah and have taken work under Food for Work projects, the problems of child care are just one additional burden for them—see Table 14.2 (Chen and Ghuznavi, 1977).

The modern extended family in rural Korea often leaves child care to the grandmother, the mother obtaining paid work outside the home (Choi, 1969). The increase of nuclear families and the decreasing availability of grandmothers or other female kin to help in child care are reflected in the sharp decline of female labour participation in Japan; from 56.5 per cent in 1960 to 44.9 per cent in 1974 for women aged 30 to 34 years, and from 54.5 per cent in 1960 to 43.4 per cent in 1974 for those aged 25 to 29 years (Willing, 1977). The proportion of working married women in Japan rose from 20.5 per cent

TABLE 14.2
Bangladesh: Women Engaged in Food for Work Activities, Problems
Associated with Child Care

Associated Problems At Home	No. of Women	Associated Problems At Site	No. of Women
Not applicable	163	Beaten by other children and disturbs work	14
No problems	44	No problem	6
No response	23	Heat affects child's health	5
Cry and get beaten by others	15	Sad and pensive	3
Fed improperly	7	Cries; fed improperly	3
Sad and pensive	7	Cannot express problem	3
Cannot express problem	5		
Disturbs family members	4		
Gives wheat to caretaker	1		
Total	269	Total	34

Source: Chen and Ghuznavi, 1977.

in 1955 to 50 per cent in 1974, most of them with grown children.
Only 12.3 per cent of mothers whose children are at private unrecog-
nized child care centres are satisfied with the care given, but 35.5
per cent are satisfied with care at public centres. In 1972,
1,284,000 children received some form of day care, but an additional
229,000 were unable to find places; in 1976, 1,560,000 children
received day care, with an additional 900,000 needing places (UNESCO,
1976). Many clerical and sales workers feel that having a job benefits them personally, but that it was bad for children, while professional workers felt both they and their children benefitted (Willing,
1977; Table 14.3).
    Very few Japanese men help their wives in the home, but among
those who do, child care is one of the acceptable chores: cooking,
dishwashing, shopping for food and ironing are not (Lebra, 1976). In
families with 3 or 4 members, most household tasks are performed by
the housewife. In households of 5 or more, a greater degree of help
comes from the mother or mother-in-law, with the wife still bearing
the major burden (Table 14.4). Contrary to what might be expected,
the least help by husbands of working women is given by younger men
of high levels of education and income. This is attributed as much
to pressure of work and long hours of travel as to the personal
failings of men.[*] Whatever the cause, the double burden on women

_____

[*]There is some indication of an ambivalent attitude towards help
from husbands, since this conflicts with a woman's autonomy and freedom of action. This is reflected in the popular saying, "A good husband is one who is healthy and absent" (Vogel, 1978).

TABLE 14.3
Japan: Working Mothers' Perceptions of the Value of Work (1973)

		Through All Workers	Clerical Workers	Sales Workers	Manufacturing and Production Line Workers	Nurses	Telephone Operators	Teachers	Others
	(Persons)	(1,185) 100	(138) 100	(87) 100	(506) 100	(121) 100	(169) 100	(97) 100	(67) 100
For the Self	Minus	2.1	3.6	3.4	1.8	0.8	2.4	1.0	3.0
	Somewhat minus	6.7	5.8	5.7	7.3	5.8	6.5	9.3	3.0
	Neither plus nor minus	30.2	32.6	33.3	36.6	21.5	23.7	13.4	29.9
	Somewhat plus	36.4	31.9	43.7	33.0	33.1	45.0	35.1	47.8
	Plus	24.6	26.1	13.8	21.3	38.8	22.5	41.2	16.4
For the Child	Minus	11.7	13.0	9.2	11.7	5.8	14.8	11.3	16.4
	Somewhat minus	20.8	22.5	33.3	18.0	17.4	22.5	20.6	23.9
	Neither plus nor minus	34.4	37.0	34.5	35.0	31.4	35.5	30.9	32.8
	Somewhat plus	20.1	21.0	18.4	18.2	31.4	17.8	23.7	14.9
	Plus	12.8	6.5	4.6	16.8	14.0	9.5	13.4	11.9

Source: Employment Research Institute, "Survey on Working Mothers with Pre-school Children"; Willing, 1977.

TABLE 14.4
Japan: Distribution of Domestic Chores, by Size of Household, 1973

Size of the household	Total	Wife Alone	Wife and Husband Together	Wife and Mother or Mother-in-law Together	Mother or Mother-in-law Alone
Through all types of household	100	84.1	1.4	4.6	10.3
2 persons	100	100.0	--	--	--
3 persons	100	97.2	1.8	--	1.1
4 persons	100	90.8	1.4	1.4	6.2
5 persons	100	66.3	1.0	11.1	22.1
6 persons and over	100	55.6	1.2	16.0	28.4

Note: Multiple answers.

Source: Employment Research Institute, "Survey on Working Mothers with Pre-school Children"; Willing, 1977.

leads to a high degree of continuous exhaustion. Those with small children sleep fewer hours on both working days and weekends than those not working outside the home (Willing, 1977). The double burden of domestic work and field activities means that women in China get less sleep than men (Whyte, 1977). Mrs. Oh Sun-joo, secretary-general of the League of Women Voters in Korea, says the average Korean housewife works 18 hours a day.

In much of Asia, while part of this burden is shared by kin, a considerable part is shared by children. Few studies exist on the contribution to family labour made by children, though many impressionistic assessments can be found. Tables 14.5 and 14.6 give the results of a detailed study in central Java. Some of the tasks performed by children, such as the cutting of fodder, relieve adult men for more productive work. Girls probably substitute for their mothers in the carrying of water, feeding livestock and looking after young children, but complement their efforts in field work to increase income. Children have an important role in freeing adults from necessary but unproductive tasks (White, 1975). Some of these tasks begin as early as the age of 6, more generally by the age of 9; more productive tasks such as weaving mats, cutting fodder, planting, harvesting, hoeing can be done by children from the age of 13 to 15 with productivity equalling that of adults. It has already been shown that much of the help given parents, especially care of younger siblings, is at the expense of children's education (Chapter 4).

TABLE 14.5
Java: Numbers of Children Engaged Regularly in Various Productive or
Useful Tasks, Age of Beginning (Youngest Case) and Average Age of
Beginning from a Sample of 146 Households

Activity	Number of Children Boys	Girls	Age of Beginning (youngest case)	Average Age of Beginning
Fetch water	29	66	5 years	8.8 years
Care of chickens/ducks	38	18	5	7.9
Care of goats/cattle	58	9	6	9.3
Cut fodder	80	4	6	9.5
Hoe sawah	41	--	8	13.0
Hoe dry field	39	--	10	13.1
Transplant rice	--	50	5	9.9
Harvest rice	8	61	7	9.7
Care of young sibs	36	35	5	8.0
Wage labor	12	8	8	12.9

Source: White, 1975.

Mechanization of rural and household tasks to relieve women of
some of the burdens of their work is a commonplace in Japan, but
elsewhere in the region this remains a distant goal. The ILO Report
on employment, growth and basic needs (1976) saw accessible water
points, rural electrification and simple technological improvements
in the processing and preparation of food in the home as the best
means of helping women. Electrification, however, also requires a
level of income sufficient to purchase and keep electrical equipment
repaired, as well as to pay for the current. New technology based on
the improvement of existing methods by simplification and reduction
of the time needed for tasks seems likely to yield greater benefits
for more women.
Mechanization and improvement of home technology may provide
increasing help to working women. The provision of child care
facilities could greatly relieve them both of the physical burden and
of the mental stress caused by the knowledge that their children are
inadequately supervised. A fundamental need, however, is to change
the attitudes of society towards the sex-typing of roles, so that men
will be ready to help in household chores and child-raising without
stigma. This involves little less than a social revolution in both
patterns of child-raising and play, and in education. A model for
suggested changes in education to achieve this aim has been drawn up
for the Philippines (Gonzalez and Hollnsteiner, 1976). Educational
materials and instruction are also being modified in Communist countries in the hope of changing the attitudes of younger generations.

TABLE 14.6
Java: Average Hours Per Day Devoted to Various Tasks by Children According to Age, Type of Activity, and Number of Siblings (N = 102 children in forty households, eight days of observation per household)[a]

Age, number of sibs in that age group, and number in the sample: / Activity:	7-12 years		13-18 years	
	0-1 sibs N = 15	2 or more sibs N = 37	0-1 sibs N = 15	2 or more sibs N = 35
A1 Care of small children	0.5	0.9	0.8	0.5
A2 Household	0.4	0.6	1.3	1.2
A3 Collect firewood	0.5	0.5	0.3	0.5
B Production outside agriculture	1.9	1.1	1.9	2.4
C Animal care and feeding	0.7	1.2	1.4	1.0
D Non-agricultural wage-labor	--	0.1	0.5	0.5
E Exchange or communal labor	--	0.1	--	0.4
F Agriculture	0.3	0.6	1.3	2.2
Total hours of "work" per day	4.3	5.1	7.5	8.7

[a]Those in the left-hand column of each age-group have one or no sibs in the potentially productive seven to eighteen age-groups; those in the right-hand columns have two or more sibs in that age-group.

Source: White, 1975.

15
Conclusions

SUB-REGIONAL VARIATION IN THE STATUS OF WOMEN

When this study began it was expected that certain clear-cut
patterns would emerge, with traditions which could be attributed to
patterns of subsistence and economic production from the land,
settled, irrigated or swidden, and to the major religions and ethnic
cultures. The text has shown that Asia may be divided into 3 main
regions in relation to the status of women, south Asia, southeast
Asia and east Asia. In south Asia up to the borders of Burma, women
originally were respected by their husbands and by their society.
They were educated before marriage, which occurred only after physical maturity. In early China too, women enjoyed an egalitarian position. But in south Asia and China, around 500 B.C., the position of
women gradually deteriorated. Their subservient role to men became
enshrined in India in the Laws of Manu, which took final form around
the third to second centuries B.C., and in China in the tenets of
Confucius which took shape progressively in the centuries after
Confucius' death. Around the same time Buddhism arose, absorbing the
prevalent atmosphere. It must be left to China scholars to determine
to what extent women's position was already deemed to be inferior in
Chinese civilization at that period, and how far the acceptance of
Buddhism influenced Chinese norms.
Among the patrilineal majority in western and eastern monsoon
Asia women had no rights to land or property; remarriage of widows
was proscribed, and a woman who divorced lost access to her children.
These customs remained so deeply entrenched in society that more
liberal faiths and modern legislation have done little to improve the
lot of rural women. In southeast Asia, among tribal groups of south
Asia and among some non-Han groups in China, women have always
enjoyed higher status in society, have been able to divorce and
remarry, have retained rights to property and the right to raise
their children.
The status of women has been attributed by many specialists,
most notably Boserup (1970), to environmental conditions and the
forms of agriculture that these permit. Undoubtedly, environment has
played a part in determining the status of women in Asia.
Most of the forests which formerly covered the countries of the

204

south Asian subcontinent and eastern China have been progressively
cleared to provide land for settled crop cultivation, dryland or
irrigated, leading to characteristic types of agrarian structure.
Outside those parts of the region which were formerly covered by
tropical or subtropical rapidly regenerating vegetation under high
rainfall, it is difficult to conceive that even the most primitive
forms of agriculture began on the basis of shifting cultivation,
fertilized by ash from burnt tree cover. This applies to the north
and northwest of south Asia, and to the non-monsoonal lands of northwest China, including the area until recently accepted as the nuclear
zone of Chinese civilization. Women worked in the fields in these
regions until the invention of the plough.

It is only relatively recently, within the last 100 or 200
years, that the forest cover of most of southeast Asia has been
cleared, first for the establishment of plantations but more recently
for widespread cultivation of padi. Up until then, there were small
groups of hunters and gatherers, and early cultivators who practised
swidden agriculture with mixtures of upland grain and other crops on
limited areas of the vast forested lands; irrigated rice was grown
only around larger centres of population in favourable areas of
valley or lowland.

We have seen that it is in swidden groups that the status of
women is high in both family and sometimes community matters. It is
suggested, therefore, that the position of women in Asia has been
largely ecologically determined (Table 15.1). The swidden way of
life, with its respect for women in family, economic, community and
religious affairs, her independence and freedom of action, is a
comparatively recent cultural memory in equatorial and tropical Asia.
If these favourable characteristics had existed under other primitive
agrarian systems, they have long since been obliterated by centuries
of settled agriculture, male ownership of land, patrilineal kinship
and female subservience in south and east Asia.

Beyond this broad level of generalization regarding the position
of Asian women, it would be unwise to proceed. There is great variation of custom within country, culture and limited geographical
areas. The choice of marriage partners traditional in one set of
villages may be quite different from that adopted only a few miles
away where mode of subsistence, ethnicity and culture are almost
identical. Conflicting reports of behaviour are common, further
complicated by class or caste differences. An educated observer from
a capital city may have quite different conceptions of the norms of
society from those of a foreigner who has lived for some time in a
remote village. Observers in Malaysia have noted the importance of
women in family decisions (see Chapter 10), but Hashimah Roose (1963)
observed that women had no power over matters affecting the family as
a whole.

The human geneticist, considering the prevalence of exogamy in
north India and China, and of endogamy and cousin-marriage in south
India and southeast Asia, will undoubtedly express concern at the
degree of inbreeding which must occur in the 2 regions. There is a
cumulative risk of mental and physical abnormalities and reduced
resistance to disease among the progeny of succeeding generations.
Anthropologists familiar with India often counter such arguments by

Status of Women and Associated Ecological and Cultural Practices

Ecosystem	Predominant Method of Subsistence/ Cultivation	Role in Production	Kinship	Land Ownership	Choice of Partner	Status in Family	Status in Community
A. Tropical rain forest	Hunting and gathering	Equal importance	Bilateral	--	Free	High	High
B. Tropical rain forest	Swidden	Equal importance	Bilateral/ matrilineal	Customary usage rights	Free	High	High
C. Dry thorn forest or scrub, and dry deciduous forest	Hoe agriculture with long fallow	Equal importance	Patrilineal?/ matrilineal?	?	Free	High	High
D. Tropical rain forest, cleared	Padi cultivation: plough, broadcast/ transplanting	Equal importance	Bilateral/ matrilineal	Male and female owner- ship	Women have say	High	Lower
E. Tropical rain forest to monsoon forest, cleared	Padi cultivation: plough, transplant- ing/sowing	Equal importance	Patrilineal	Male	No say	Lower	Low
F. Tropical monsoon or subtemperate forest, cleared	Wheat/millets on dry or irrigated land. Plough and drill seeding	Lesser role	Patrilineal	Male	No say	Lower	Low
G. As F.	As F.	Restricted by purdah to processing of crop	Patrilineal	Male	No say	Low	Low

Note: Density of population increases from ecosystems A to E and into F and G if crops are irrigated. Cereal cultivation on dryland with low rainfall is characterized by low population density.

Source: Whyte and Whyte, 1978.

claiming that cousin-marriage may be the preferred form, but it is in fact adopted less frequently than might be anticipated. Conclusions can be reached only by comparative study of the incidence of abnormalities and of disease in communities which have traditionally been exogamous and those which have long practised endogamy and marriage with close kin. This would involve investigations by a geneticist, a medical practitioner and an anthropologist.

A major factor of change in rural Asia is the reduction of available land for cultivation, bringing about constant modification of social relations within the group of kin with which a family relates, based upon what can be contributed in exchange of land and labour. Changes in cropping systems, whether from swidden to settled agriculture, dryland to irrigated cropping or the adoption of new cash crops or high-yielding crop varieties, cause changes in social relations and often in the position of women within their families and in their communities. The family itself may disintegrate under the strains of extreme poverty, as revealed by higher proportions of female heads of household among lower socio-economic groups.

SOME MEASURES OF IMPROVEMENT

It may be asked whether the lot of women has in fact improved at all over recent decades. Undoubtedly, life has improved for large numbers of women. Even if preference is still expressed among Chinese, Indian, Pakistani and Korean families for sons, for both religious and economic reasons, there is no longer female infanticide, nor the giving away of girls during times of acute distress. The adoption of daughters, to be brought up as future brides for sons among lower socio-economic groups unable to afford the cost of major marriage in Taiwan and China is no longer practised (Wolf, A., 1975; Wolf, M., 1975; Smith, 1899/1970). The mortality rate among girl infants and children in Taiwan was higher than that for boys, largely accounted for by deaths of adopted girls (Wolf, M., loc. cit.).

Costly medical care may still be sought more swiftly for a sick boy than for his sister, as neonatal death rates in India show--74 male, 76 female deaths per 1,000; in the 0 to 4 age group, 58 male and 70 female deaths (ICSSR, 1975). A study in Punjab showed the growth curves of female children were consistently below those of males, and morbidity was 2:1 female to male (Neumann, 1969). An Expert Committee of the Indian Council of Social Science Research has noted in a special memorandum to the government that the mortality rate for girls is from 30 to 60 per cent higher than that for boys (see Chapter 3, Status and the Life Cycle). However, prosperity gained under the green revolution in a Rajput village in Uttar Pradesh has improved the quality of medical care for girls, and the sex ratio has improved from 66 per cent male/33 per cent female in 1954 to 55 per cent male/45 per cent female in the 1970's (Minturn, 1976). It seems likely that a study of the health of Asian females would provide a valuable indicator of their status within their families and socio-economic groups, but no systematic investigation has yet been undertaken.

Levels of literacy are slowly rising, especially in the

countries of southeast Asia and eastern Asia where girls are likely
to attend at least some years of primary school (Chapter 4). In
these same countries the age of marriage is also rising (Chapter 5).
In east Asia where a woman who left or was cast out from her husband's home lost access to her children and was often left destitute,
she is today given protection, if she knows how to seek it. This is
true also for the south Asian subcontinent, though the numbers
involved are still very small. The situation of women in southeast
Asia in these respects has never been so disadvantaged; they have
commonly held property independently, have been able to divorce and
take their children with them. In the People's Republic of China,
women's rights were protected in the Marriage Act of 1950, but while
divorce and remarriage are sanctioned, a woman still receives no
share of the property for which she worked during the marriage, and
still loses her sons to her husband's family (Parish and Whyte, 1978)
(see also Chapter 7).

Superficially, it is easy to discern the continuity of tradition
in rural Asia, since change is slower and less dramatic than in urban
areas. Yet even where custom seems most entrenched, changes in
women's attitudes over the past hundred years have been profound. A
Bangladeshi woman whose husband was unable to work was able to overcome her fear of the stigma of abandoning purdah to work when financial problems had become overwhelming:

> I decided that I would take the only recourse left to me. I
> would find work and support my family. And so I did. I
> accepted any kind of work I could find just so long as it helped
> us to survive. I have not been able to send my children to
> school as before but there was nothing I could do about that
> . . . Perhaps some day. . . . When I first heard of earthwork I
> was hesitant about going for it. I was not sure I would be able
> to do those long hours of arduous work. Look at me today. I
> cannot only do it but do it well. I earn enough wheat for my
> family's consumption. I even manage to save a little. It is
> not work that I am afraid of, but the lack of it (quoted by Chen
> and Ghuznavi, 1977).

This is a far cry from the helplessness of a Chinese woman
nearly a hundred years ago, who told Ida Pruitt (1945):

> Day after day I sat at home. Hunger gnawed. What could I do?
> My mother was dead. My brother had gone away. When my husband
> brought home food I ate it and my children ate with me. A woman
> could not go out of the court. If a woman went out to service
> the neighbours all laughed. They said "So and so's wife has
> gone out to service". . . . I did not know enough even to beg.
> So I sat at home and starved. . . . How could I know what to do?
> We women knew nothing but to comb our hair and bind our feet and
> wait at home for our men. When my mother had been hungry she
> had sat at home and waited for my father to bring her food, so
> when I was hungry I waited at home for my husband to bring me
> food.

Few Asian women today would remain so ineffective in the protection of themselves and their children. The change has been imperceptible, but real in those societies which are modernizing by means of evolution. In those which are modernizing by means of revolution, change has been dramatic, but tradition still remains significant.

MAJOR FUTURE NEEDS

In this study we have tried to examine the position of women in Asian societies and in their own families. It has not been part of our brief to suggest how their lives might be improved. This is best done by people sharing their own culture, even though it has been seen that there is a severe shortage of female professionals in most countries. Only women are able to penetrate female society and gain the confidence and trust of rural women.

Certain conclusions appear to indicate the directions in which special efforts are needed to improve the lives of women. Legislation is not lacking in most countries for the protection of women in the fields of personal rights and in the labour market. Tradition still strongly affects the operation of these legal rights within the family, and the supply of and demand for labour affects the enforcement of laws relating to employment and equality of pay. It is clear that an educational thrust aimed at changing attitudes towards the sexual division of labour, however slow it may be to take effect, would do much to relieve women of the exhaustion characteristic of the double role performed by most within and outside the home. Adequate facilities for child care are a matter of vital concern to rural women obliged to work outside the home, but so far only the Communist countries have given systematic attention to this need. The National Committee on the Status of Women in India recommended that laws be revised to ensure the provision of child care services wherever 20 or more women are employed (the present minimum is 50). Such provision should also be made for casual or contract labour. It is admitted that even in the organized sector to which these laws apply at present, this regulation is inadequately observed. Poor working women have said that though they would prefer child care to be free, they would be prepared to pay (INCCU, 1977).

In many Asian countries there are significant proportions of women who are heads of households; these are in an especially vulnerable position, since rates of pay for women so often fall well below those of men.

Techniques of family planning are probably adequate to meet national requirements for fertility control; what is needed above all in most countries is more effective coverage--more clinics, more vehicles, which can travel to villages in which women have no time to leave their daily tasks, and more trained staff. There is still much to be learned of the motivation for accepting and continuing to practise contraception.

Education

Educational developments have tended to respond to social demand rather than to strategies for equal education. It has been recognized that in order to meet some of the shortcomings in educational systems, particularly as they affect girls, a more innovative approach is necessary (UNESCO, 1978a). Poverty is the chief obstacle to female education. Asian countries have devised a variety of measures to assist some of their most underprivileged groups. Malaysia offers a textbook loan scheme; India pays stipends to children of Scheduled Castes and Tribes to cover costs of attending school. Girls in remote areas of Nepal are given preference in the distribution of textbooks. Hostel accommodation has been started in Rajasthan, India and Nepal, to overcome parental resistance to their daughters' attending school and to avoid the cost of transport from remote areas. Inadequate numbers of female teachers in the rural areas of countries practising segregation are a great obstacle to female enrolment; Bangladesh has started a scheme to recruit local female teachers, providing free clothing, books, food and medical care.

Many children are quite simply beyond the reach of primary schools. This applies particularly to nomadic groups, and while no special measures have been taken in monsoonal Asia, the teachers of Afghanistan who travelled with the nomads, or the schools which were provided along the main routes of migration in Iran, may serve as models of what might be done. Some children of cattle herdsmen in Nepal are taught informally in their fields, though boys are more likely than girls to benefit. Elementary boarding schools have been started for the hill tribes of Thailand; 3 grades of primary school are available at medical posts in jungle areas for some of the children of Malaysia's tribal (Orang Asli) groups.

Non-formal programmes have been devised to give at least part-time education to Asian children who are unable to attend school regularly; Indonesia, the Philippines, India and Pakistan all have schemes in progress, characterized by flexible time schedules and short hours for girls fully involved in household chores, with curricula suited to community needs. The use of modern media to supplement local education facilities is expected to expand in the future (UNESCO, 1978a).

Nepal, with its high, remote areas and difficulties of access, presents particular problems in raising levels of female education. An innovative programme aimed at increasing the number of female teachers in rural areas began in 1970, with the help of UNESCO, UNICEF and the U.N. Development Programme (UNDP). Rural girls who have not completed school are recruited, helped to complete secondary education and provided with teacher training at high schools with special hostel accommodations. Stipends, travel allowance, medical care, books and clothing are provided, although it is acknowledged that financial incentives cannot be regarded as a permanent measure. It is hoped that attitudes will gradually change to a point where parents will be willing to cover costs. Teachers trained in this way are expected to return to their own areas to teach. A mid-term evaluation of this project showed that there had been an increase in enrolment of girls in primary schools in all 8 districts surveyed, with the proportion of girls in the 40 schools where teachers trained under the scheme ranging from 14.2 to 43.8 per cent of total enrolment. At the same time the ratio of women teachers has also increased somewhat; the national average is 4 per cent, while within the areas served by the project the ratio ranges from 5.2 to 8.8 per cent (UNESCO, 1978c).

Opportunities for Supplementing Family Income

Perhaps the most important conclusion reached from this study is that agriculture is no longer able to offer a satisfactory standard of living to vast numbers of rural families, particularly the landless and those with small holdings (Whyte, 1982). This trend will continue ineluctably as the cultivated land capable of sustaining high-yielding crop varieties is fully utilized, as monocrop regions reach production plateaux--many have already done so--and, above all, as population growth makes progressively less land available per head with each succeeding generation.

The availability of non-farm employment near farms in Taiwan has been responsible for increased rural incomes, particularly of households owning less than 0.5 hectares. This has been a means of offsetting disparities in income between larger and smaller landholdings. Moreover, employment has provided capital for farm investment, further increasing productivity (Chinn, 1979).

Unless there is, throughout Asia, widespread development of rural industry to provide opportunities to the rural young now increasingly being educated away from their family setting, these young people will flock to the primate cities. Urban opportunities for employment are scarce, and living conditions less favourable than in the villages, where friendly neighbours and kin help both in bridging family crises and providing trusted companionship for daily tasks and leisure. Paradoxically, the outward flow of rural youth can give rise to labour shortages at peak seasons in the agricultural cycle.

We have seen that unemployment and underemployment are greater for women than for men. Men move out of agricultural employment more easily than women (Devadas, 1978; Palmer, 1978). Moreover, increasing the efficiency of agriculture has been widely shown to have adverse effects on the employment of women, due to the realignment of tasks in the sexual division of labour. Only now is it beginning to be realized that plans for development must have components aimed specifically at women, if women are to benefit from them. An ILO seminar on the status and role of women in the organized sector (1978) recommended the adoption of innovative types of approaches to female education to reach those who never get a chance to break away from the village milieu. Such education should aim at providing women with skills leading to employment. In the labour-surplus countries of Asia, policies have to be geared to promoting opportunities for self-employment without reducing efforts to increase openings for wage-employment. Skills imparted must be of high quality, so that they are marketable. Organizations at district or state levels should take over co-ordination of both marketing and training in accounting and business skills, and in management and the provision of credit so that women entrepreneurs can set up their own businesses.

The proportions of women engaged in traditional rural industries in India are given by Devadas (1978), while suitable activities designed to increase the employment of women in rural areas are discussed by Dixon (1980).

It has been suggested that the upgrading of women's productive activities by the provision of income-generating employment outside the home may intervene in the cycle of rural poverty and high fertility characteristic of economically stagnant rural economies (Dixon, 1978). Eight prerequisites are proposed for such employment: women should have control over the income generated; jobs should be in villages and small towns; they should be outside agriculture; they should focus on small-scale, labour intensive light industries; work should be centrally located away from the home; jobs should attract only or primarily women in early reproductive years; production should be organized on principles of economic and social co-operation; additional social services and incentives should be provided.

In 1977, a project designed by T. Scarlett Epstein of the University of Sussex and Ranjit Senaratne of Sri Lanka initiated 8 micro-studies of the role of women in rural development, 2 each in Bangladesh, India, Sri Lanka and Pakistan. Studies covering different socio-economic strata aim at the eventual formulation of measures to include women in rural development and the training of local personnel in the introduction of appropriate technologies to increase both agricultural and non-agricultural activities.

Until the considerable technological and administrative changes such recommendations imply can be brought about on an adequate scale, there is a pressing need for the creation of jobs that women can do near or in their homes, and the organization of advice and channels for providing raw materials for rural handicrafts and their sale, such as has been attempted in Malaysia. Rural embroidery schools have been established in Pakistan to meet this need, though on a small scale so far. Women are more anxious to learn marketable skills than to acquire literacy (Khan and Bilquees, 1976), and this has given rise to the concept of training for "functional literacy" in Bangladesh. Small amounts of credit and training could help the promotion of cottage industries in Java in which the landless engage, although it is acknowledged that methods for doing this successfully are nowhere well understood. "If village handicraft products were more competitive price-wise in the urban markets, it would be a catalyst to small-scale industrial development" (Collier, 1978). The difficulties involved in organizing cottage industries, and ensuring that proceeds go to workers and not to middlemen, have led many to discount handicrafts as a means of supplementing family income. Workers in Bangladesh regard cottage industries as they now operate as "essentially non-productive" (McCarthy, Sabbah and Akhter, 1978a). Sewing groups in Sri Lanka have failed to arouse enthusiasm because they are not income-generating (Wijeratne, 1978).

Women in Thailand said they wanted to know more about nutrition, health, family planning, better agricultural practices, improved

212

animal husbandry, crafts and literacy. If training were to be
limited to only one area, however, 31 per cent selected sewing
instruction, 20 per cent training in better crop management and 19
per cent improved animal care. Only 9 per cent chose literacy training. The low esteem accorded handicrafts is attributed to the lack
of a market for such products (Nantanee et al, 1977).

PLANS AND ACTIVITIES: NATIONAL

A series of seminars was held in the states of the Indian Union
to prepare a national analysis of current women's needs for presenta-
tion at the regional meeting of the Economic and Social Council in
New Delhi in November, 1979. It was noted from the composition of
delegations to these meetings that women's leaders in India continue
to come from higher socio-economic groups. While participation in
politics and trade union activities, improvements in health services
and education were considered important by each state, employment
opportunities for women are the most vital concern throughout the
country (Awasty, 1979).
The Janata Government of India planned the removal to rural
areas of the manufacture of all products of village consumption which
can be cheaply produced without sophisticated technology or costly
infrastructure. Agricultural produce was also to be processed in
rural areas. This is similar to the commune self-sufficiency which
has long been attempted in China. It gives rise to a two-tier industrial structure, with quality control of sophisticated products in
the large industrial centres, requiring transportation networks to
the regional, national or international markets, and the manufacture
of products for local consumption in the rural areas. Here quality
may not be high, but it is hoped to keep costs lower and, above all,
to create employment.
An Expert Committee of the Indian Council of Social Science
Research in 1978 addressed a memorandum to the government expressing
its disquiet at recent trends in women's employment, and the "erosion
of women's productive roles (which) emphasizes women's position
primarily as consumers and bearers of children." The Committee has
recommended that at least 25 per cent of investment and promotional
activities in the small scale and cottage industries sectors, and
public works and services in the trading and commercial sector be
earmarked to increase economic opportunities for women. Stress is
laid on extension services aimed at women, and on the need to train
rural women (ICSSR, 1978). There are 218 small-scale units throughout the country giving training to women in handicrafts, handlooms,
agro-units, small-scale industries and ancillary units to larger
industries (INCCU, 1977). The scale of such operations needs greatly
to be increased.
It has been recognized in the Draft Five Year Plan 1978-1983
(India: Planning Commission, 1978a) that women have lost employment
because of changes which have transferred jobs from homes and cot-
tages to factories and machines, while family and community power
structure prevents their seeking adequate education and outside
employment. A policy for female employment recognizes that the need

of the majority of women is for part-time or seasonal employment. It is hoped to expand and diversify training for women, and to stimulate occupations preferred by women, especially in food processing--grain-milling, oil crushing and the manufacture of dairy products; the spinning and weaving of textiles, the manufacture of coir and bidi products and domestic, laundry and sanitation services. In the allo-cation of co-operative and commercial bank credit and other aid (training, technical assistance, marketing facilities and hire/ purchase of machinery) a reasonable share is to be made available for potential women entrepreneurs and women's co-operatives employing a majority of women workers. Manpower budgeting of the female labour force is to be a component of all area development schemes. A Working Group of the Planning Commission will study all aspects of female employment, and sub-groups will deal with: existing pro-grammes for women; the development of self-employment and entre-preneurship among women; and the development of cadres for promoting the employment of women.

Individual states in the Indian Union undertake activities to help women. The state government of Uttar Pradesh is setting up a training-cum-shelter workshop for destitute women of some hill areas in the Himalayan foothills. Grants-in-aid are given to poor women to purchase sewing, knitting and weaving machines. Nari Niketans are being established in 5 tribal blocks where 250 women and girls will be trained in gainful trades (Uttar Pradesh State Planning Depart-ment, 1977).

Proposals have been made for reinforcing Pakistan's Rural Development Programme, stressing the training of suitable women for leadership and developing special skills, and increasing opportuni-ties for rural women to raise their earning ability, especially in food processing and rural agro-industries, as well as in small businesses (Rashid, 1977).

Considerable work is necessary on refining the implements used by women in agriculture, in processing and within the home. The installation of tubewells in Bangladesh has been enthusiastically welcomed, although it is not known whether this is because they facilitate work, because the water is pure, or because they make the observation of purdah easier. Similarly, water-sealed latrines from the Comilla project are welcomed because increased population pres-sure makes seclusion in the fields more and more difficult (Abdulla, 1976).

It is found in Bangladesh that, despite the restrictions of purdah, women are willing to come to some central place for func-tional education classes, for mothers' clubs and paramedical ser-vices. Women will work and harvest a plot collectively with other women, and are willing to work in family planning and on functional education both within their own and other villages. Women walk miles to attend classes they see as useful, and will even travel outside their locality for training (Abdulla, loc. cit.). Women can be encouraged to design and implement development activities. Urban women can be induced to work in rural areas. Even relatively inex-perienced women, given sufficient training, can plan, design, imple-ment and monitor a development programme. Social constraints can be overcome if females work in pairs or teams. Women will leave their

homes to attend meetings and will voice opinions. Some activities
do not succeed: programmes which address welfare needs without
economic or tangible benefit; programmes which do not take account of
felt needs; imported or imposed ready-made programmes which do not
evolve from the participants themselves; and programmes which do not
take into account problems of training, supervision, management,
procurement and marketing. The Bangladesh Institute of Education and
Research is developing functional educational materials for their
programmes (Abdulla, loc. cit.).

The Rubber Smallholders Development Authority of Malaysia
(RISDA) has so far concentrated on improving agricultural practices
and marketing, but has now realized that women need help in running
their families and managing households on a low budget. Twenty-five
field workers, themselves mostly from smallholder families, have been
trained to advise women on the best use of their budgets for improved
family nutrition, and to make suggestions on what can be produced by
the women themselves.

The Malaysian Farmers Organization Authority (FAMA) is drawing
up a new system of group farming, with special courses for rural
women to show them how they may increase their incomes through group
activities. Between 2 and 10 farmers are to cultivate 2 or 3 crops
together, as well as rearing poultry and livestock. In 1977, 222
units of farmers' co-operatives carried out 331 group schemes of this
kind.

Tengku Maziedah Khaulah Ahmad, director of women's activities at
the Farmers Organization Authority (FAMA), states that women's participation has been steadily increasing since the department was
founded in 1975. Guidebooks are distributed describing typical projects, but women themselves must take the initiative; they may submit
a proposal to the FAMA for capital to start the project, but it is
then expected to become self-sustaining. There are 1,000 agro-based
co-operatives in Malaysia with a combined membership of over 300,000.
Wives of farmers and fishermen engage in poultry-rearing co-
operatives, cottage industries, tailoring and the making of kerepok
(fish and tapioca crisps).

A long scheme designed by the Johore State Economic Development
Corporation is aimed specifically at young, single girls from families which depend mostly on rubber and coconut for income, over 80
per cent of which is spent on food, with 10 per cent spent on education and the remainder on transport and clothing. Most girls have
been educated up to Standard Six, although some possess a Lower
Certificate of Education. The main crop on the land scheme is oil
palm, and each participant receives an allowance of M.$30 per month,
plus an additional average of M.$20, depending on the price received
at the time of sale of the crop. Men assist in harvesting the fruits
and weeding. Accommodation, recreational and sporting facilities and
classes in domestic science and religion are provided; there is a
small town 2 miles away, and a larger one 17 miles distant. It may
be difficult to maintain the emphasis on employment of women, however, since girls leave upon marriage; separate accommodations for
couples are being constructed to counteract this. It may be asked
whether schemes which include divorced women, requiring special child
care facilities, might not meet a great need in Islamic southeast

215

Asia.
The U.N. Asian and Pacific Centre for Women and Development has
embarked on a project with the government of Thailand to train
"multi-purpose field workers who can undertake activities in agriculture, nutrition, health/disease and public health" (UNAPCWD, 1978).
Nine groups, each composed of 450 women from rural areas, have
received four-month training courses in community development
regional centres under a scheme devised by the Thai Government to
teach women how most productively to use their time, with training in
special skills in cottage industries, agriculture and nutrition
(Vichai, 1978).
The Institute of Philippine Culture sought to design a programme
to improve the situation of rural women in the Philippines on the
basis of careful analysis of their present economic status and outlook in a sample region in the Bicol River Basin (Illo, 1977). Three
different projects have been evolved, relating respectively to women
with a wholly traditional role, those who occupy a more transitional
position and the few non-traditional, career women. The first project stresses home and family management and the improvement of
community services; the second stresses adult education and the
training of women in skills likely to generate income; the last
stresses skills at a higher level, including tasks generally performed by men, involvement in leadership and the setting up of day
care centres.
A woman's leadership training course has been planned by the
Korean Women's Institute of Ewha University, and the first course on
women's studies began in autumn, 1977 (Kim, 1977). Under the Saemaul
Undong village development schemes, villagers elect 2 leaders, one
male, one female, to organize activities (Kim, 1978).
The Home-Living Improvement Section of the Ministry of Agriculture and Forestry, Japan, has, since 1948, been advising farm women
on improved technology relating to clothing, food, housing and home
management. Today there are over 2,000 female home advisers. These
receive instruction at a central institute in Tokyo, which also provides refresher courses and a forum for experiments designed to
further improve techniques. The functioning of this institute would
be of great interest to those in other Asian countries responsible
for instructing rural women on better practices in and around the
home.
Japan has taken the lead in attempting to incorporate into
national policy measures decisions by the World Conference of International Women's Year, by setting up the Headquarters for the Planning and Promoting of Policies Relating to Women, headed by the Prime
Minister (Japan, 1977). It is seeking to clarify targets and formu-
late a plan of action.

INTERNATIONAL ACTIVITIES

The period 1976-1985 has been designated the U.N. Decade for
Women: Equality, Development and Peace, with the subthemes: employment, education and health. A three-week meeting to review progress
was held in Copenhagen in July, 1980, against a background of a world

economic situation which had deteriorated since the first meeting in
1975. Delegates to the 1980 meeting agreed that the situation of
women in employment had also deteriorated since 1975, and educational
gains by middle-class women were not matched by increased opportunities for employment. A report presented to the meeting hoped that
links could be established between women's advancement and the solution of major problems of recession and inflation. Many delegates
signed a convention forbidding discrimination on the basis of sex; it
is difficult to see how this convention can be enforced. In common
with many international conferences, politics displaced the more
substantive considerations for which the delegates had been convened.
Various aspects of the practical side of women's lives were discussed
at a non-governmental conference which took place in Copenhagen at
the same time.

    In 1977, the Economic and Social Council of the United Nations
invited its regional commissions to consider ways of contributing
effectively to the 1980 Copenhagen meeting; the Asian and Pacific
Commission held a regional preparatory conference in November, 1979,
in New Delhi, in which 26 member countries participated and presented
national views. Methods for involving women in development were
described, and critical issues, short-range strategies and long-term
plans discussed. Four workshops concentrated on problems relating
to: (1) employment; (2) health; (3) education; and (4) (a) equality,
development and peace, and (b) policy, mechanisms, monitoring and
appraisal. The conference concluded that equality must mean greater
access to power over the allocation of resources, and stressed the
importance of grass-roots organization of women in sustaining
national political will to help them.

    International Women's Year showed that the inclusion of women in
schemes for development could not be taken for granted, but must be
planned for. A set of criteria for evaluating development projects
involving women has been prepared (American Council of Voluntary
Agencies for Foreign Service, 1975). A programme of international
action aimed at promoting the advancement of women and their integration in development has been suggested by FAO (FAO, 1973; FAO, Home
Economics and Social Programmes Service, 1975). An inventory of FAO
activities relating to women is available (FAO, 1977). A model for
extension programmes in home economics aimed at rural women in southeast Asia has been proposed (Purvis, 1976). Above all, greater
attention needs to be paid to agricultural extension aimed specifically at women, preferably conducted by women. This is especially
true in the field of animal husbandry; it has been seen that women
are, to a large extent, responsible for the care of domestic animals
in Asia, yet extension is aimed usually only at men. The Applied
Nutrition Program of FAO, WHO and UNICEF does stress poultry care and
production as an important component. Much more could be achieved if
existing extension services giving advice on better husbandry of
large and small farm animals were to reach women.

    Planners have long placed much faith in the "trickle-down"
theory, whereby improved techniques would slowly penetrate to the
village from larger centres, such as small towns (Whyte, 1982). The
U.N. Center for Regional Development considers that evidence shows
the theory to be erroneous, and is now strongly in favour of greater

emphasis on work at the village level. It must be admitted, however, that the number of people with some degree of training which would be required, and the logistics and organization involved, represent daunting obstacles. Moreover, as has been shown, there is abundant evidence that efforts even at the village level may not help women. It has been demonstrated, however, that there is a great potential for improving women's lot within the framework of current village life by means of trained village women and co-operative work done by women's clubs (for example, in Bangladesh and Korea).

Food aid has been shown to have considerable potential for improving women's status, providing a means of bringing in new ideas, particularly to rural areas, and offering possibilities to women for assuming new roles. Food for Work projects in Bangladesh have been one example (World Food Program, 1977).

The Protein Advisory Group of the United Nations, considering the vital role of women in food and nutrition, undertook a two-year study in Africa to assess "the adequacy of conceptual and methodological orientations of current research on women's role in food production, food handling and nutrition; indicating linkages between food and nutritional status and various aspects of women's role in food production; using information from research in both nutrition and the social sciences, and identifying new directions in research to provide a better basis for planning and implementation of practical programmes" (PAG Bulletin 7[3-4]:40-49, 1977). Conclusions reached in this study are applicable to most parts of the developing world, and guidelines have been drawn up for examining women's activities (PAG, 1977).

A consultative group from the United Nations University is to study the role of women in post-harvest conservation, with special attention to the technologies used, as well as to the social background of village, market and district, the time women devote to such activities and the degree to which their families benefit, nutritionally and economically.

Participants at the Wingspread Workshop on Women and Development, convened by the Center for Research and Development of Wellesley College in 1976, formed working groups to assess current research, to identify research practices and new methodologies and to suggest ways of creating new research institutions and networks to advance knowledge in the following fields: (1) labour force participation of women; (2) education and training as they affect women; (3) women and health; (4) women and the family; (5) ideology, values and religion; (6) women and political participation; and (7) women and the world economic order. The working group on labour force participation recommended the establishment of regional centres to co-ordinate future research. In Asia, Dr. Vina Mazumdar of the Indian Council of Social Science Research, New Delhi, is regional co-ordinator (Casal et al, 1976). An international directory of women's development organizations has been prepared to enable women in different parts of the world to establish contact (U.S. AID, 1977).

In 1977, the United Nations Asian and Pacific Centre for Women and Development was set up in Teheran, moving to Bangkok in 1979. It aims at working with women for a more equitable distribution of

resources and opportunities for participation in decision-making and
to achieve better understanding of the effect of development on
women. An Expert Group Meeting on the Identification of Basic Needs
of Women held in December, 1977, stressed the importance of changing
the attitudes of society--of both men and women--towards women, and
the need for redesigning the workforce to include opportunities for
part-time work, more flexible hours and job sharing to benefit women.
Women need to be trained in the making of consumer goods from locally
available resources, for both rural and urban markets, to increase
their incomes. There was a call for greater participation of women
in community decisions, which would require training, and for the
creation of pressure groups on specific aspects of importance to
women.

The new Centre will concentrate initially on identifying
priority needs, and will attempt to intervene at the planning stage
of development projects likely to affect women. It will study the
effect of mechanization on the displacement of women from the labour
market. Training, technical and advisory activities will be carried
on, and links created with women's organizations throughout the
region. The meeting drew up guidelines for the activities of the
Institute (UNAPCWD, 1977).

We have been able to give here examples of only some of the
innumerable activities under way in Asia, aimed at a better understanding of the needs and goals of women, and at bringing about practical improvements to their ways of life.

CHANGING ATTITUDES

Other less tangible problems present greater difficulty, particularly those relating to status. The application of the new household economics (Chapter 11), and its concomitant integration of
market and non-market activities into economic analyses, should
enhance women's status among policy-makers by giving more value to
non-wage earning activities in the home. Women's status at community
levels will, however, not improve rapidly. It has long been held
that progress is evolutionary, and modernization would, of itself,
bring about female emancipation. In fact, modernization may well
have an adverse rather than a salutary impact on the status of women
(Youssef, 1977) (see also Chapter 13).

Much faith is placed in the effect of education on changing
traditional attitudes, and it has been seen in India, Taiwan and
Japan that the educated daughter-in-law has an edge over her conser-
vative, sometimes tyrannical mother-in-law, which was undreamed of by
her mother. Yet the education of girls continues to remain subsidiary to that of boys, and the need for their help in the rural home is
not likely to change this situation in the foreseeable future. Even
in Japan, where universal education has long been in force and the
majority of girls receive some form of higher education, attitudes
towards child-raising remain traditional. In a recent survey, 74.9
per cent of women thought boys should be trained to be "strong and
courageous" and girls "tender and gentle." Only 19.4 per cent
thought boys and girls should be trained in the same way (UNESCO,

1976).

It will take much time to eradicate the acceptance of a secondary, submissive role for females, which automatically assigns to
males a greater right to education and prevents women from taking the
initiative to improve their own lot, or that of the family, by
activities at the village level or in leadership roles. The weak,
passive, home-oriented woman, less intelligent and capable than men,
is enshrined in mythology, symbolism and stereotypical ideals, and
the picture is perpetuated in school textbooks, adult literature and
all forms of visual entertainment. It will, above all, take time to
change the unconscious assumption of preordained privilege which may
be encountered among Asian men at every socio-economic level.

Yet in the short period since worldwide prominence was given to
the needs of women during International Women's Year, 1975, much has
been achieved. Some Asian governments have appointed female ministers, or at least advisers at cabinet level, on women's affairs.
And, throughout the region, there are many individual educated women
who are no longer willing to tolerate injustice in the treatment of
their sex, nor are they content to be passive participants in
national development.

The efforts of these leaders will receive support and understanding from rural women only when economic conditions give them
adequate income and leisure to participate in community decisions.
Then they may hope to gain recognition from men for their rights and
abilities, without which equality in daily life will never be
attained.

It must, however, be recognized that as long as total income in
most of the rural communities of Asia is inadequate to maintain
acceptable standards of living for the family as a whole, attempts to
improve the position specifically of women are not likely to proceed
far beyond the realm of good intentions. Increased prosperity for
the family may improve the status of its women members, though this
cannot be taken for granted. It will be very difficult to emphasize
the needs of women in the socio-economic environment of poverty and
under-employment in which most rural households live.

Bibliography

ABDULLA, Tahrunnessa A. (1976). Village women as I saw them. Bangladesh Academy for Rural Development, Comilla. 36 pp.

ABDULLA, Tahrunnessa A., and ZEIDENSTEIN, S. (1976). Finding ways to learn about rural women: experiences from a pilot project in Bangladesh. Ford Foundation, Dacca. 32 pp.

_____. (1977). "Rural women and development." In Role of women in socio-economic development in Bangladesh, pp. 94-102. Bangladesh Economic Association, Dacca.

ADAMS, J. W., and KASAKOFF, A. B. (1976a). "Factors underlying endogamous group size." In Regional analysis (ed. C. Smith), vol. 2, pp. 149-173. Academic Press, New York, London.

_____. (1976b). "Central place theory and endogamy in China." In Regional analysis (ed. C. Smith), vol. 2, pp. 175-187. Academic Press, New York, London.

ADNAN, S., ISLAM, R., and the VILLAGE STUDY GROUP. (1977). "Social change and rural women: possibilities of participation." In Role of women in socio-economic development in Bangladesh, pp. 80-93. Bangladesh Economic Association, Dacca.

AIYAPPAN, A. (1975). "Social change in rural India." In Seminar on approaches to rural development, pp. 225-341. Asian Centre for Development Administration, Kuala Lumpur.

ALAM, B. A. (1975). "Women in nursing." In Women for women (ed. Women for Women Research and Study Group), pp. 121-153. University Press, Dacca.

ALTEKAR, A. S. (1959). The position of women in Hindu civilization from prehistoric times to the present day. 2nd ed. Motilal Banarsidass, Delhi. 380 pp.

ALVI, Salim. (1977). Women's rights in Pakistan. Gemini News, reprinted by Action for Development.

AMERICAN COUNCIL OF VOLUNTARY AGENCIES FOR FOREIGN SERVICE (ACVAFS). (1975). Criteria for evaluation of development projects involving women. Technical Assistance Information Clearing House, New York. 40 pp.

ANDORS, P. (1976). "Politics of Chinese development: the case of women, 1960-66." Signs 2: 89-119.

APPLETON, S. (1979). "Sex, values and change on Taiwan." In Value change in Chinese society (eds. R. W. Wilson, A. A. Wilson and S. L. Greenblatt), pp. 185-203. Praeger, New York.

ARISHIMA, Takeo. (1919). *Aru Onna*. Translated 1979 by Kenneth Strong as *A Certain Woman*, University of Tokyo Press.

ARNOLD, F. *et al*. (1975). *The value of children: a cross national study. 1. Introduction and comparative analysis*. East-West Population Institute, Honolulu. 251 pp.

ASHRAF, K. (1963). *Some land problems in tribal areas of West Pakistan*. Board of Economic Enquiry, Peshawar University, Peshawar. 191 pp.

AWASTY, I. (1979). *National and state level conferences on women and development, December, 1978-May, 1979*. UNDP, New Delhi. Tss. 108 pp.

AWE, Bolanle. (1977). "Reflections on the Conference on Women and Development: 1." *Signs* 3: 314-319.

BAKER, H. D. R. (1968). *A Chinese lineage village: Sheung Shui*. Cass, London. 237 pp.

BANDO, M. (1977). *The women of Japan - past and present*. Foreign Press Center, Tokyo. 36 pp.

BANGLADESH ECONOMIC ASSOCIATION. (1977). *Role of women in socio-economic development in Bangladesh*. Bangladesh Economic Association, Dacca. 197 pp.

BANISTER, J. (1977). "Mortality, fertility and contraceptive use in Shanghai." *China Quarterly* no. 70: 254-295.

_____. (1978). Psycho-social factors in rapid fertility transition - The People's Republic of China. Paper to Workshop on Psycho-Social Factors in Population Research, Population Association of America meeting, Atlanta, Georgia. 27 pp.

BARKOW, J. H. (1978). "Culture and sociobiology." *American Anthropologist* 80: 5-20.

BASHAM, A. L. (1954). *The wonder that was India: a survey of the culture of the Indian sub-continent before the coming of the Muslims*. Sidgwick and Jackson, London. 568 pp.

BAUTISTA, G. (1977). "Socio-economic conditions of the landless rice workers in the Philippines: the landless of Barrio St. Lucia as a case in point." In *Hired labor in rural Asia* (ed. S. Hirashima), pp. 106-126. Institute of Developing Economies, Tokyo.

BEALS, A. R. (1962). *Gopalpur: a south Indian village*. Holt, Rinehart and Winston, New York, London. 99 pp.

BEAN, L. L. (1968). "Utilization of human resources: the case of women in Pakistan." *International Labour Review* 97: 391-410.

BEAUVOIR, S. de. (1949). *Le deuxième sexe. 1. Les faits et les mythes*. Gallimard, Paris. 395 pp.

BECKER, G. (1965). "A theory of the allocation of time." *Economic Journal* 75: 493-517.

BEFU, H. (1971). *Japan: an anthropological introduction*. Chandler, San Francisco, London, Toronto. 210 pp.

BERGMAN, A. E. (1975). *Women of Vietnam*. People's Press, San Francisco. 255 pp.

BERNSTEIN, G. L. (1976). Changing roles of women in rural Japan. Paper to Association of Asian Studies Annual Conference, Toronto. 19pp.

BERREMAN, G. D. (1977). "Ecology, demography and social strategies in the western Himalaya: a case study." In Himalaya: ecologie, ethnologie, pp. 453-480. C.N.R.S., Paris.

BERTOCCI, P. J. (1974). "Rural communities in Bangladesh: Hajipur and Tinpara." In South Asia: seven community profiles (ed. C. Maloney), pp. 81-130. Holt, Rinehart and Winston, New York, Toronto, London.

BETEILLE, A. (1975). "The position of women in Indian society." In Indian Women (ed. Devaki Jain), pp. 59-68. Ministry of Information and Broadcasting, New Delhi.

BHATIA, J. C. (1978). "Ideal number and sex preference of children in India." J. Family Welfare 24(4): 3-16.

BIRD, I. L. (1883). The Golden Chersonese and the way thither. John Murray, London. 384 pp. Reprinted by Oxford University Press, Kuala Lumpur, 1967.

BLAIKIE, P. (1976). "Family planning programmes and the growth of population in Kosi." In The Kosi symposium (ed. J. L. Joy and E. Everitt), pp. 249-255. Institute of Development Studies, University of Sussex.

BLUMBERG, R. L. (1976). "Fairy tales and facts: economy, family, fertility and the female." In Women and world development (ed. I. Tinker and M. B. Bramsen), pp. 12-21. Overseas Development Council, Washington.

BOONLERT, L., and COOK, M. J. (1976 and 1977). Labour force participation, village characteristics and modernism and their influence on fertility among rural Asian women. Institute of Population and Social Research, Mahidol University, Bangkok. 29 and 164 pp.

BOONSANONG, Punyodyana. (1971). Thai selective social change: a study with comparative reference to Japan. Ph.D. Thesis, Cornell University. University Microfilms, Ann Arbor. 397 pp.

BOSE, A. B., and SEN, M. L. A. (1966). "Some characteristics of the widows in rural society." Man in India 46: 226-232.

BOSERUP, E. (1970). Woman's role in economic development. Allen and Unwin, London. 283 pp.

BRANDAUER, F. P. (1977). "Women in the Ching-hua yüan: emancipation towards a Confucian ideal." Journal of Asian Studies 36: 657-660.

BRANDT, V. R. (1971). A Korean village: between farm and sea. Harvard University Press, Cambridge, Mass. 252 pp.

BRAY, F. (1977). Report for the British Academy, the Royal Society and the East Asia History of Science Trust on a year's field trip to southeast Asia: a comparative study of padi cultivation in Kelantan, Malaysia. Cambridge. 18 pp.

BUCK, J. L. (1937). Land utilization in China. Commercial Press, Shanghai. 494 pp. Reprinted Paragon Books, New York, 1964.

BULATAO, R. A. (1974). "Philippines." In Social and psychological aspects of fertility in Asia (ed. H. P. David and S. J. Lee), pp. 35-38. Transnational Family Research Institute, Washington.

BURIPAKDI, C. (1974). "Thailand." In Social and psychological aspects of fertility in Asia (ed. H. P. David and S. J. Lee), pp. 31-34. Transnational Family Research Institute, Washington.

BURNS, P. L., and COWAN, C. D. (1975). Sir Frank Swettenham's Malayan journals, 1874-1876. Oxford University Press, Kuala

Lumpur. 347 pp.

BUVINIC, M. (1976). <u>Women and world development: an annotated bibliography</u>. Overseas Development Council, Washington. 162 pp.

BUXBAUM, D. C. (ed.). (1977). <u>Chinese family law and social change in historical and comparative perspective</u>. University of Washington Press, Seattle. 544 pp.

CAPLAN, L. (1974). "A Himalayan people: Limbus of Nepal." In <u>South Asia: seven community profiles</u> (ed. C. Maloney), pp. 173-201. Holt, Rinehart and Winston, New York, Toronto, London, Sydney.

CAREY, I. (1976). <u>Orang Asli: the aboriginal tribes of peninsular Malaysia</u>. Oxford University Press, Kuala Lumpur, London, New York, Melbourne. 376 pp.

CASAL, L., JOSEPH, Suad, PALA, Achola and SEIDMAN, A. (eds.). (1976). <u>Report of a Wingspread Workshop on woman and development</u>. The Johnson Foundation, Racine, Wisconsin. 40 pp.

CASTILLO, G. T. (1976a). <u>The Filipino woman as manpower: the image and the empirical reality</u>. Council for Asian Manpower Studies, Quezon City. 263 pp.

_____. (1976b). The changing role of women in rural societies: a summary of trends and issues. Paper summarizing Seminar at Fourth World Congress for Rural Sociology, Torun, Poland. 23 pp.

CASTILLO, G. T., and PUA, J. F. (1963). "Research notes on the contemporary Filipino family: findings in a Tagalog area." <u>Philippine J. Home Economics</u> 14(3): 4-35.

CHA Jae-ho, CHUNG Bom-mo, and LEE Sung-jin. (1977). "Boy preference reflected in Korean folklore." In <u>Virtues in conflict</u> (ed. S. Mattielli), pp. 113-127. Royal Asiatic Society, Korea Branch, Seoul.

CHAMIE, M. (1977). "Sexuality and birth control decisions among Lebanese couples." <u>Signs</u> 3: 294-312.

CHAN, A. (1974). "Rural Chinese women and the Socialist revolution: an enquiry into the economics of sexism." <u>Journal of Contemporary Asia</u> 4: 197-208.

CHAUDHURI, Nirad C. (1951). <u>The autobiography of an unknown Indian</u>. Jaico, Bombay. 528 pp.

CHEN, M., and GHUZNAVI, R. (1977). <u>Women in food-for-work: the Bangladesh experience</u>. World Food Program Committee on Food Aid Policies and Programmes, FAO, Rome. (WFP/CFA:4/INF/5). 49 pp.

CHEN, P. S. J. (1974). "Singapore." In <u>Social and psychological aspects of fertility in Asia</u> (ed. H. P. David and S. J. Lee), pp. 39-49. Transnational Family Research Institute, Washington.

CHENG Siok-hwa. (1977). "Singapore women: legal status, educational attainment and employment patterns." <u>Asian Survey</u> 17: 358-374.

CHINN, D. L. (1979). "Rural poverty and the structure of farm household income in the developing countries: evidence from Taiwan." <u>Economic Development and Cultural Change</u> 27: 283-301.

CHODOROW, N. (1974). "Family structure and feminine personality." In <u>Woman, culture and society</u> (ed. M. Rosaldo and L. Lamphere), pp. 43-66. Stanford University Press, Stanford.

CHOI, J. S. (1969). "Role structure of Korean rural family." <u>Chintan Hakpo</u> 32: 275-276. (English summary.)

CHUNG, Betty J. (1972). "Costs and benefits of children in Hong Kong." In The satisfactions and costs of children: theories, concepts, methods (ed. J. T. Fawcett), pp. 210-230. East-West Center, Honolulu.
_____. (1974). "Hongkong." In Social and psychological aspects of fertility in Asia (ed. H. P. David and S. J. Lee), pp. 23-30. Transnational Family Research Institute, Washington.
CHUNG, B. J., and NG, S. M. (1977). The status of women in law: a comparison of four Asian countries. Occasional Publication no. 59. Institute of Southeast Asian Studies, Singapore. 63 pp.
CHUNG, B. J., PALMORE, J. A., LEE, S. J., LEE, S. J. (1972). Psychological perspectives: family planning in Korea. Hollym, Seoul. 532 pp.
COLLIER, W. L. (1977). Agricultural evolution in Java: the decline of shared poverty and involution. Mimeo, Bogor. 38 pp.
_____. (1978). "Food problems, unemployment and the green revolution in rural Java." (English translation of original in Indonesian, Prisma, February 1978, pp. 20-37). Mimeo. Bogor.
COLLIER, W. L., WIRADI, Gunawan, and SOENTORO. (1973). "Recent changes in rice harvesting methods." Bulletin of Indonesian Economic Studies 9(2): 36-45.
CONTADO, M. S. (1978). M.S. Thesis, East Samar, reported in Monitor. (Philippines Council for Agricultural and Resources Research.)
COOK, M. J. (1977). Female labour force participation, modernity and fertility in rural Thailand. Ph.D. Thesis, Brown University. 299 pp.
COOMBS, C. H., COOMBS, L. C., and McCLELLAND, G. H. (1975). "Preference scales for number and sex of children." Population Studies 29: 273-298.
CORTES, I. R. (1977). "Philippine law and status of women." In Law and the status of women, pp. 229-261. U.N. Centre for Social Development and Humanitarian Affairs, New York.
CRISSMAN, L. W. (1976). "Spatial aspects of marriage patterns as influenced by marketing behaviour in west central Taiwan." In Regional analysis (ed. C. Smith), pp. 123-148, vol. 2. Academic Press, New York, London.
CROLL, E. (1974). The women's movement in China: 1949-73. Anglo-Chinese Educational Institute, London. 150 pp.
_____. (1976). Female solidarity groups as a power base in rural China. Paper to Fourth World Congress for Rural Sociology. 14 pp.
_____. (1979). Women in rural development: the People's Republic of China. International Labour Office, Geneva. 61 pp.
DAS, Veena. (1975). "Marriage among the Hindus." In Indian Women (ed. Devaki Jain), pp. 69-86. Ministry of Information and Broadcasting, New Delhi.
DASGUPTA, B. (1977). "New technology and the agricultural labourers in India." In Hired labor in rural Asia (ed. S. Hirashima), pp. 9-31. Institute of Developing Economies, Tokyo.
DAVID, H. P., and LEE, S. J. (eds.). (1974). Social and psychological aspects of fertility in Asia. Transnational Family Research Institute, Washington. 128 pp.

226

DAVIN, D. (1975). "Women in the countryside of China." In Women in Chinese society (ed. M. Wolf and R. Witke), pp. 243-273. Stanford University Press, Stanford.

DAVIS, M. (1976). "The politics of family life in rural West Bengal." Ethnology 15: 189-200.

DELVERT, J. (1961). Le paysan cambodgien. Mouton, Paris, The Hague. 740 pp.

DENICH, B. S. (1974). "Sex and power in the Balkans." In Woman, culture and society (ed. M. Z. Rosaldo and L. Lamphere), pp. 243-262. Stanford University Press, Stanford.

DEUCHLER, M. (1977). "The tradition: women during the Yi dynasty." In Virtues in conflict (ed. S. Mattielli), pp. 1-47. Royal Asiatic Society, Korea Branch, Seoul.

DEVADAS, R. P. (1978). The Integration of women in agrarian reform and rural development in India and Sri Lanka. Paper to World Conference on Agrarian Reform and Rural Development, FAO, Rome. 78 pp.

DEWEY, A. (1962). Peasant marketing in Java. Free Press of Glencoe, New York. 238 pp.

DIAMOND, N. (1969). K'un Shen: a Taiwan village. Holt, Rinehart and Winston, New York, Toronto, London. 111 pp.

_____. (1975). "Collectivization, kinship and the status of women in rural China." Bulletin of Concerned Asian Scholars 7: 25-32.

DIXON, R. B. (1971). "Explaining cross-cultural variations in age at marriage and proportions never marrying." Population Studies 25: 215-233.

_____. (1978). Women's co-operatives and rural development: a policy proposal. Johns Hopkins Press, Baltimore. 315 pp.

_____. (1980). Jobs for women in rural industry and services. Ford Foundation, Dacca, Report no. 50. 78 pp.

DJAMOUR, J. (1965). Malay kinship and marriage in Singapore. Athlone Press, London. 153 pp.

DJERASSI, C. (1974). "Some observations on current fertility control in China." China Quarterly 57: 40-62.

DOERIAT, F. (1976). "Overpopulation, population growth and the status of Indonesian women." In Indonesian women: some past and current perspectives (ed. B. B. Hering), pp. 151-155. Centre d'Etude du Sud-Est Asiatique et de l'Extreme Orient, Bruxelles.

DORE, R. P. (1965). Education in Tokugawa Japan. Routledge and Kegan Paul, London. 346 pp.

DUBE, Leela. (1978a). "Sex roles in contrasting family systems." Paper to World Congress of Sociology, Uppsala. 12 pp.

_____. (1978b). The seed and the earth: symbolism of human reproduction in India. Paper to session on symbolism of biological reproduction and its correlation with patterns of production, Xth International Congress of Anthropological and Ethnological Sciences, New Delhi. 11 pp.

DUBE, S. C. (1963). "Men's and women's roles in India: a sociological review." In Women in the new Asia (ed. B. E. Ward), pp. 174-203. UNESCO, Paris.

DUNBAR, Sir George. (1949). A history of India. Nicholson and Watson, London. 2 volumes. 659 pp.

DWYER, J. (1976). "Nutrition education at the village level." Food and Nutrition 2(2): 2-7.

EBER, I. (1976). "Images of women in recent Chinese fiction: do women hold up half the sky?" Signs 2: 24-34.

EDMUNDSON, W. C. (1977). "Two villages in contrast, 1971-76." Bulletin of Indonesian Economic Studies 13: 95-110.

ELLICKSON, J. (1975). "Rural women." In Women for women (ed. Women for Women Research and Study Group), pp. 81-89. University Press, Dacca.

_____. (1976). Women of rural Bangladesh. Variation in problems of self-perception. Paper to Women and Development Conference, Wellesley College, Wellesley, Mass. 23 pp.

ELLIOTT, C. M. (1977). "Theories of development: an assessment." Signs 3: 1-8.

ELWIN, V. (1975, reprinted from 1958 volume). "Tribal women." In Indian women (ed. Devaki Jain), pp. 205-213. Ministry of Information and Broadcasting, New Delhi.

EMBREE, J. F. (1950). "Thailand - a loosely structured social system." American Anthropologist 52: 181-193.

ENCARNACION, J. (1973). "Family income, educational level, labour force participation and fertility." Philippine Economic Journal 12: 536-549.

EPSTEIN, T. S. (1973). South India: yesterday, today and tomorrow. Macmillan, London. 273 pp.

ESTIOKO-GRIFFIN, A. A., and GRIFFIN, P. B. "Woman the hunter." In Woman the gatherer (ed. F. Dahlberg), forthcoming.

FAROUK, A., and MUHAMMAD, A. (1977). The hardworking poor: a survey on how people use their time in Bangladesh. Bureau of Economic Research, University of Dacca. 196 pp.

FAWCETT, J. T. (1972). The satisfactions and costs of children: theories, concepts, methods. East-West Center, Honolulu. 324 pp.

FIELD, C. E., and BABER, F. M. (1973). Growing up in Hong Kong. Hong Kong University Press. 178 pp.

FIRTH, Rosemary. (1966). Housekeeping among Malay peasants. Athlone Press, London/Humanities Press Inc., New York. 242 pp.

FLIEGER, W., and SMITH, P. C. (eds.). (1975). A demographic path to modernity. University of the Philippines Press, Quezon City.

FLORES, E. P. (1970). Child rearing among a Moslem group in the Sulu Archipelago, Philippines. Ph.D. Thesis. University Microfilms, Ann Arbor. 206 pp.

FLORES, P. M. (1969/1970). Socio-psychological development of Filipino children. (No publisher given.) 199 pp.

FONG Chan-onn. (1976). Attitudes of local leaders and family planning in peninsular Malaysia. SEAPRAP Research Report no. 8, Kuala Lumpur. 51 pp.

FONG, M. S. (1975). Female labor force participation in a modernizing society: Malaya and Singapore 1921-57. Papers of East-West Population Institute no. 34. Honolulu. 39 pp.

FOOD AND AGRICULTURE ORGANIZATION OF THE UNITED NATIONS (FAO). (1973). Status of rural women, especially agricultural workers. Programme of concerted international action to promote the advancement of women and their integration in development. Doc. no. E/CN/6/583/Add.2. FAO, Rome.

_____. (1977). An inventory of FAO activities as related to women. FAO, Rome. 61 pp.

FAO, Home Economics and Social Programmes Service. (1975). Promoting the increased participation of rural women in the development process. FAO, Rome. 8 pp.

FOX, R. (1963). "Men and women in the Philippines." In Women in the new Asia (ed. B. E. Ward), pp. 342-364. UNESCO, Paris.

FRANKEL, F. (1971). India's green revolution: economic gains and political costs. Princeton University Press, Princeton. 232 pp.

FREDERICKS, L. J. (1977). "Some socio-economic characteristics of rural labor with special reference to a rice double-cropping area in Selangor, West Malaysia." In Hired labor in rural Asia (ed. S. Hirashima), pp. 170-190. Institute of Developing Economies, Tokyo.

FREEDMAN, M. (1958). Lineage organization in southeastern China. Athlone Press, London. 151 pp.

_____. (1966). Chinese lineage and society: Fukien and Kwangtung. Athlone Press, London/Humanities Press, New York. 207 pp.

_____ (ed.). (1970a). Family and kinship in Chinese society. Stanford University Press, Stanford. 269 pp.

_____. (1970b). "Ritual aspects of Chinese kinship and marriage." In Family and kinship in Chinese society (ed. M. Freedman), pp. 163-187. Stanford University Press, Stanford.

FREEDMAN, R., and COOMBS, L. C. (1974). Cross-cultural comparisons: data on two factors in fertility behaviour. Population Council, New York. 94 pp.

FRIED, M. H. (1953). Fabric of Chinese society: a study of the social life of a Chinese county seat. Farrar, Straus and Giroux, New York. 243 pp.

FRIEDLANDER, S., and SILVER, M. (1967). "A quantitative study of the determinants of fertility behaviour." Demography 4: 38-55.

FULLER, C. J. (1976). The Nayars today. Cambridge University Press, Cambridge. 173 pp.

von FÜRER-HAIMENDORF, C. (1974). "A central Indian tribal people: the Raj Gonds." In South Asia: seven community profiles (ed. C. Maloney), pp. 202-257. Holt, Rinehart and Winston, New York, Toronto, London.

GANI, Amna. (1963). "Combining marriage and career in Karachi." In Women in the new Asia (ed. B. E. Ward), pp. 323-339. UNESCO, Paris.

GEERTZ, H. (1961). The Javanese family. Free Press of Glencoe, New York. 176 pp.

GEERTZ, H., and GEERTZ, C. (1975). Kinship in Bali. University of Chicago Press, Chicago and London. 213 pp.

GERMAIN, A. (1976). Women's roles in Bangladesh development: a program assessment. Ford Foundation, Dacca, report no. 39. 18 + 30 pp.

GILLE, H., and PARDOKO, H. (1966). "A family life study in east Java: preliminary findings." In Family planning and population programs: a review of world developments (ed. Berelson et al), pp. 503-521. Chicago University Press, Chicago and London.

GLUCKMAN, M. (1953). "Bridewealth and the stability of marriage."

Man 53: 141-143.
GOLDSTEIN, M. C. (1978). "Pahari and Tibetan polyandry revisited." Ethnology 17: 325-337.
GOLDSTEIN, S. (1972). "The influence of labor force participation and education on fertility in Thailand." Population Studies 26: 419-435.
GONZALEZ, A. M. (1976). Filipino women in development, the impact of poverty. Paper to National Convention of the Philippine Sociology Society on Poverty: the Illusion and the Reality. Quezon City, January 23-25.
_____. (1977). "Filipino women in development: the impact of poverty." Philippine Sociological Review 25: 97-104.
GONZALEZ, A. M., and HOLLNSTEINER, M. R. (1976). Filipino women as partners of men in progress and development. A survey of empirical data and statement of goals fostering male and female membership. Institute of Philippine Culture, Ateneo de Manila University, Quezon. 48 pp. + 107 pp. appendix.
GOODY, J. (ed.). (1958). The developmental cycle in domestic groups. Cambridge University Press, Cambridge. 145 pp.
_____. (1976). Production and reproduction: a comparative study of the domestic domain. Cambridge University Press, Cambridge. 157 pp.
GOODY, J., and TAMBIAH, S. J. (1973). Bridewealth and dowry in Africa and Eurasia. Cambridge University Press, Cambridge. 169 pp.
GOUGH, K. (1977). "India and Vietnam compared: family planning and everyday life." Bulletin of Concerned Asian Scholars 9(2): 42-51.
_____. (1978). "The green revolution in south India and north Vietnam." Bulletin of Concerned Asian Scholars 10(1): 13-23.
GOULD, H. A. (1974). "Cities on the north Indian plain: contrasting Lucknow and Kanpur." In South Asia: seven community profiles (ed. C. Maloney), pp. 258-293. Holt, Rinehart and Winston, New York, Toronto, London.
GRAHAM, H. M., and GRAHAM, J. K. (1959). Some changes in Thai family life: a preliminary study. Thammasat University, Bangkok. 53 pp.
GRAHAM, W. A. (1908). Kelantan, a state of the Malay Peninsula. MacLehose, Glasgow/Macmillan, London. 139 pp.
GRONAU, R. (1976). Leisure, home production and work - the theory of the allocation of time revisited. National Bureau of Economic Research, Inc., Working Paper no. 137. Stanford. 50 pp.
_____. (1977). Home production - a forgotten industry. Mimeo. 34 pp.
GUILLAUME, A. (1954). Islam. Penguin Books, Harmondsworth. 210 pp.
GULATI, I. (1976). "Unemployment among female agricultural labourers." Economic and Political Weekly 11(13): A-13 - A-39.
GUTHRIE, G. M., and JACOBS, P. J. (1966). Child rearing and personality development in the Philippines. Pennsylvania State University Press, University Park. 223 pp.
HALPERN, J. M. (1964). Economy and society of Laos. Southeast Asia Studies, Yale University Press, New Haven. 178 pp.
HANKS, L. M., Jr., and HANKS, J. R. (1963). "Thailand: equality

230

between the sexes." In Women in the New Asia (ed. B. E. Ward), pp. 424-451. UNESCO, Paris.

HART, G. P. (1977). Patterns of household labor allocation in a Javanese village. Paper to ADC Workshop in Household Studies, Singapore 1976. Cornell University, Ithaca. 41 pp.

_____. (1978). Labor allocation strategies in rural Javanese households. Ph.D. Thesis. Cornell University, Ithaca. 349 pp.

HASHIMAH ROOSE. (1963). "Changes in the position of Malay women." In Women in the new Asia (ed. B. E. Ward), pp. 287-294. UNESCO, Paris.

HAYAMI, Y., and HAFID, Anwar. (1979). "Rice harvesting and welfare in rural Java." Bulletin of Indonesian Economic Studies 15(2): 94-112.

HERING, B. B. (1976). "Law of the Republic of Indonesia no. 1 of the year 1974 on marriage." In Indonesian women (ed. B. B. Hering), pp. 91-114. Centre d'Etude du Sud-Est Asiatique et de l'Extreme Orient, Bruxelles.

HINTON, W. (1972). Fanshen: a documentary of revolution in a Chinese village. Penguin Books, Harmondsworth. 757 pp.

HIRASHIMA, S. (ed.). (1977). Hired labor in rural Asia. Institute of Developing Economies, Tokyo. 282 pp.

HIRSCHMAN, C., and AGHAJANIAN, A. (1980). "Women's labour force participation and socioeconomic development: the case of penin-sular Malaysia, 1957-1970." Journal of Southeast Asian Studies 11: 30-49.

HOANG VAN CO. (1955). La femme vietnamienne. Son Hai, Saigon. 136 pp.

HOLLNSTEINER, M. R., and BURCROFF, R. (1975). The role of women in the Philippines. Technical paper presented at International Conference on Women, Mexico City.

HOSSAIN, N. (n.d.). "Third world craftsmen and development: the Bangladesh experience." Women's Cooperative Federation, Dacca. Mimeo.

HSIA, C. T. (1963). "Residual feminity: women in Chinese Communist fiction." China Quarterly no. 13: 158-179.

HU Chi-hsi. (1974). "The sexual revolution in the Kiangsi Soviet." China Quarterly 59: 472-490.

HULL, T. H. (1976). The influence of social class on the need and effective demand for children in a Javanese village. Population Institute, Gadjah Mada University, Yogyakarta. 23 pp.

HULL, T. H., and HULL, V. J. (1976). The relation of economic class and fertility. Population Institute, Gadjah Mada University, Yogyakarta. 39 pp.

HULL, V. J. (1976a). The positive relation between economic class and family size in Java. Population Institute, Gadjah Mada University, Yogyakarta. 115 pp.

_____. (1976b). Women in Java's rural middle class: progress or regress? Paper for Fourth World Congress of Rural Sociology, Torun. 26 pp.

HUSIN ALI, S. (1975). Malay peasant society and leadership. Oxford University Press, Kuala Lumpur, London. 192 pp.

HUTT, C. (1972). Males and females. Penguin Books, Harmondsworth. 158 pp.

HYDER, Q. (1975). "Muslim women of India." In Indian women (ed. Devaki Jain), pp. 187-202. Ministry of Information and Broadcasting, New Delhi.

IHROMI, T. O. (1973). The status of women and family planning in Indonesia. Research Team on the Status of Women and Family Planning, Jakarta. 174 pp.

ILLO, J. F. I. (1977). Involvement by choice: the role of women in development. Institute of Philippine Culture, Quezon City. 207 pp.

_____. (1979). "Constraints to rural women's participation in Philippine development: a report from the field." Philippine Studies 27: 198-209.

IMTIAZ, Ahmed. (1975). "Women in politics." In Indian women (ed. Devaki Jain), pp. 301-312. Ministry of Information and Broadcasting, New Delhi.

INDIA, Government of, Planning Commission. (1978a). Draft Five Year Plan 1978-83. Controller of Publications, Delhi. 276 pp.

_____. (1978b). Study of the special programmes for girls' education. Programme Evaluation Organisation, Planning Commission, New Delhi. 181 pp.

INDIA, National Committee on the Status of Women. (1974). Towards equality. Department of Social Welfare, Ministry of Education and Social Welfare, New Delhi.

INDIAN COUNCIL OF SOCIAL SCIENCE RESEARCH (ICSSR). (1975). Status of women in India. Allied Publishers, New Delhi. 188 pp.

_____. (1978). Critical issues on the status of women. Memorandum submitted to Government.

INDIAN NATIONAL COMMISSION FOR CO-OPERATION WITH UNESCO (INCCU)/ National Institute of Public Co-operation and Child Development. (1977). Role of working mothers in early childhood education. UNESCO, Paris. 200 pp.

INFANTE, T. R. (1969). The women in early Philippines and among the cultural minorities. University of Santo Tomas, Manila. 196 pp.

INNES, E. (1885). The Chersonese with the gilding off. Bentley, London. 273 + 250 pp. Reprinted by Oxford University Press, Kuala Lumpur, 1974.

INTERNATIONAL LABOUR OFFICE (ILO). (1970). Conditions of work of women and young workers on plantations. Report to Committee on Work on Plantations, Sixth Session. ILO, Geneva. 95 pp.

_____. (1976). Employment, growth and basic needs: a one-world problem. Report of the Director-General. ILO, Geneva. 177 pp.

_____. (1977). Report on the Expert Group meeting on the identification of the basic needs of women of Asia and the Pacific and on the formulation of a programme of work. ILO, Geneva.

_____. (1978). Report of ILO Sub-Regional Seminar on status and role of women in the organized sector. ILO, Bangkok. Discontinuous pagination.

ISLAM, M. (1975). "Women at work in Bangladesh." In Women for women (ed. Women for Women Research and Study Group), pp. 93-120. University Press, Dacca.

ISLAM, S. (1977a). "Women, education and development in Bangladesh: a few reflections." In Role of women in socio-economic development in Bangladesh, pp. 121-130. Bangladesh Economic Association, Dacca.

_____. (1977b). Women's education in Bangladesh: needs and issues. Foundation for Research on Educational Planning and Development, Dacca. 145 pp.

JACOBS, S. E. (1974). Women in perspective: a guide for cross-cultural studies. University of Illinois Press, Urbana. 312 pp.

JACOBSON, D. (1977). "The women of north and central India: goddesses and wives." In Women in India (ed. D. Jacobson and S. S. Wadley), pp. 17-111. Manohar, New Delhi.

_____. (1978). Insights into individual experience: the life history of a village woman of central India. Paper to Annual Meeting of Association of Asian Studies. 16 pp.

JAHAN, Rounaq. (1975). "Women in Bangladesh." In Women for women (ed. Women for Women Research and Study Group), pp. 1-30. University Press, Dacca.

JAIN, D. (ed.). (1975). Indian women. Ministry of Information and Broadcasting, New Delhi. 312 pp.

JALAL, Khurshid. (1975). "Women in politics." In Women for women (ed. Women for Women Research and Study Group), pp. 204-214. University Press, Dacca.

JANCAR, B. W. (1976). "Women's lot in Communist societies." Problems of Communism 25(6): 68-73.

JAPAN, Headquarters for the Planning and Promoting of Policies Relating to Women. (1977). National Plan of Action. Tokyo. 15 pp.

JAPAN, Prime Minister's Secretariat. (1976a). Report of the Advisory Council to the Prime Minister on Women's Affairs. Tokyo. 45 pp.

_____. (1976b). Information relating to women. Tokyo. 57 pp.

_____. (1978). Actual status of women and present situation of women's policies. Tokyo. 350 pp. (In Japanese.)

JAPAN, Statistics Bureau, Prime Minister's Office. (1979). A report on the household economy survey. Averages in 1978. Foreign Press Center, Tokyo. 26 pp.

JAQUETTE, J. S. (1977). "Politics and institutions: introduction." Signs 3: 190-192.

JAY, R. R. (1969). Javanese villagers: social relations in rural Modjokuto. MIT Press, Cambridge, Mass. and London. 468 pp.

JAYAWARDENA, C. (1977). "Achehnese marriage customs." Indonesia 23: 157-173.

JAYME-HO, T. (1976). Time allocation, home production and labor force participation of married women: an explanatory survey. Discussion Paper 76-78. Institute of Economic Development and Research, University of the Philippines, Quezon City. 39 pp.

JOCANO, F. L. (1969). Growing up in a Philippine barrio. Holt, Rinehart and Winston, New York, Toronto, London. 121 pp.

JOHNSON, E. (1975). "Women and childbearing in Kwan Mun Hau village: a study of social change." In Women in Chinese society (ed. M. Wolf and R. Witke), pp. 215-241. Stanford University Press, Stanford.

JOHNSON, E. H. (1967). "Status changes in hamlet structure accompanying modernization." In Aspects of social change in modern

Japan (ed. R. P. Dore), pp. 153-183. Princeton University Press, New Jersey.

JONES, H. J. (1976). "Japanese women and party politics." Pacific Affairs 49: 213-234.

_____. (1977). "Japanese women and the dual-track employment system." Pacific Affairs 49: 589-606.

JONES, R. L., and JONES, S. K. (1976). The Himalayan woman. Mayfield, Palo Alto. 155 pp.

JOY, J. L., and EVERITT, E. (eds.). (1976). The Kosi Symposium: the rural problem in north-east Bihar: analysis, policy and planning in the Kosi area. Institute of Development Studies, University of Sussex. 277 pp.

KABIR, K., ABED, A., and CHEN, M. (1976). Rural women in Bangladesh: exploding some myths. Ford Foundation, Dacca, report no. 42. 17 + 23 pp.

KAHN, J. S. (1977). Social structure and agricultural productivity in Negri Sembilan. Social Science Research Council, London. 45 pp.

KAKAR, S. (1978). The inner world: a psycho-analytic study of childhood and society in India. Oxford University Press, Delhi, Oxford, New York. 213 pp.

KANNANGARA, I. (1966). "Women's employment in Ceylon." International Labour Review 93: 117-126.

KAPADIA, K. M. (1962). "Caste in transition." Sociological Bulletin 12: 73-90.

_____. (1966). Marriage and family in India. 3rd edition. Oxford University Press, Delhi. 395 pp.

KAPUR, P. (1972). Marriage and the working woman in India. Vikas, Delhi. 415 pp.

_____. (1973). Love, marriage and sex. Vikas, Delhi. 302 pp.

_____. (1974). The changing status of the working woman in India. Vikas, Delhi. 178 pp.

KATZ, J. S., and KATZ, R. S. (1975). "The new Indonesian marriage law: a mirror of Indonesia's political, cultural and legal systems." American Journal of Comparative Law 23: 653-681.

KATZENSTEIN, M. F. (1978). "Towards equality? Cause and consequence of the political prominence of women in India." Asian Survey 78: 473-486.

KENDALL, L. (1979). "Korean ancestors: from the woman's side." Paper to Annual Meeting of Association for Asian Studies Panel on Korean Women: View from the Inner Room, in Los Angeles.

KHAN, Seemin Anwar, and BILQUEES, Faiz. (1976). The environment, attitudes and activities of rural women: a case study of Jhok Sayal. Research Report no. 98, Pakistan Institute of Development Economics, Islamabad. 69 pp.

KHARE, R. S. (1976). The Hindu hearth and home. Vikas, Delhi. 315 pp.

KHATUN, S. (1977). "Equal educational opportunity for women: a myth." In Role of women in socio-economic development in Bangladesh, pp. 132-145. Bangladesh Economic Association, Dacca.

KHATUN, S., and BEGUM, K. (1975). "Life of urban middle class widows." In Women for women (ed. Women for Women Research and Study Group), pp. 180-203. University Press, Dacca.

234

KHATUN, S., and RANI, Gita. (1977). Bari-based post harvest operations and livestock care: some observations and case studies.
Ford Foundation, Dacca. 24 pp.
KIM Joon Kyu. (1978). "Republic of Korea." In Rural development
strategies in selected member countries, pp. 12-20. Asian Productivity Organization, Tokyo.
KIM Mo-Im. (1974). "Age at marriage and fertility of women in three
selected areas in Korea." In Population and family planning in
the Republic of Korea, pp. 451-461. Korean Institute of Family
Planning, Seoul.
KIM Young-chung. (1977). "Women's studies." The Woman 13(2): 42-
48.
KLEINMAN, A. et al (eds.). (1975). Medicine in Chinese cultures:
comparative studies of health care in Chinese and other societies.
Fogarty International Center, N.I.H., U.S. Government Printing
Office, Washington. 803 pp.
KNAPP, R. (1971). "Marketing and social patterns in rural Taiwan."
Annals of Association of American Geographers 61: 131-155.
KOENTJARANINGRAT, R. M. (1960). "The Javanese of south central
Java." In Social structure in southeast Asia (ed. G. P. Murdock),
pp. 88-115. Quadrangle Books, Chicago.
KOH Hesung-chun. (1978). Korean women: conflict and change: an
approach to development planning. Paper to annual meeting of
Association for Asian Studies. 26 pp.
KOLENDA, P. (1967). "Regional differences in Indian family struc-
ture." In Regions and regionalism in South Asian studies (ed.
R. I. Crane), pp. 147-226. Duke University, Durham.
KOMALIG, Aske Theo. (1975). The relationship of socio-economic
factors with fertility and attitudes towards family planning in
North Sulawesi. SEAPRAP, Singapore. 45 pp.
KOMANYI, M. I. (1973). The real and ideal participation in
decision-making of Iban women: a study of a longhouse community
in Sarawak, East Malaysia. Ph.D. Thesis, New York University.
University Microfilms, Ann Arbor. 143 pp.
KONG Chung-ja and CHA Jae-ho. (1974). "Boy preference in Korea: a
review of empirical studies." In Population and Family Planning
in the Republic of Korea, pp. 302-329. Korean Institute of Family
Planning, Seoul.
de KONINCK, R. (1979). "The integration of the peasantry: examples
from Malaysia and Indonesia." Pacific Affairs 52: 265-293.
KRESSEL, G. M. (1977). "Bride-price reconsidered." Current Anthropology 18: 441-450.
KRIPPENDORFF, S. (1977). Women's education in Bangladesh: needs
and issues: content analysis. Foundation for Research on Educational Planning and Development, Dacca. 58 pp.
KUCHIBA, M. (1978). "Socio-economic changes in a Malay padi-growing
community (Padang Lalang) in Kedah." South East Asian Studies 16:
198-215.
LANCASTER, C. S. (1976). "Women, horticulture and society in sub-
Saharan Africa." American Anthropologist 78: 539-564.
_____. (1977). "Cultivation intensiveness, population and
women's status." American Anthropologist 79: 910-911.
LANG, O. (1968). Chinese family and society. Archon, Hamden, Conn.

395 pp. Reprint of 1946 edition, Yale University Press.
LAPUZ, L. V. (1973). A study of psychopathology. University of
Philippines Press, Quezon. 313 pp.
_____. (1977). Filipino marriages in crisis. New Day, Quezon.
136 pp.
LEACH, E. R. (1953). "Bridewealth and the stability of marriage."
Man 53: 179-180.
_____. (1960). "The Sinhalese of the Dry Zone of Sri Lanka."
In Social structure in southeast Asia (ed. G. P. Murdock), pp.
116-126. Quadrangle, Chicago.
_____. (1961). Pul Eliya: a village in Ceylon. Cambridge
University Press, London. 344 pp.
LEACOCK, E. (1978). "Women's status in egalitarian society:
implications for a social evolution." Current Anthropology 19:
247-255.
LEBAR, F. M. (ed.). (1972). Ethnic groups of insular southeast
Asia. 1. Indonesia, Andaman Islands and Madagascar. HRAF Press,
New Haven. 226 pp.
_____. (1975). Ethnic groups of insular southeast Asia. 2.
Philippines and Formosa. HRAF Press, New Haven. 167 pp.
LEBAR, F. M., HICKEY, G. C., and MUSGRAVE, J. K. (1964). Ethnic
groups of mainland southeast Asia. HRAF Press, New Haven. 288 pp.
LEBRA, Takie Sugiyama. (1976). "Sex equality for Japanese women."
Japan Interpreter 10: 284-295.
_____. (1976). Japanese Patterns of Behavior. University of
Hawaii Press, Honolulu. 295 pp.
LEDESMA, A. J. (1977). "The Sumagaysay family: a case study of
landless rural workers." Land Tenure Center Newsletter 55: 14-
30.
LEE Byung-tae. (1977). "Discrimination between men and women in
labor and means for correction." The Woman 13(2): 23-28.
LEE Hyo-chai and CHO Hyoung. (1976). Fertility and women's labour
force participation in Korea. Report to Interdisciplinary Communications Program, Smithsonian Institution. Occasional Monograph
Series no. 7. 39 pp.
LEE Hyo-chai, and KIM Joo-sook. (1976). The status of Korean women
today. Women's Resources Development Research Institute, Ehwa
Womens University, Seoul. 16 pp.
_____. (1977). (Same title as above.) In Virtues in conflict
(ed. S. Mattielli), pp. 147-155. Royal Asiatic Society, Korea
Branch, Seoul.
LEE Myong-sop. (1977). "Population policy and revision of family
law." The Woman 13(1):29-32.
LEE, S. J. (1974). "Korea." In Social and psychological aspects of
fertility in Asia (ed. H. P. David and S. J. Lee), pp. 8-15.
Transnational Family Research Institute, Washington.
LEONARD, K. I., and LEONARD, J. G. (1981). "Social reform and
women's participation in political culture: Andhra and Madras."
In Women and political participation in South Asia (ed. G.
Minault). South Asia, U.S.A., and Manohar, India.
LEVY, Banyen Phimmasone. (1963). "Yesterday and today in Laos: a
girl's autobiographical notes." In Women in the new Asia (ed.
B. E. Ward), pp. 244-265. UNESCO, Paris.

236

LEWIS, O. (1951). Life in a Mexican village: Tepoztlán restudied. University of Illinois Press, Urbana. 512 pp.
LICUANAN, P. B., and GONZALEZ, A. M. (1976). Filipino women in development. Draft of final report. Institute of Philippine Culture, Ateneo de Manila University, Quezon. Typescript.
LIPPITT, Noriko Mizuta. (1978). "Literature, ideology and women's happiness: the autobiographical novels of Miyamoto Yuriko." Bulletin of Concerned Asian Scholars 10(2): 2-9.
LIU, W. T. (1971). "Fertility patterns in Cebu." In Acculturation in the Philippines (ed. P. G. Gowing and W. H. Scott), pp. 167-205. New Day, Quezon City.
LONDON, H., and LONDON, I. D. (1979). Hunger in China: the failure of a system? Paper to Cornell Workshop on Agricultural and Rural Development in the P.R.C., Cornell University, Ithaca. 24 pp.
LUECHAI Chulasai. (1975). The roles of husbands and fathers in family planning in Chiang Mai. SEAPRAP, Singapore. 20 pp.
McCARTHY, F. E., SABBAH, S., and AKHTER, R. (1978a). Rural women workers in Bangladesh. Women's Section, Planning and Development Division, Ministry of Agriculture and Forests, Dacca. 57 pp.
_____. (1978b). Bibliography and selected references. Rural women in Bangladesh. Women's Section, Planning and Development Division, Ministry of Agriculture and Forests, Dacca. 44 pp.
MACCOBY, E., and JACKLIN, C. (1974). The psychology of sex differences. Stanford University Press, Stanford. 634 pp.
MacFARQUHAR, E. (1977). "Making China work." The Economist, December 31: 23-32.
McHALE, J., and McHALE, M. C. (1978). Basic human needs: a framework for action. Transaction Books, New Brunswick.
MADIGAN, F. C. (ed.). (1967). Human factors in Philippine rural development. Xavier University, Cagayan de Oro. 318 pp.
MAEDA, N. (1978). "The Malay family as a social circle." South East Asian Studies 16: 216-248.
MAKALI. (1974). Upah buruh tani pada tanaman padi dikaitkan dengan kenaikan produksi dan harga padi selama lima tahun di dua puluh desa sampel Intensifikasi Padi Sawah di Jawa (Relations between wages in rice agriculture, increased yields and rice prices over five years in twenty Javanese villages in the Rice Intensification Study Sample). Survey Agro Ekonomi, Bogor.
MALAYSIA, Federation of Family Planning Associations (FFPA). (1976). Women today. Federation of Family Planning Associations, Kuala Lumpur. 47 pp.
MALAYSIA, National Family Planning Board. (1966-1967). Annual Report.
_____. (1970). Annual Report. 62 pp.
_____. (1974). (1967-1970). Annual statistical report. Kuala Lumpur. 352 pp.
MALAYSIA, Pusat Pembinaan Sumber daya Manusia. (1977). Peserta Seminar Wanita-Se-Jawa. Kuala Lumpur. Discontinuous pagination.
MALIK, Ashraf. (1977). "Notes on the role of rural Pakistani women in farming in the Northwest Frontier Province." Land Tenure Center Newsletter 55: 10-13.
MANDELBAUM, D. G. (1972). Society in India. I. Continuity and change. II. Change and continuity. University of California

237

Press, Berkeley, Los Angeles, London. 665 pp.
MANDERSON, L. (1977a). "The shaping of the Kaum Ibu (Women's section) of the United Malays National Organization." Signs 3: 210-228.
_____. (1977b). "Malay women and development in peninsular Malaysia." Kabar Sekarang 2: 61-84.
_____. (1977c). Women in politics: change or continuum? The case of Malay women in peninsular Malaysia. Paper to 7th Conference of International Association of Historians of Asia, Bangkok. 41 pp.
_____. (1978a). "The development and direction of female education in peninsular Malaysia." Journal of the Malayan Branch of the Royal Asiatic Society 51: 100-122.
_____. (1978b). "Women and work: continuities of the past and present." Asia Teachers Bulletin, June: 6-24.
_____. (1980). Women, politics and change: the development of the Pergerakan Kaum Ibu, UMNO Malaysia, 1945-1972. Oxford University Press, Kuala Lumpur, London, New York, Melbourne. 260 pp.
MANGAHAS, Mahar, and JAYME-HO, T. (1976). Income and labor force participation rates of women in the Philippines. Discussion Paper no. 76-3. Institute of Economic Development and Research, University of Philippines, Quezon City. 157 pp.
MARTIN, R. (1975). "The socialization of children in China and on Taiwan: an analysis of elementary school textbooks." China Quarterly 62: 242-262.
MARTIUS von HARDER, G. (1975). "Women's role in rice-processing." In Women for women (ed. Women for Women Research and Study Group), pp. 66-80. University Press, Dacca.
_____. (1977). Frauen im Ländlichen Bangladesh. Eine empirische Studie in vier Dörfern im Comilla Distrikt. Verlag der ssip-Schriften Breitenbach, Saarbrücken.
MATHPAL, Y. (1978). Prehistoric rock paintings of Bhimbetka, central India. Ph.D. Thesis. University of Poona. 507 pp.
MATHUR, P. B. (1974). Status of women and Hindu divorce. Michigan State University, East Lansing. Mimeo.
MATTIELLI, S. (ed.). (1977). Virtues in conflict: tradition and the Korean woman today. Royal Asiatic Society, Korea Branch, Seoul. 214 pp.
MAZUMDAR, V. (1977). "Reflections on the Conference on Women and Development. IV." Signs 3: 323-325.
MEAD, M. (1976). "A comment on the role of women in agriculture." In Women and world development (ed. I. Tinker and M. B. Bramsen), pp. 9-11. Overseas Development Council, Washington.
MEHRA, R. (1975). The divorced Hindu woman. Vikas, Delhi. 173 pp.
MEHTA, U. H., and BILLIMORIA, R. N. (1977). "Political status of women in India." ICSSR Research Abstracts Quarterly 6(3 and 4): 100-105.
MEIJER, M. J. (1972). Marriage law and policy in the Chinese People's Republic. Hongkong University Press/Oxford University Press, London. 369 pp.
MENDEZ, P. P., and JOCANO, F. L. (1974). The Filipino family in its rural and urban orientation. Two case studies. Centro Escolar University Research and Development Center, Manila. 394 pp.

238

MI MI KHAING. (1963). "Burma: balance and harmony." In Women in
the new Asia (ed. B. E. Ward), pp. 104-137. UNESCO, Paris.
_____. (1976). Women in Burmese economic life. Paper to
annual meeting of Association for Asian Studies. 8 pp.
MINTURN, L. (1976). The Rajputs restudied. Paper to annual meeting
of Association for Asian Studies. 5 pp.
MINTURN, L., and HITCHCOCK, J. T. (1966). The Rajputs of Khalapur,
India. Wiley, New York, London, Sydney. 158 pp.
MODY, S., and MHATRA, S. (1975). "Slum women of Bombay." In Indian
women (ed. Devaki Jain), pp. 237-250. Ministry of Information and
Broadcasting, New Delhi.
MONTEIL, C., and HOLLNSTEINER, M. R. (1976). The Filipino woman:
her role and status in Philippine society. Final report. Ateneo
de Manila University, Quezon City. 52 pp.
MOSLEY, W. H. (1979). "Health, nutrition and mortality in Bangla-
desh." In Research in human and capital development (ed. I.
Sirageldin), pp. 77-94. JAI Press, Inc., Greenwich, Connecticut.
MOSQUEDA, R. P. (1977). Marriage and its dissolution. Quis
Publishing, Manila. 682 pp.
MOUGNE, C. (1978). "An ethnography of reproduction. Changing
patterns of fertility in a northern Thai village." In Nature and
man in southeast Asia (ed. F. A. Stott), pp. 68-106. London
University Press.
MUECKE, M. A. (1974). A cultural view of Thai conjugal family
relationships. Paper to annual meeting of American Anthropologi-
cal Association, Mexico. Mimeo.
MUKHERJEE, B. N. (1974). "Status of married women in Haryana, Tamil
Nadu and Meghalaya." Social Change 4: 1.
MURATA, Y. (1978). "Education and rural development: a comparative
study of Thai and Malay villages." South East Asian Studies 16:
274-296.
MURDOCK, G. P. (1949). Social structure. Macmillan, New York.
377 pp.
MURRAY, F., Jr. (1971). Local groups and kin groups in Tagalog rice
farmers' barrio. Ph.D. Thesis, University of Pittsburgh. University Microfilms, Ann Arbor. 290 pp.
MYRDAL, J., and KESSLE, G. (1973). China: the revolution continued. Penguin Books, Harmondsworth. 155 pp.
NAG, M. (1972). "Economic value of children in agricultural societies: evaluation of existing knowledge and an anthropological
approach." In The satisfactions and costs of children: theories,
concepts, methods (ed. J. T. Fawcett), pp. 58-94. East-West
Center, Honolulu.
NAG, M., WHITE, B. N. F., and CREIGHTON PEET, R. (1978). "An
anthropological approach to the study of the economic value of
children in Java and Nepal." Current Anthropology 19: 293-301.
NAKAGAWA, Y. (1979). "Japan, the welfare super-power." Journal of
Japanese Studies 5: 5-51.
NAKANE, C. (1967). Kinship and economic organization in rural
Japan. Athlone Press, London/Humanities Press, New York. 203 pp.
NANDA, B. R. (ed.). (1976). Indian women: from purdah to modern-
ity. Vikas, New Delhi. 187 pp.
NANDI, S. B. (1977). "Status of women in polyandrous society." Man

in India 57: 137-151.
NANTANEE, J., CHIRA, S., LUKHANA, S., NATCHAI, T., CHALIT, T., DIREK,
T., and WOODBURY, C. (1977). Status of Thai women in two rural
areas. National Council of Women of Thailand, Bangkok. 34 pp.
NARENDRAN, V. M. (1975). The women of Perupuk: an economic study.
Ph.D. Thesis. Universiti Sains, Penang. Microfilm.
NASH, M. (1965). The golden road to modernity: village Life in
contemporary Burma. Wiley, New York, London, Sydney. 333 pp.
_____. (1974). Peasant citizens: politics, religion and
modernization in Kelantan, Malaysia. Ohio University Center for
International Studies, Athens, Ohio. 153 pp.
NEEDHAM, R. (1973). "Rethinking kinship and marriage." American
Anthropologist 75: 1783-1784.
NEUMANN, C. G. (1969). "Nutritional and anthropometric profile of
young rural Punjabi children." Indian J. Medical Research 57:
1122-1149.
NIBHON, Debavalya. (1977). Female employment and fertility: cross-
sectional and longitudinal relationships from a national sample of
married women. Institute of Population Studies, Chulalongkorn
University, Paper no. 24. 88 pp.
NOONE, R. (1972). Rape of the dream people. Hutchinson, London.
211 pp.
NOOR, Y. R. (1976). "Indonesian women's participation in development." In Indonesian women (ed. B. B. Hering), pp. 156-163.
Centre d'Etude du Sud-Est Asiatique et l'Extreme Orient, Bruxelles.
NORHALIM bin Hj. Ibrahim. (1977). "Social change in Rembau."
Journal Malayan Branch Royal Asiatic Society 50: 136-149.
NYDEGGER, W. F., and NYDEGGER, C. (1966). Tarong: an Illocos
barrio in the Philippines. Wiley, New York, London, Sydney.
180 pp.
O'BARR, J. (1976). Third world women: factors in their changing
status. Occasional Paper no. 2, Center for International Studies,
Duke University, Durham. 94 pp.
O'HARA, A. R. (1971). The position of women in early China. Mei
Ya, Taipei. 302 pp.
OLIN, U. (1976). "A case for women as co-managers: the family as a
general model of human social organization." In Women and world
development (ed. I. Tinker and M. B. Bramsen), pp. 105-128. Over-
seas Development Council, Washington.
OMRAN, A. R., and STANDLEY, C. C. (eds.). (1976). Family formation
patterns and health. An international collaborative study in
India, Iran, Lebanon, Philippines and Turkey. World Health Organ-
ization, Geneva. 564 pp.
ORLEANS, L. A. (1978). "China's population growth: another
perspective." Current Scene 16(2 and 3): 1-24.
PADAN-EISENSTARK, D. (1975). "The uneven pace of equality." Kidma
7: 24-29.
PALMER, I. (1978). The integration of women in agrarian reform and
rural development in Asia and the Far East. Paper to World
Conference on Agrarian Reform and Rural Development, FAO, Rome.
70 pp.
PALMORE, J. A., HIRSCH, P. M., and ARIFFIN bin MARZK. (1971).
"Interpersonal communication and the diffusion of family planning

PAPANEK, H. (1971). "Purdah in Pakistan: seclusion and modern occupations for women." Journal of Marriage and the Family 33: 517-530.

_____. (1973). "Purdah: separate worlds and symbolic shelter." Comparative Studies in Society and History 15: 289-325.

_____. (1976). "Women in cities: problems and perspectives." In Women and world development (ed. I. Tinker and M. B. Bramsen), pp. 54-69. Overseas Development Council, Washington.

_____. (1977). "Development planning for women." Signs 3: 14-21.

PAPANEK, H., IHROMI, T. O., and RAHARDJO, Y. (1974). Changes in the status of women and their significance in the progress of social change: Indonesian case studies. Paper to 6th International Conference on Asian history. 41 pp.

PARISH, W. L., Jr. (1975). "Socialism and the Chinese peasant family." Journal of Asian Studies 34: 613-630.

PARISH, W. L., Jr., and WHYTE, M. K. (1978). Village and family in contemporary China. University of Chicago Press, Chicago and London. 419 pp.

PARKER, S., and PARKER, H. (1979). "The myth of male superiority: rise and demise." American Anthropologist 81: 289-309.

PARTHASARATHY, G. (1977). "Employment, wage and poverty of hired labor within Indian agriculture." In Hired labor in rural Asia (ed. S. Hirashima), pp. 32-47. Institute of Developing Economies, Tokyo.

PASTERNAK, B. (1972). Kinship and community in two Chinese villages. Stanford University Press, Stanford. 174 pp.

PASTNER, C. M. (1974). "Accommodations to purdah: the female perspective." Journal of Marriage and the Family 36: 408-414.

PELZEL, J. C. (1970). "Japanese kinship: a comparison." In Family and kinship in Chinese society (ed. M. Freedman), pp. 227-248. Stanford University Press, Stanford.

PENBROOK, J. F. (1976). "The role of women in traditional Bali." In Indonesian women (ed. B. B. Hering), pp. 67-79. Centre d'Etude du Sud-Est Asiatique et l'Extreme Orient, Brussels.

PHARR, S. J. (1981). Political women in Japan. University of California Press, Berkeley and Los Angeles. 275 pp.

PHILIPPINES, Department of Labour, Bureau of Women and Minors. (1974). Status of working women in the Philippines. Bureau of Women and Minors, Manila.

_____. (1976). Strategy for change: seminar on women workers. Sponsored by Department of Labour, Personnel Management Association, Philippines Association of Secretaries, Philippines Association of Trade Union Women and Manila Community Services, Manila. 110 pp.

PHILIPPINES, National Committee on Role of Filipino Women. (1976). Annual Report. Manila. 44 pp.

PHILLIPS, H. P. (1966). Thai peasant personality. University of California Press, Berkeley and Los Angeles. 231 pp.

PIKER, S. (1969). "'Loose structure' and the analysis of Thai social organization." In Loosely structured social systems: Thailand in comparative perspective (ed. H. D. Evers), pp. 61-76.

_____. (1975). "The post-peasant village in central plain Thai society." In Change and persistence in Thai society (ed. G. W. Skinner and A. T. Kirsch), pp. 298-323. Cornell University Press, Ithaca and London.

POFFENBERGER, T. et al. (1975). Fertility and family life in an Indian village. University of Michigan Papers on South and South-east Asia no. 10. Ann Arbor. 114 pp.

POFFENBERGER, T., and SEBALY, K. (n.d.). The socialization of family size values: youth and family planning in an Indian village. University of Michigan Papers on South and Southeast Asia no. 12. Ann Arbor. 156 pp.

POPKIN, B. (1978). "Economic determinants of breast feeding behaviour: the case of rural households in Laguna, Philippines." In Nutrition and reproduction (ed. H. Mosley), pp. 461-497. Plenum Press, New York.

POPKIN, B., and HART, G. P. (1975). A note on the interdependence between economics and welfare factors in the rural Filipino house-holds. Discussion Paper no. 75-5. University of the Philippines School of Economics. Quezon City. 27 pp.

POPKIN, B., and SOLON, F. (1976). Income, time, the working mother and child nutriture. Discussion Paper no. 75-9. Institute of Economic Development and Research, University of Philippines, Quezon. Also published in Environmental Child Health, August, pp. 156-166.

POTTER, J. M. (1969). Capitalism and the Chinese peasant: social and economic change in a Hong Kong village. University of California Press, Berkeley and Los Angeles. 215 pp.

_____. (1976). Thai peasant social structure. University of Chicago Press, Chicago and London. 249 pp.

POTTER, S. H. (1977). Family life in a northern Thai village: a study in the structural significance of women. University of California Press, Berkeley and Los Angeles. 137 pp.

PROTEIN ADVISORY GROUP OF THE UNITED NATIONS. (1977). Women in food production, food handling and nutrition. United Nations, New York. Discontinuous pagination.

PRUITT, I. (1945). A daughter of Han. Yale University Press, New Haven. 249 pp.

PURCAL, J. T. (1971). Rice economy: a case study of four villages in West Malaysia. University of Malaya Press, Kuala Lumpur. 248 pp.

PURVIS, B. M. (1976). Extension programmes for rural women: a model for southeast Asia. FAO Home Economics and Social Programmes Services. FAO, Rome. 20 pp.

QUINN, N. (1977). "Anthropological studies in women's status." In Annual Review of Anthropology 6: 181-225.

RANA, Kamal. (1978). "Status and role of women in the organized sector: Nepal." In ILO Sub-regional Seminar on Status and Role of Women in the Organized Sector. 33 pp. ILO, Bangkok. Discontinuous pagination.

RAO, Kamala G. (1978). "Status of women: factors affecting status of women in India. In ILO Sub-regional Seminar on Status and Role of Women in the Organized Sector. 60 pp. ILO, Bangkok.

RASHID, R. (1977). "Women's leadership and integrated rural

development in Pakistan." <u>Integrated Rural Development Review</u> 2: 53-57.

REPETTO, R. (1973). "Son preference and fertility behaviour in developing countries." <u>Studies in Family Planning</u> 3: 70-76.

RHI Bhou-yong. (1977). "Psychological problems among Korean women." In <u>Virtues in Conflict</u> (ed. S. Mattielli), pp. 129-146. Royal Asiatic Society, Korea Branch, Seoul.

RIHANI, M. (1978). <u>Development as if women mattered: an annotated bibliography with a third world focus</u>. New Transcentury Foundation, Washington. 137 pp.

ROBINSON, W. C., SOMBOONSUB, N., and SUWANNAPIROM, S. (1975). "Changing Thai attitudes toward fertility and family size." <u>Southeast Asian Journal Social Science</u> 4: 19-28.

RODGERS, G. B. (1976). "The conceptualization of poverty in the Kosi area." In <u>The Kosi Symposium</u> (ed. J. L. Joy and E. Everitt), pp. 5-42. Institute of Development Studies, University of Sussex.

ROGERS, M. L. (1977). <u>Sungai Raya: a sociopolitical study of a rural Malay community</u>. Center for South and Southeast Asia Studies Research Monograph no. 15. University of California, Berkeley. 108 pp.

ROGERS, S. C. (1978). "Woman's place: a critical review of anthropological theory." <u>Comparative Studies in Society and History</u> 20: 123-162.

ROSALDO, M. Z. (1974). "Woman, culture and society: a theoretical overview." In <u>Woman, culture and society</u> (ed. M. Z. Rosaldo and L. Lamphere), pp. 17-42. Stanford University Press, Stanford.

ROSALDO, M. Z., and LAMPHERE, L. (eds.). (1974). <u>Woman, culture and society</u>. Stanford University Press, Stanford. 352 pp.

ROY, M. (1975). <u>Bangali women</u>. University of Chicago Press, Chicago and London. 205 pp.

RUDRA, A. (1975). "Cultural and religious influences." In <u>Indian women</u> (ed. Devaki Jain), pp. 37-49. Ministry of Information and Broadcasting, New Delhi.

SACHCHIDANANDA. (1978). "Social structure, status and mobility patterns: the case of tribal women." <u>Man in India</u> 58: 1-12.

SACKS, K. (1976). "State bias and women's status." <u>American Anthropologist</u> 78: 565-569.

SAFA, H. I. (1977). "Changing modes of production: introduction." <u>Signs</u> 3: 22-24.

SAGHIR AHMAD. (1974). "A village in Pakistani Panjab: Jalpana." In <u>South Asia: seven community profiles</u> (ed. C. Maloney), pp. 131-172. Holt, Rinehart and Winston, New York, Toronto, London.

SAJOGYO, P. (1974). Modernization without development in rural Java. Paper to Study Seminar on Changes in Agrarian Structures (FAO), Bogor.

SAJOGYO, P., HASTUTI, E. L., WIGNA, W., SURKATI, S., WHITE, B., and SURYANATA, K. (1980). <u>The role of women in different perspectives</u>. Center for Rural Sociological Research, Bogor Agricultural University. Discontinuous pagination.

SALAFF, J. W. (1973). "The emerging conjugal relationship in the People's Republic of China." <u>Journal of Marriage and the Family</u> 35: 705-717.

SANDAY, P. A. (1973). "Toward a theory of the status of women."

American Anthropologist 75: 1683-1700.

——————. (1974). "Female status in the public domain." In _Woman, culture and society_ (ed. M. Z. Rosaldo and L. Lamphere), pp. 189-206. Stanford University Press, Stanford.

SARKAR, L. (1977). "Law and the status of women in India." In _Law and the status of women_, pp. 95-121. U.N. Centre for Social Development and Humanitarian Affairs, New York.

SARMA, J. (1963). "Three generations in my Calcutta family." In _Women in the new Asia_ (ed. B. E. Ward), pp. 216-228. UNESCO, Paris.

SATTAR, M. E. (1975). "Village women's work." In _Women for women_ (ed. Women for Women Research and Study Group), pp. 33-65. University Press, Dacca.

——————. (1978). "Status and role of women in the organized sector in Bangladesh." In _ILO Sub-regional Seminar on Status and Role of Women in the Organized Sector_. 26 pp. ILO, Bangkok.

SCHIEFFELIN, O. (ed.). (1967). _Muslim attitudes towards family planning_. Population Council, New York. 145 pp.

SCHNEIDER, D. M. (1953). "A note on bridewealth and the stability of marriage." _Man_ 53: 55-57.

SCHWARTZ, T. (ed.). (1976). _Socialization as cultural communication. Development of a theme in the work of Margaret Mead_. University of California Press, Berkeley and Los Angeles. 251 pp.

SEBO, K. A. (1975). A comparison of the study of women in India and Pakistan. Paper for annual meeting of Association for Asian Studies. 30 pp.

SEHGAL, J. M. (1978). "Role and status of women in the organized sector. ILO activities." In _ILO Sub-regional Seminar on Status and Role of Women in the Organized Sector_. ILO, Bangkok. Discontinuous pagination.

SEN, K. M. (1961). _Hinduism_. Penguin Books, Harmondsworth. 160 pp.

SHAH, N. M. (1978). "Female participation in selected occupations within the organized sector: Pakistan." In _ILO Sub-regional Seminar on Status and Role of Women in the Organized Sector_. 30 pp. ILO, Bangkok.

SHARMA, U. M. (1978). "Women and their affines: the veil as a symbol of separation." _Man_ 13: 218-233.

SHEPHER, J. (1971). _Self-imposed incest avoidance and exogamy in second generation kibbutz adults_. Ann Arbor Xerox Monograph series nos. 72-871.

SHIH, H. Y. (1974). "The archaeology of the Yangtze delta." _Journal of the Hong Kong Archaeological Society_ 5: 82-84.

SIDEL, R. (1972). _Women and child care in China_. Hill and Wang, New York/Sheldon Press, London (1974). 207 pp.

SINGARIMBUN, M. (1974). "Indonesia." In _Social and psychological aspects of fertility in Asia_ (ed. H. P. David and S. J. Lee), pp. 50-55. Transnational Family Research Institute, Washington.

SINGARIMBUN, M., and MANNING, C. (1974). "Marriage and divorce in Mojolama." _Indonesia_ 17: 67-82.

SIRIWARDENA, B. S. (1963). "The life of Ceylon women." In _Women in the new Asia_ (ed. B. E. Ward), pp. 150-172. UNESCO, Paris.

SKINNER, G. W. (1964/1965). "Marketing and social structure in rural China." _Journal of Asian Studies_ 24: 3-43 and 195-228.

‿ _____. (1971). "Chinese peasants and the closed community: an open and shut case." Comparative Studies in Society and History 13: 270-281.

‿ SMITH, A. H. (1899, reprinted 1970). Village life in China. Little, Brown and Co., Boston. 278 pp.

SMITH, J., and GASCON, F. (1979). "The effect of the new rice technology on family labor utilization in Laguna." IRRI Saturday Seminar, Aug. 11, 1979. Department Paper no. 79-10. International Rice Research Institute, Manila. 12 pp. + 16 tables + 7 figures.

SOEWONDO, N. (1977). "Law and the status of women in Indonesia." In Law and the status of women, pp. 123-140. U.N. Centre for Social Development and Humanitarian Affairs, New York.

SOON Young S. Yoon. (1977a). "The role of Korean women in national development." In Virtues in conflict (ed. S. Mattielli), pp. 157-167. Royal Asiatic Society, Korea Branch, Seoul.

_____. (1977b). "Occupation, male housekeeper: male-female roles on Cheju island." In Virtues in conflict (ed. S. Mattielli), pp. 191-207. Royal Asiatic Society, Korea Branch, Seoul.

de SOUZA, A. (ed.). (1975). Women in contemporary India. Manohar, Delhi. 264 pp.

SPIRO, M. E. (1975). "Marriage payments: a paradigm from the Burmese perspective." J. Anthropological Research 31: 89-115.

_____. (1977). Kinship and marriage in Burma. University of California Press, Berkeley and Los Angeles. 313 pp.

SRINIVAS, M. N. (1968). Social change in modern India. University of California Press, Berkeley and Los Angeles. 194 pp.

_____. (1976). The remembered village. Oxford University Press, Delhi. 356 pp.

_____. (1977). "The changing position of Indian women." Man 12: 221-238.

STEWARD, V. H. (1968). "Causal factors and processes in the evolution of pre-farming societies." In Man the hunter (ed. R. B. Lee and I. deVore), pp. 321-334. Aldine, Chicago.

STOKES, O. (1975). "Women of rural Bihar." In Indian women (ed. Devaki Jain), pp. 215-228. Ministry of Information and Broadcasting, New Delhi.

STOLER, A. (1975). "Some socio-economic aspects of rice harvesting in a Javanese village." Masyarahat Indonesia 2(1): 51-87.

_____. (1976). Class structure and female autonomy in rural Java. Paper to Women and Development Conference, Wellesley College, Wellesley, Mass. 43 pp.

_____. (1977). "Class structure and female autonomy in rural Java." Signs 3: 74-89.

_____. (1978). "Garden use and household economy in rural Java." Bulletin of Indonesian Economic Studies 14(2): 85-101.

STRANGE, H. (1971). The weavers of Rusila: working women in a Malay village. Ph.D. Thesis, New York University. University of Michigan Microfilms, Ann Arbor. 501 pp.

_____. (1976a). "Continuity and change: patterns of mate selection and marriage ritual in a Malay village." Journal of Marriage and the Family 38: 561-571.

_____. (1976b). Education and employment patterns of rural
Malay women, 1965-75. Paper to annual meeting of Association for
Asian Studies. 25 pp.

STRATHERN, M. (1978). Review article. RAIN, October, pp. 4-7.

STYCOS, J. M., and WELLER, R. H. (1967). "Female working roles and
fertility." Demography 4: 210-217.

SWANN, N. L. (1932). Pan Chao: foremost woman scholar of China.
Century, New York, London. 179 pp.

SWIFT, M. (1963). "Men and women in Malay society." In Women in
the new Asia (ed. B. E. Ward), pp. 268-286. UNESCO, Paris.

TAEUBER, I. (1970a). "Family, migration and industrialization in
Japan." In Readings in the sociology of migration (ed. C.
Jansen), pp. 367-383. Pergamon, Oxford.

_____. (1970b). "The families of Chinese farmers." In Family
and kinship in Chinese society (ed. M. Freedman), pp. 63-85.
Stanford University Press, Stanford.

TAKAHASHI, A. (1977). "Rural labor and agrarian changes in the
Philippines." In Hired labor in rural Asia (ed. S. Hirashima),
pp. 97-105. Institute of Developing Economies, Tokyo.

TAMBIAH, S. J. (1973). "Dowry and bridewealth, and the property of
women in south Asia." In Bridewealth and dowry in Africa and
Eurasia (ed. J. Goody and S. J. Tambiah), pp. 59-169. Cambridge
University Press, Cambridge.

TANAKA, Y. (1979). "Japanese society through the eyes of three
generations. (2) The plight of the elderly: scenes of indigence
in an affluent land." Japan Quarterly 26: 63-74.

TANNER, N. (1974). "Matrifocality in Indonesia and Africa and among
Black Americans." In Women, culture and society (ed. M. Z.
Rosaldo and L. Lamphere), pp. 129-156. Stanford University Press,
Stanford.

TANNER, N., and ZIHLMAN, A. (1976). "Women in evolution: innovation and selection in human origins." Signs 1: 585-608.

TEXTOR, R. B. (1977). "The 'loose structure' of Thai society: a
paradigm under pressure." Pacific Affairs 50: 467-472.

THIENCHAY, Kirananda. (1977). An economic analysis of fertility
determination among rural and urban Thai women. Institute of
Population Studies, paper no. 20. Chulalongkorn University,
Bangkok. 17 pp.

THOMPSON, S. I. (1977). "Women, horticulture and society in
tropical America." American Anthropologist 79: 908-910.

TIFFANY, S. W. (1978). "Models and the social anthropology of
women: a preliminary assessment." Man 13: 34-51.

TIGER, L., and SHEPHER, J. (1977). Women in the kibbutz. Penguin
Books, Harmondsworth. 334 pp.

TINKER, I. (1976a). "Women in developing societies: economic
independence is not enough." In Economic independence for women:
the foundation for equal rights (ed. J. R. Chapman), pp. 113-135.
Sage, Beverly Hills/London.

_____. (1976b). "The adverse impact of development on women."
In Women and world development (ed. I. Tinker and M. B. Bramsen),
pp. 22-34. Overseas Development Council, Washington.

TINKER, I., and BRAMSEN, M. B. (eds.). (1976). Women and world

development. Overseas Development Council, Washington. 228 pp.
TOPLEY, M. (1975). "Marriage resistance in rural Kwangtung." In Women in Chinese society (ed. M. Wolf and R. Witke), pp. 67-88. Stanford University Press, Stanford.
de TRAY, D. N. (1977). Household studies workshop. Agricultural Development Council, New York. 8 pp.
TSUBOUCHI, Y. (1972). "Marriage and divorce among Malay peasants in Kelantan." South East Asian Studies 10: 390-408.
_____. (1978). "The changing function of religion among rural Malays." South East Asian Studies 16: 249-259.
UCHIDA, Y. (1978). "Aspects of family planning in Japan." Feminist 1(4): 25-27.
UNITED NATIONS ASIAN AND PACIFIC CENTRE FOR WOMEN AND DEVELOPMENT (UNAPCWD). (1977). Report of Expert Group meeting on the identification of the basic needs of women. 1. The critical needs of women. 2. Guidelines for a work programme. Teheran. 20 pp.
_____. (1978). Women's resource book 1978. Teheran. 328 pp.
UNITED NATIONS CENTRE FOR SOCIAL DEVELOPMENT AND HUMANITARIAN AFFAIRS (1977). Law and the status of women. New York. 371 pp.
UNITED NATIONS EDUCATIONAL, SCIENTIFIC AND CULTURAL ORGANIZATION (UNESCO). (1976). Exchange programme of information and experience between member states of UNESCO. Inventory of the result of experience of Japan in developing successful approaches to improving the status of women. UNESCO, Paris. 87 pp.
_____. (1978a). Status of girls in primary education in some Asian countries, and prospects. UNESCO, Paris. 42 pp.
_____. (1978b). Disparities in enrolment by sex in primary education in twelve Asian countries (a statistical review). UNESCO, Paris. 39 pp.
_____. (1978c). Experimental project for equal access of girls and women to education in Nepal. Background paper for Asian Regional Seminar on Access of Girls to Primary Education in Rural Areas. UNESCO, Paris. 26 pp.
_____. (1979). Final report of the Asian Regional Seminar on Access of Girls to Primary Education, Kathmandu, Nepal, October 2-6, 1978. UNESCO, Paris. 33 pp.
UNITED STATES AGENCY FOR INTERNATIONAL DEVELOPMENT (U.S. AID). (1977). International directory of women's development organizations. U.S. AID, Washington. 311 pp.
UTSUMI, A. (1978). "Feminism in Indonesia." Feminist 1(4): 46-48.
UTTAR PRADESH STATE PLANNING DEPARTMENT. (1977). Fifth Five Year Plan. Draft annual plan, 1978-79. Lucknow. 320 pp.
VALEX, M. C. (1975). Images of the Filipina. (Bibliography.) 219 pp.
VICHAI Thamchob. (1978). "Thailand." In Rural development strategies in selected member countries, pp. 167-177. Asian Productivity Organization, Tokyo.
VIETNAM RESOURCE CENTER. (1974). Vietnamese women in society and revolution. VRC, Cambridge, Mass. 207 pp.
VISID, Prachuamboh, KNODEL, J., and ALERS, J. O. (1974). "Preference for sons, desire for additional children, and family planning." Journal of Marriage and the Family 36: 601-614.
VOGEL, E. F. (1967). "Kinship structure, migration to the city, and

modernization." In Aspects of social change in modern Japan (ed. R. P. Dore), pp. 91-111. Princeton University Press, New Jersey.

VOGEL, S. H. (1978). "Professional housewife: the career of urban middle class Japanese women." The Japan Interpreter 12: 17-43.

de VOS, G. (ed.). (1973). Socialization for achievement: essays on the cultural psychology of the Japanese. University of California Press, Berkeley, Los Angeles, London. 597 pp.

de VOS, G., and WAGATSUMA, H. (1973a). "Status and role behaviour in changing Japan: psychocultural continuities." In Socialization for achievement (ed. G. de Vos), pp. 10-60. University of California Press, Berkeley, Los Angeles, London.

_____. (1973b). "Value attitudes towards role behaviour of women in two Japanese villages." In Socialization for achievement (ed. G. de Vos), pp. 110-143. University of California Press, Berkeley, Los Angeles, London.

VREEDE De STUERS, G. (1968). Parda: A study of Muslim women's life in northern India. van Gorcum, Assen. 128 pp.

WADLEY, S. S. (1977). "Women and the Hindu tradition." Signs 3: 113-125.

WARD, B. E. (ed.). (1963). Women in the new Asia. The changing social roles of men and women in south and south-east Asia. UNESCO, Paris. 529 pp.

_____. (1970). "Women and technology in developing countries." Impact of Science on Society 20: 93-101.

WASHBURN, S. L., and LANCASTER, C. S. (1968). "The evolution of hunting." In Man the hunter (ed. R. B. Lee and I. DeVore), pp. 293-303. Aldine, Chicago.

WEE, A. E. (1963). "Chinese women of Singapore: their present status in the family and in marriage." In Women in the new Asia (ed. B. E. Ward), pp. 376-409. UNESCO, Paris.

WEERAKOON, G. (1978). "The status and role of women in the organized sector in Sri Lanka." In ILO Sub-regional Seminar on Status and Role of Women in the Organized Sector. 17 pp. ILO, Bangkok.

WEISNER, T. S., and GALLIMORE, R. (1977). "My brother's keeper: child and sibling caretaking." Current Anthropology 18: 169-190.

WELLESLEY EDITORIAL COMMITTEE (ed.). (1977). "Women and national development: the complexities of change." Signs 3: 1-346.

WHITE, B. N. F. (1967). Production and reproduction in a Javanese village. Ph.D. Thesis, Columbia University, New York.

_____. (1973). "Demand for labor and population growth in colonial Java." Human Ecology 1: 217-236.

_____. (1974). "Reply to Geertz and van de Walle." Human Ecology 2: 63-65.

_____. (1975). "The economic importance of children in a Javanese village." In Population and social organization (ed. M. Nag), pp. 127-146. Mouton, The Hague and Paris.

_____. (1976). "Population, involution and employment in rural Java." Development and Change 7: 267-290.

WHITE, M. I., and MOLONY, B. (eds.). (1979). Proceedings of the Tokyo Symposium on women. International Group for the Study of Women, Tokyo. 188 pp.

WHYTE, M. K. (1973). "The family." In China's developmental

248

experience (ed. M. Oksenberg), pp. 174-192. Praeger, New York.
_____. (1977). "Rural marriage customs." Problems of
Communism 26(4): 41-55.
WHYTE, R. O. (1974). Rural nutrition in monsoon Asia. Oxford
University Press, Kuala Lumpur, London, New York. 296 pp.
_____. (1976). The Asian village as a basis for rural moderni-
zation. Institute of Southeast Asian Studies, Occasional Paper
no. 44. Singapore. 77 pp.
_____. (1981). "Employment for Asia's rural labour." SPAN 24:
57-59.
_____. (1982). The spatial geography of rural economies.
Oxford University Press, Delhi.
WHYTE, R. O., and WHYTE, P. (1978). Rural Asian women: status and
environment. Institute of Southeast Asian Studies, Research Note
and Discussion Series no. 9. Singapore. 34 pp.
WICKRAMASEKARA, P. (1977). "Aspects of the hired labour situation
in rural Sri Lanka: some preliminary findings." In Hired labor
in rural Asia (ed. S. Hirashima), pp. 71-94. Institute of
Developing Economies, Tokyo.
WIJERATNE, D. J. D. (1978). "Sri Lanka." In Rural development
strategies in selected member countries, pp. 156-166. Asian
Productivity Organization, Tokyo.
WILLIAMSON, N. E. (1978). "Boys or girls? Parents' preferences and
sex control." Population Bulletin 33(1): 1-35.
WILLING, A. Shinoda. (1977). "The social influences on the employ-
ment of Japanese women." Paper presented at second New Zealand
Conference on Asian Studies, Christchurch, 1977. 30 pp.
WILSON, C. S. (1970). Food beliefs and practices of Malay fisher-
men: an ethnographic study of diet on the east coast of Malaya.
Ph.D. Thesis, University of California, Berkeley. University
Microfilms, Ann Arbor. 1975. 497 pp.
WILSON, P. J. (1967). A Malay village and Malaysia. HRAF Press,
New Haven. 171 pp.
WINZELER, R. L. (1976). "Ethnic differences and economic change in
a local Malaysian setting." Journal of South East Asian Studies
14: 309-333.
WOLF, A. P. (1975). "The women of Hai-shan: a demographic por-
trait." In Women in Chinese society (ed. M. Wolf and R. Witke),
pp. 89-110. Stanford University Press, Stanford.
WOLF, M. (1970). "Child training and the Chinese family." In
Family and kinship in Chinese society (ed. M. Freedman), pp. 37-
62. Stanford University Press, Stanford.
_____. (1972). Women and the family in rural Taiwan. Stanford
University Press, Stanford. 233 pp.
_____. (1975). "Women and suicide in China." In Women in
Chinese society (ed. M. Wolf and R. Witke), pp. 111-141. Stanford
University Press, Stanford.
WOLF, M., and WITKE, R. (eds.). (1975). Women in Chinese society.
Stanford University Press, Stanford. 315 pp.
WONG, A. K. (1973). "Rising social status and economic participa-
tion of women in Hongkong." Southeast Asian Journal Social
Science 1(2): 11-26.
_____. (1974). The continuous family revolution in China -

249

ideology and changing family patterns. Working Paper no. 31,
Department of Sociology, University of Singapore. 39 pp.
_____. (1975). _Women in modern Singapore_. University Educa-
tion Press, Singapore. 137 pp.
WOOLF, V. (1928:1945). _A room of one's own_. Penguin Books,
Harmondsworth. 112 pp.
WORLD FOOD PROGRAM, Executive Director. (1977). _Interim evaluation
and terminal reports: women in food-for-work: the Bangladesh
experience_. FAO, Rome. 6 pp.
WU Tsong-shien. (1972). "The value of children, or boy preference."
In _Satisfactions and costs of children_ (ed. J. T. Fawcett), pp.
293-299. East-West Center, Honolulu.
WYON, J. B., and GORDON, J. E. (1971). _The Khanna study: popula-
tion problems in the rural Punjab_. Harvard University Press,
Cambridge.
YANG, C. K. (1959). _The Chinese family in the Communist revolution_.
Technology Press, Cambridge, Mass. 246 pp.
YANG, K. S. (1974). "Taiwan." In _Social and psychological aspects
of fertility in Asia_ (ed. H. P. David and S. J. Lee), pp. 16-22.
Transnational Family Research Institute, Washington.
YANG, M. C. (1945). _A Chinese village: Taitou, Shantung Province_.
Columbia University Press, New York. 275 pp.
de YOUNG, J. E. (1966). _Village life in modern Thailand_. Univer-
sity of California Press, Berkeley and Los Angeles. 225 pp.
YOUNG, M. (ed.). (1973). _Women in China_. Michigan Papers in China
Studies no. 15. University of Michigan, Ann Arbor. 259 pp.
YOUSSEF, N. H. (1977). "Methodology and data collection: introduction." _Signs_ 3: 275-277.
ZAINAL ABIDIN bin Ahmad. (1949). "Malay festivals: and some
aspects of Malay religious life." _Journal of the Malayan Branch
of the Royal Asiatic Society_ 22: 94-106. Reprinted in centenary
volume, 1977, pp. 166-178.
ZIHLMAN, A. (1978a). "Women and evolution. II. Subsistence and
social organization among early hominids." _Signs_ 4: 4-20.
_____. (1978b). "Motherhood in transition: from ape to
human." In _The first child and family formation_ (ed. W. B. Miller
and L. F. Newman), pp. 35-50. University of North Carolina,
Chapel Hill.
ZIHLMAN, A., and TANNER, N. (1978). "Gathering and the hominid
adaptation." In _Female hierarchies_ (ed. L. Tiger and H. Fowler),
pp. 163-194. Beresford Book Service, Chicago.

Glossary of Terms and Abbreviations

Adat:	Traditional custom, governing behaviour (Malaysia, Indonesia).
ADB:	Asian Development Bank.
Ani-ani:	Small blade for harvesting rice (Indonesia).
Baht:	Unit of currency (Thailand).
Bari:	Village (Bangladesh).
Bawon:	Villagers' right to harvest on large holdings within their village, in return for portion of grain they gather (Indonesia.)
Belachan:	Preserved paste of dried, ground shrimps and salt (Indonesia).
Biahdari:	Endogamous group (India).
Bidi:	Cigarette, made from tree leaves.
Birdari:	Patrilineage (Pakistan).
Burqa:	Loose garment covering woman's entire body, to preserve purdah outside home (South Asia).
Ceblokan:	Workers transplant without pay in exchange for right to harvest, for which they receive portion of grain they gather (Indonesia).
Chamar:	Leather workers, a Scheduled Caste (India).
Chula:	Cooking range (South Asia).
Dehi:	Yoghurt (South Asia).
Dharma:	Right-living, deriving from moral law (Hinduism).
Dōzoku:	Extended kin group (Japan).
ESCAP:	Economic and Social Council for Asia and the Pacific.
FAO:	Food and Agriculture Organization of the United Nations.
Food for Work:	Relief employment, usually public works, in time of famine. Paid in grain supplied by the World Food Program.
Gotong Royong:	Mutual help, especially at times of peak labour demand such as planting or harvesting.
Gula Jawa:	Brown sugar.
Guru:	Teacher (South Asia).
Hadith:	Body of traditions relating to Mahomet; supplement to Koran (Islam).
ICSSR:	Indian Council of Social Science Research.
Ie:	Household, sometimes including non-family members (Japan).
ILO:	International Labour Office.

251

Imam: Leader of prayers in mosque (Islam).
Jati: Endogamous caste group (India).
Kampong: Village (Indonesia, Malaysia).
Kaoliang: A millet, Sorghum bicolor (People's Republic of China).
Katchcha: Makeshift, temporary, not durable (South Asia).
Kaum Ibu: Women's wing of the United Malays' National Party
            (Malaysia).
Kelumbong: Shawl (Malaysia).
Kepang: Plaited natural fibre ware (Indonesia, Malaysia).
Kerepok: Crisp made of pounded shrimps (Indonesia, Malaysia).
Khsatriya: Second of four major caste divisions of India, formerly
            warrior caste.
Khutbah: Form of sermon given at Friday service (Islam).
Kosei Nenkin: National Welfare Annuity Scheme (Japan).
Longhouse: Hamlet where separate family units live in rooms sub-
            divided under one long roof, opening on common platform
            (Borneo).
Lontong: Steamed rice dumplings (Indonesia).
Machismo: Cultivation of image of dominant male (by male).
Maund: 82 lb. = 37 kg. (South Asia).
Miai: Formal meeting of two families, at which prospective bride
            and groom may see if they wish to embark on an engagement
            (Japan).
Nari Niketan: Women's hostel (India).
Nat: Spirit, usually anthropomorphic (Burma).
NCNA: New China News Agency.
Padi: Rice field.
PAG: Protein Advisory Group of the United Nations.
Panchayat: Village Council (South Asia).
Pandanus: Pandanus pandan, the screw pine (esp. southeast Asia).
Parang: Large chopping blade (Indonesia, Malaysia).
Picul: 133-1/3 lb. = 60 kg. (China).
Purdah: Seclusion of women.
Sagod: Right given to labourers who weed crop to participate in
            harvest for which they are paid portion of grain they
            gather (Philippines).
Sari-Sari Store: General provisions shop (Philippines).
Sarong: Length of patterned material worn as skirt.
Sawah: Irrigated rice field (Indonesia).
Scheduled Caste: Those falling outside four major caste groups,
            formerly known as Untouchables, called by Gandhi,
            Harijans, Children of God. Given preferential treatment
            under Indian Constitution.
Seer: About 2 lb. = 0.9 kg. (South Asia).
Sudra: Lowest of four major caste groups (India).
SWB: Summary of World Broadcasts, monitored by the British
            Broadcasting Corporation.
Swidden: Shifting cultivation.
Tebasan: Rice crop sold in field to middleman, who is responsible
            for harvesting (Indonesia).
Tehsil: Administrative subdivision of a district (South Asia).
Tempe: Soybean curd (Indonesia).

Thana:	Police station and territory within its jurisdiction (Bangladesh).
Tikar:	Mat made of nipa palm or bamboo.
UNAPCWD:	United Nations Asian and Pacific Centre for Women and Development.
UNDP:	United Nations Development Programme.
UNESCO:	United Nations Educational, Scientific and Cultural Organization.
USAID:	United States Agency for International Development.
Wat:	Buddhist temple.
Zat:	Caste (Pakistan).

Index of
Geographical Terms

Subject Index

Acculturation, 12, 37, 38, 127
Adat, 108
Agricultural Development Council,
  186
Agriculture
  dryland, 19, 153, 204, 205, 206
  and employment of women, 131–
    157, 164–165
  mechanization in, 156, 183,
    184, 185, 186, 189, 200
  modernization of, 183–191
  plough, 18, 19, 204, 205
  See also Gathering; Harvesting;
    High-yielding varieties;
    Horticulture
Agta Negritos, 6
Ambilocality, 21
Ancestral spirits, 28, 29
Animal husbandry, 2, 19, 131,
  133, 134, 135, 138, 140,
  145, 146, 152, 155, 160,
  169, 172, 214, 216
Ashraf, 71
Asian and Pacific Centre for
  Women and Development. See
  United Nations, Asian and
  Pacific Centre for Women and
  Development
Auditory-perceptual ability, 11
Autonomy, female, 6, 9, 17, 18,
  20, 21, 82, 181. See also
  Decision making; Heads of
  household, female
Avoidance patterns, Hindu, 23

Bangladesh Institute of Education and Research, 214

Basic needs, 200, 218. See also
  Subsistence
Bawon, 187
Bilateral societies, 7, 22, 24,
  65, 91, 109, 180, 205
Biographies of Women, 19
Biological determinism, 10. See
  also Cultural determinism;
  Environmental determinism
Birth control, 7, 113, 114, 115,
  116, 120, 122, 127–129, 208.
  See also Contraception
Bogor Agricultural University,
  148, 149
Brides
  adoption of, as children, 18,
    108, 206
  and bride price, 32, 33, 34, 73.
    See also Dower; Dowry;
    Marriage
  and bridewealth, 33
Buddhism, 27, 45, 118, 203. See
  also Religion
Burqa, 22, 125, 140, 170, 171

Caste, 12, 26, 110. See also
  Class
Ceblokan, 187
Center for Regional Development.
  See United Nations, Center for
  Regional Development
Centre for Social Development and
  Humanitarian Affairs. See
  United Nations, Centre for
  Social Development and Humani-
  tarian Affairs
Chen Mu-hua, 52

257

258

Chien Cheng-ying, 52, 114
Child care, 6, 13, 14, 114, 152,
    154, 155, 157, 173, 176, 193,
    194, 195, 196, 197, 208
Childlessness, 93, 95. See also
    Fertility
Childraising, 5, 6, 9, 11, 12
Children
    contribution to labour, 126,
        148, 152, 155, 199, 200, 201
    ideal number of, 120-122
    number of, 14, 43, 113-129
    value of, 124-127
    See also Child care; Child-
        raising; Education
Ch'ing dynasty, 19
Ch'ing-lian-kiang culture, 19
Christianity, 27, 28, 91, 92,
    127. See also Religion
Class, 6, 8, 19, 164. See also
    Caste
Colonialism, 3
Communism, women under, 14, 15,
    41, 52, 132, 194
Concubines, 77, 93
Conference on Women in Inter-
    national Development, 7, 8
Confucian tradition, 19, 20, 27,
    48, 80, 89, 93, 145, 203
Contraception, 113, 114, 115,
    116, 121, 127, 128, 208.
    See also Birth control
Cultural determinism, 10. See
    also Biological determinism;
    Environmental determinism

Decision making, 19, 20, 131,
    138, 140, 143, 145, 146,
    147, 148, 149, 150-152, 153,
    155, 157, 161, 179, 180,
    181. See also Autonomy,
    female
Decade for Women. See United
    Nations, Decade for Women
Division of labour, 6, 19, 23,
    131-157. See also Child-
    raising; Housework; Labour
Divorce, 19, 32, 33, 68, 83, 90-
    96, 113, 140, 207, 214
Dower, 33. See also Brides;
    Marriage
Dowry, 32, 33, 34, 35, 73, 84.
    See also Brides, and bride

price; Marriage
Dozoku, 20

Economic and Social Council. See
    United Nations, Economic and
    Social Council
Education
    attitudes towards, 12, 30,
        44-51, 116, 200, 218
    higher, 12, 13, 43, 45, 48
    innovation in, 209-210, 215
    levels of, 8, 12, 20, 44-51, 92,
        111, 115, 117, 122-123, 127,
        138, 201, 218. See also
        Kindergartens and nurseries;
        Teachers; Textbooks
Egalitarianism, 6, 8, 9, 20, 21,
    27, 79, 127, 140, 145, 150
Elopement, 69. See also Marriage
Employment
    after marriage, 12, 13, 123-124,
        196, 197, 198
    off-farm, 169, 170, 181, 185,
        210, 211, 213
    See also Children, contribution
        to labour; Labour; Underem-
        ployment; Unemployment
Endogamy, 65, 70, 72. See also
    Marriage
Entrepreneurs, 210, 211
Environmental determinism, 203,
    204. See also Biological
    determinism; Cultural deter-
    minism
Evolution of women's role, 5, 19,
    204
Exogamy, 5, 70, 71. See also
    Marriage

FAMA. See Malaysian Farmers
    Organization Authority
Fertility, 113, 114, 117, 122,
    123-124. See also Birth con-
    trol; Childlessness; Contra-
    ception
Fishing villages, 20, 147
Food and Agricultural Organization
    (FAO). See United Nations,
    Food and Agricultural Organi-
    zation
Food for Work, 88, 140, 171, 196,
    197, 207, 217
Footbinding, 19, 22, 153, 154, 207

Friendship, 12, 124

Gathering, 5, 19, 204, 205. See also Agriculture; Harvesting
Gonds, 35, 137
Great Leap Forward, 154
Green revolution, 181, 183, 184, 185, 206

Han, 19, 20
Handicrafts, 131, 146, 150, 160, 169, 189, 211, 212
Harvard School of Public Health, 29
Harvesting, 133, 146, 148, 168, 173, 186. See also Agriculture; Gathering
Heads of household, female, 173, 208. See also Autonomy, female; Decision making
Health care
  rural, 30, 113
  and status, 20, 206
Heian period, 27
High-yielding varieties, 184, 185, 186, 188, 189, 190, 206. See also Agriculture
Hinduism, 23, 26, 45, 87, 92, 95. See also Religion
Historical dialectical approach, 6
Hominids
  role of females, 6
  social structure, 6
Horticulture, 5, 168
Household help, 13, 193-201
Housework, 13, 14, 131-157, 167, 194, 196. See also Division of labour
Hunting, 5, 6, 19, 204, 205
Hypergamy, 29. See also Caste; Class; Marriage

Iban, 131, 147
Income, women's contribution, 13, 22, 27, 131, 140, 159-177, 210-212
India
  National Committee on the Status of Women, 208
  Planning Commission, 47, 170, 213
Indian Council of Social Science

Research, 212
Individuality, 9, 12. See also Personality
Indonesia, Co-ordinating Body for Welfare of the Family and Children, 74, 75
Infanticide, 5, 206. See also Mortality, infant
International Women's Year (1975), 7, 216, 219
Irrigation, 18, 20, 205, 206. See also Agriculture
Islam
  societies, 23, 25
  traditions, 24, 26, 29, 33, 45, 46, 47, 68, 70, 71, 76, 88, 91, 92, 95, 116-117, 136. See also Religion

Jakun, 147
Japan
  Labour Standards Law, 41
  Ministry of Agriculture and Forestry, Home-Living Improvement Section, 215
  National Welfare Annuity Scheme, 89
  pension scheme, 89
Johor State Economic Development Corporation, 215
Joint households, dissolution, 110-112

Kaira Milk Union, 160
Kibbutzim, 10, 11, 108, 132
Kindergartens and nurseries, 194. See also Education, levels of
Koran, 26, 76
Korea
  Association of Confucian Scholars, 42
  Civil Code, 42
  Family Law of 1977, 42
Kyoto, Center of South-East Asian Studies, 49

Labour
  exchange of, 146, 160, 168, 169
  participation, female, 12, 14, 19, 20, 43, 94, 123-124, 131-158, 159, 160, 163, 167, 168, 169, 170, 186
  See also Children, contribution